Revolution in Rojava

Revolution in Rojava

Democratic Autonomy and Women's Liberation in Syrian Kurdistan

Michael Knapp, Anja Flach,
and Ercan Ayboğa

Foreword by David Graeber
Afterword by Asya Abdullah
Translated by Janet Biehl

www.plutobooks.com

First published 2016 by Pluto Press
345 Archway Road, London N6 5AA

www.plutobooks.com

British Library Cataloguing in Publication Data
A catalogue record for this book is available from the British Library

ISBN   978 0 7453 3664 0   Hardback
ISBN   978 0 7453 3659 6   Paperback
ISBN   978 1 7837 1987 7   PDF eBook
ISBN   978 1 7837 1989 1   Kindle eBook
ISBN   978 1 7837 1988 4   EPUB eBook

Typeset by Stanford DTP Services, Northampton, England

Simultaneously printed in the United Kingdom and United States of America

Contents

List of Figures

Translator's Note

Revolution in Rojava, the first full book to appear on the democratic, gender-equal, cooperative revolution under way in northern Syria, was originally published in German in March 2015 by VSA Verlag. This English version began as a direct translation, but over the course of 16 months, it has been extensively revised and updated, so that in many respects it is a new book. I would like to thank Pluto Press for editorial support and for bringing the book to the wide audience it deserves; Sherko Geylani, for early help with translation; and New Compass Press for solidarity.

Janet Biehl

Foreword

David Graeber

Even many ostensible revolutionaries nowadays seem to have secretly abandoned the idea that a revolution is actually possible.

Here I am using "revolution" in its classical sense, let's say: the overthrow of an existing structure of power and the ruling class it supports by a popular uprising of some sort, and its replacement by new forms of bottom-up popular organization. For most of the twentieth century this was not the case: even those revolutionaries who hated the Bolsheviks, for example, supported the revolution itself, even popular uprisings that came to be led by ethno-nationalists were not simply condemned if they were seen to be genuinely popular. There was an obvious reason for this. For most of that time, revolutionaries felt that, whatever temporary complications, history was flowing inevitably in the direction of greater equality and freedom. Those rising up to shake off some form of tyranny, however temporarily confused or distracted, were clearly the agents of that greater movement of liberation.

It's understandable that it's hard to maintain that kind of blind optimism anymore. It often led to extraordinarily destructive naiveté. But neither is it particularly helpful to replace naiveté with cynicism, and it must be admitted that in many quarters, this is what has happened. A very large portion of those who at least think of themselves as the revolutionary left now seem to have adopted a politics which leads to the instant and near automatic condemnation of pretty much any even moderately successful revolutionary movement that actually takes place on planet earth. Certainly this is what has happened in the case of Rojava. While a large number of people have been utterly astounded, and deeply moved, to see a popular movement dedicated to direct democracy, cooperative economics, and a deep commitment to ecology emerge in that part of the world they'd long been informed was the very most authoritarian and benighted, let alone to witness thousands of armed feminists literally defeating the forces of patriarchy on the battlefield, many either refused to believe any of this was actually happening, or tried to come up with any reason they could for why there must be something deeply insidious lying behind it. One expects this kind of reaction from the mainstream media, or US and European politicians. After lecturing the world for generations about how the peoples of the Middle East were desperately backwards, and how their traditional and supposedly uncompromising hostility towards liberal values like formal democracy and women's rights justified both the support of extreme right-wing regimes like Saudi Arabia ("what else can you expect from people like that?") and endless bombing and massacres against the population unfortunate enough to live under whichever regimes the Empire's guns happened to be trained on, it's hardly surprising that the emergence of popular movements embracing forms of democracy far more radical, and not just women's rights but genuine full women's equality, in all aspects of life, would be a topic they'd prefer to avoid. But the left?

These reactions I should stress went well beyond mere skepticism, which of course is healthy (indeed necessary): I have former friends, English activists who had never taken a strong interest in Middle Eastern affairs, who on learning of the Rojava Revolution decided the appropriate response was to appear at any event about the region in London to distribute pamphlets condemning the revolution and urging people not to help it. What on earth would move someone to conclude that, of all the things they could be doing to further the cause of universal freedom and equality in the limited days they had left upon this planet, this would be the best usage of their time?

*   *   *

In my unkinder moments, I am tempted to label such elements "the Loser Left"—by which I mean, not that they are personally inadequate in any way, but that they have embraced a politics which tacitly assumes the inevitability of ultimate defeat. Admittedly, this attitude has always been with us. Consider the phrase "fighting the good fight"—it seems to carry within it an assumption that of course one will not win. But since the end of the Cold War the Loser Left has ballooned enormously. I would suggest that, as currently constituted, it has two main divisions: purists, and extreme anti-imperialists. The first have taken the old Marxist vanguardist idea that anyone who doesn't adopt every detail of my particular form of doctrine isn't really a revolutionary, and pushed it just a step further to conclude that any revolution that doesn't fit my theory of what a real revolution should look like is worse than no revolution at all. In anarchist and some Marxist circles, this attitude converges around a kind of cool-kid clubbism: many, one suspects, are unconsciously horrified at the prospect of a revolution, since that would mean everyone, even hairdressers and postal workers, would be debating *Théorie Communiste* or *Aufheben* and there would be nothing special about them anymore.

The anti-imperialists are a stranger case. I am not obviously speaking here of anyone who opposes the global dominance of North Atlantic military powers: it's hard to imagine how one could be a revolutionary and not do so. "Financialized" capitalism is essentially military capitalism; the power of JP Morgan Chase or even Standard & Poor's is entirely dependent on the power of the US military; even the inner workings of capitalist profit extraction increasingly work through simple coercive force. These things are not extricable. What I am speaking of here instead is the feeling that foiling imperial designs—or avoiding any appearance of even appearing to be on the "same side" as an imperialist in any context—should always take priority over anything else. This attitude only makes sense if you've secretly decided that real revolutions are impossible. Because surely, if one actually felt that a genuine popular revolution was occurring, say, in the city of Kobanî and that its success could be a beacon and example to the world, one would not also hold that it is better for all those revolutionaries to be massacred by genocidal fascists than for a bunch of rich white intellectuals to sully the purity of their reputations by suggesting that US imperial forces already conducting airstrikes in the region might wish to direct their attention to the fascists' tanks. Yet, astoundingly, this was the position that a very large number of self-professed "radicals" actually did take.

* * *

I support the revolution in Rojava because I would like to see the revolutionaries win. The Kurdish freedom movement has evolved in stunningly dramatic ways since the beginning of the current round of armed struggle in the 1970s. Old-fashioned Marxist dogmas and debates have been replaced by a welter of new ideas, arguments, and commitments. The demand for a separate Kurdish state has been replaced by a rejection of the very notion of the state, and an embrace of a principle of Democratic Confederalism based on a synthesis of the ideas of American anarchist and social ecologist Murray Bookchin and other authors, Kurdish tradition, and wide-ranging experience in the pragmatics of revolutionary organization. These changes were not simply the collective brainchild of Abdullah Öcalan—they build on debates that were already well underway in some quarters of the Kurdish movement long before his capture and imprisonment, and the flurry of new writings that has followed. They also sparked very lively further debate, including many debates that are by no means definitively concluded. One of the co-chairs of the KCK, for instance, told me that the formal consensus-finding process that followed the proposal to abandon the demand for a separate Kurdish state took over 18 months, and prompted quite a number of indignant resignations, though most of those who had originally resigned rather than accept the new policy had since returned. There was a clash not only of ideas, but of sensibilities, generations, institutional cultures. Progress has been in many areas extremely uneven. In Rojava, it is hard to find anywhere untouched by the Kurdish women's movement; in some parts of Turkey and Iraq, even areas with ardent and well-nigh universal support for the PKK, patriarchy remains unquestioned. Even in Rojava, there is opposition, even if much of it takes covert form. "No man dares challenge the principle of gender equality in public," one organizer for Yekîtiya Star, the Rojava women's union, told me. "But physical attacks on women nearly doubled in the first years of the revolution." This was one of the main reason for creating women's courts, and women's justice committees that regularly increased the penalties of men found guilty of such assaults by the neighborhood "peace and consensus" committees. I point this out only to emphasize that no real, revolutionary change is won without a struggle, and much of the internal, social struggle is invisible to the outside eye.

*   *   *

I'm an anthropologist and I only visited Rojava very briefly—for a little over a week—not knowing any of the languages; but being an anthropologist at least gave me a keen sense for everything I didn't know. It would have taken years for me to have a sense for what was really going on and by then, much would have been entirely different. But what I did see was enough to understand, not just that this was a legitimate popular revolution, in the sense that there was an obvious sense of newfound freedom, of both dignity and cheerful playfulness, among the people we encountered that could not possibly have been put on for show, but that I was witnessing what was in some ways a rare, almost best-case scenario for mass revolutionary mobilization. The ruling class had, after all, largely fled, the government had dismantled itself, clearing out their offices, computers, files, and instruments of torture; a large percentage of the most important buildings, mills, and arable land were already technically public property; yet key salaries were still being paid by the largely absent central government; and even many of the most socially conservative families saw revolutionary organizers as part of a legitimate movement of national liberation. Of course, in other ways, it was almost a worst case: Rojava was under total embargo, surrounded on all sides by hostile forces—a Turkish government that would stop at nothing to destroy them, a right-wing Kurdish government in Iraq willing to starve their Syrian kin even of basic medical supplies to please their Turkish allies, a Ba'athist government biding its time to restore secret police power, a rebel alliance determined to exclude them, an Islamic State willing to throw everything at its disposal to conquer them, cynical world powers such as the United States and Russia willing to exploit their courage and sacrifice in opposing the Islamic State for precisely as long as it suited their purposes, whereon, everyone knew, they would instantly stab them in the back. (The only strategic question here was which one was likely to do it first.) The fact that Rojava has survived, and thrived, and even grown, despite all this is a testimony to the outpouring of energy, courage, creativity, and sheer human brilliance that can be unleashed in a revolutionary situation, where suddenly, that 95 percent or so of most human populations that is normally told their perspectives count for nothing are suddenly free to find out what they're actually good at, and say whatever they want. Any mass of humans instantly witnesses an outpouring of collective intelligence when the mechanisms keeping them scared and stupid are suddenly taken away.

* * *

In terms of revolutionary theory, I would say that the case of Rojava is in certain ways unique. What we find is essentially a dual power situation.

On the one hand, there is the democratic self-administration, which looks very much like a government, replete with ministries, parliament, and higher courts. If you simply read the formal constitution of the Rojava cantons you would have very little sign this was anything other than an enlightened social democratic, or perhaps at most democratic socialist, state. It includes numerous political parties but was largely set up by the PYD. On the other there's the bottom-up structures, organized by TEV-DEM, the Movement for a Democratic Society, many of whose members are also PYD or former PYD, where initiative flows entirely from popular assemblies. The balance of power between these two institutional structures appears to be fluid and under constant renegotiation. This is what one would expect in a revolutionary dual power situation; one might draw an analogy here, for instance, between the relation of MAS, the socialist party in Bolivia, and the popular assemblies of urban centers like El Alto. The unique thing is that this seems to be the only known case of a dual power situation where both sides are not just in alliance, as in Bolivia, but were actually set up by the same movement, even, in some cases, the same individuals.

This very unusual situation seems to be a direct effect of the tumultuous circumstances in which Rojava's revolutionaries find themselves: the realities of civil war, refugees, foreign aid, embargo . . . There was, two years ago at least, a very large number of Ezidi refugees living in camps in Cezîrê, the easternmost canton of Rojava. These people were in a desperate situation because, while local collectives could supply them with bread and gasoline, which is abundant in Cezîrê, they had little means to supply them with anything else. The UN refugee agency at first refused even to provide tents, arguing that, since Rojava was still technically part of the sovereign Syrian government, they could do nothing until they'd received permission from the appropriate authorities. (Needless to say this was not forthcoming.) Eventually tents were finagled, and some generators, but virtually nothing else. Trade having been cut off, except for very unpredictable smuggling and one bridge that occasionally opened to Iraq, Rojava was more or less forced to look to international NGOs for anything from educational materials to spare parts for dialysis machines; to work with an NGO, however, you have to look and be organized at least a little like a government. Certainly to be taken seriously by international powers one has to have ministers, diplomats, the trappings of formal liberal democracy. But at the same time, everyone I talked to insisted—often quite indignantly—that this apparatus in no sense constituted a state.

How did this make sense? Essentially, because "state", for them, schooled as so many were in anarchist-inspired theory, meant structures of systematic coercion. "In this part of the world," the familiar joke went, "to ask for your own state is basically to say 'I demand the right to be tortured by secret police speaking my *own* language!'" Not only had the Ba'athist police and secret police been entirely eliminated, the Asayîş, the popular security forces put in their place, were not, ultimately, answerable to the self-administration, but to the local assemblies, which worked on a combination of consensus-finding (for important decisions) and majority vote. In fact, one of the clearest signs, for me, that these assemblies were real decision-making bodies and not just for show was the fact that the first one we visited broke down into a major argument, with much shouting and waving of hands. When I later asked what all the fuss was about, I was told that there had been a problem with a local merchant who some suspected of hoarding sugar to jack up the price. The neighborhood justice committee had called in some local Asayîş to go into the house and investigate, but the Asayîş explained they couldn't do so without clearance from their commanding officers. This caused outrage. "Commanding officers!?! They work for us! This is exactly how creeping bureaucratization sets in!" "So what do we have to do?" said another, "Make up some kind of special hat? A big badge? Maybe that will impress them."

It seemed a strong matter of principle that anyone with a gun should ultimately be answerable to the bottom-up structures, and not the top down—and if not, there was something terribly wrong. Even soldiers in the YPJ sometimes rankled at the suggestion they were given "commands" by their commanders. This is why, they insisted, this was not a state. And liberation from structures of violence and coercion were seen as flowing all the way down. When we asked about the origins of the women's militias, we were often greeted by the same formulae. "Well, we're anti-capitalist. One thing we think the twentieth century has shown us is that you can't get rid of capitalism without getting rid of the state. And you can't get rid of the state without eliminating patriarchy." The implication: giving all women access to automatic weapons seems a fairly obvious place to start.

*   *   *

At the end of our trip, some activists from TEV-DEM asked us for criticisms. "We don't just want to hear how great we are. We need outside insights about things we might be overlooking, things we're miscon-struing, things that might still go terribly wrong." We all tried to offer what we could—again, we'd been there so briefly, we didn't really have the means to make a genuine critical analysis. Of course I particularly remember what I said, though it wasn't just my own ideas, but based on long conversations the group had had together. It might not be a bad idea to end with them here, since these are all issues which, I think, may well become major problems in the future. These are the things I think we need to worry about:

1. The question of class. Part of the Kurdish movement's rejection of the Marxist legacy has been a sidelining of the entire issue of social class. As one organizer put it to me when I asked, "Do we really have to go on about those old conversations about what's feudalism, what's capitalism, what's a comprador elite, what's a national elite . . . ? Isn't it better to talk about other issues for a change: the oppression of women, for example?" Put in those terms it was hard to argue with. But in some ways, the fact that the revolution in Rojava was almost too easy, with the regime authorities and their closest local allies simply fleeing the area and leaving their most significant properties to be expropriated without violence or even legal opposition, allowed certain other structural features to be overlooked. To move from Marxist terminology to that popularized by Pierre Bourdieu: economic capital had been partly expropriated, social capital had been somewhat rearranged, but cultural capital—and particularly class habitus—had barely been affected. Drivers looked and acted remarkably like Parisian cab drivers, university students looked and acted, at least half of them, remarkably like university students in Paris too. During a moment of revolutionary ferment such as we witnessed this didn't seem to make a huge amount of difference (though I don't know, I was only there for a week and a half). But unless these structures are directly addressed, they will always tend to reassert themselves. And while the system of academies definitely seemed to be designed to disseminate forms of knowledge that could undercut existing structures of social and cultural capital, it was not clear to me how sustained and self-conscious that aspect of their work was.

2. *The question of time.* The form of direct democracy adopted in Rojava is very time-consuming. Local assemblies confederate to neighborhood assemblies, by sending two delegates each, male and female (each attached working group such as health, education, security, also sends its own two delegates and so does the all-women group associated with each), and then those neighborhood groups each likewise send two delegates to municipal assemblies. These are delegates, it was emphasized, not representatives. They must consult about everything, they cannot make decisions on their own. But this means that anyone in a municipal assembly has to engage in three different groups, on three different levels, and if they are in a municipal working group at least six! Since meetings are long, it's hard to imagine how anyone not free to dedicate a very large percentage of their daylight hours to meetings could manage this. Surely this limits the kind of people who can take an active political role, and runs the danger of creating a class of politicians—precisely what the system is meant to avoid.

3. *The integration of top-down and bottom-up structures.* The difficulty of creating a balance between the democratic self-organization, effectively the formal government, and the bottom-up structures of democratic confederalism, is that there is enormous pressure from outside to turn the former into something resembling a state. This pressure comes from all directions. For instance, one early report by Human Rights Watch, called *"Under Kurdish Rule,"* condemned Rojava for failing to provide those accused of crimes with trials that met international standards. In fact, Rojava uses an elaborate consensus process, at least at the first level, which was designed to combine traditional Kurdish means of dispute resolution with principles of restorative justice, while eliminating the principle of retribution or revenge. If injury is proved, both culprit and victim, and their families, have to come to collective agreement on the punishment or other response. By the standards of HRW however this is a human rights abuse because such trials do not meet "international standards." A harsh judgment from a respected human rights NGO in turn will almost certainly mean it will be harder for Rojava to import weapons (hence, the death of more young men and women on the

battlefield), and likely make it more difficult to make deals with other NGOs that would allow the import of, say, insulin, which will in turn mean diabetics will also die. This begins to give a sense of the kind of moral dilemmas faced by those trying to create new, revolutionary institutions under the circumstances that now exist.

On a gentler note, when I was in Qamişlo, there were a few limited zones still under Syrian government control. One surrounded the Post Office and a nearby Armenian neighborhood. The biggest, though, was the local airport. I always wondered about this. But then one day I asked: Are there any other airports in Rojava itself? The answer was, no. The regime used to use the airport to fly very sick people to hospitals in Damascus, but in the last year they'd stopped. And suddenly it became clear. The Asayîş and YPG/J could easily take over the airport. But what would be the point? They had no military aircraft. And as for commercial aircraft: Where could they fly? Obviously not to anywhere in Syria. But to be allowed to arrange a flight outside the country, one would have to be signatory to an endless variety of treaties and agreements: security agreements, customs agreements, health and safety agreements, commercial agreements . . . Only states could make such arrangements. Unless the democratic self-organization declared itself a state, and got someone else to recognize it as such, there would be nothing for them to do.

The only possible response is twofold: first of all, to try to find the minimal degree of state-like organizational structure one can, short of an actual state, that will meet the standards of the "international community" and thus be able to interact with it; and second, to create a kind of membrane, a means to communicate information and move resources back and forth between those formal structures and the bottom-up structures created in the spirit of democratic confederalism, that nonetheless does not cause those bottom-up structures to be compromised.

The problem with the first is that if Rojava does formalize its situation, either as an autonomous region in a decentralized Syria, or as three cantons in a democratic confederalist Syria, the problem of foreign pressure is only going to get worse. And then the problem of social class (and also secondarily, that of time) is likely to kick in as well. Educated would-be technocrats with foreign educations or the means to get them, savvy businesspeople, if those still exist—and it seems some will in the anticipated mixed economy—those with greater social or cultural capital more generally, will add to the pressure to integrate into international institutions. One can imagine all sorts of scenarios where this could lead to very bad results. The problem with the second is that no one has ever really tried this before, and there's no clear way to know how, or even if, it would work.

*　*　*

I don't want to end on a pessimistic note because I'm not actually pessimistic. It might seem unlikely that Rojava and the Kurdish movement more generally will sort these problems out. But the very existence of Rojava is extremely unlikely. If one had told almost anyone who wasn't part of the Kurdish movement in 2010 that by 2015 there would be an armed feminist uprising demanding direct democracy across a significant swath of the Middle East, they would probably have thought you were insane. Yet there it is.

Revolutions are messy, confusing; almost unimaginably terrible things happen, and even in the best of them authoritarian elements, bigots, and cynics find their way into the cracks and crevices; even the best people can do things that are stupid and unjust; but they also allow for an unleashing of pure happiness that can itself become a material force in history. You could see it in the way people held themselves, in where they put their eyes. And in the sudden musing over possibilities ("Is it possible that most disease is ultimately made possible by subtle ambient depression due to the absence of sufficient numbers of trees?" "Rights? What's a right? And how can I 'have' something if I don't even know what it is?" "But cannot women also defend the honor of men?").

When we were leaving, we apologized to our hosts that there wasn't more that we could bring them. They were under embargo, almost everything was in short supply. One woman answered, speaking, she said, only for herself. "Don't worry about that too much," she said. "I have something that no one can give me. I have my freedom. In a day or two you have to go back to a place where you don't have that. I only wish there was some way I could give what I have to you."

Introduction

Not long ago, few observers could have foreseen the emergence of a democratic revolution in northern Syria, or even believed it could happen. So in the spring of 2011, when the Kurdish freedom movement declared its aim to build a society around a concept called "Democratic Confederalism," few noticed. Nor were many paying attention when the Democratic Union Party (PYD), part of the Kurdish freedom movement, established the People's Council of West Kurdistan as a participatory-democratic umbrella for diverse peoples and political actors. Few noticed either, in July 2012, when popular uprisings, one by one, liberated the cities and villages of Rojava, which are mostly populated by Kurds, from the Ba'ath dictatorship and established a democratic system.

Yet those uprisings marked the beginning of a profoundly important contemporary revolution. In January 2014, the three cantons of Rojava—Cizîre, Kobanî and Afrîn—went on to issue a declaration of Democratic Autonomy and thereby created "democratic-autonomous administrations" to ensure that their new system would be inclusive and pluralistic. It would constitute a "third way," associated with neither the Ba'ath regime nor the chauvinist and Islamist opposition.

Then, between September 2014 and January 2015, the revolution's defense forces waged a stunning resistance to the Islamic State (IS) at Kobanî—and defeated it. The world finally noticed. Today, many revolutionary, democratic, leftist, socialist, libertarian, and human rights groups are aware of the existence in northern Syria of a free region known as Rojava.[1]

Contrary to all expectations, Democratic Autonomy has proved to be successful and realistic in northern Syria. In 2015-16, the liberation of Girê Spî (Til Abyad), Hesekê, and the Tishrin Dam, the creation of the Syrian Democratic Forces and the Syrian Democratic Council, and the Manbij operation suggested that the system could be a feasible alternative for all of Syria.

The Syrian war has killed hundreds of thousands of people, and ever more perish on a daily basis; it is destroying both urban and rural spaces, the country's infrastructure, and the natural environment. It has forcibly displaced millions of Syrians, accounting for much of the present "refugee crisis" in Europe. Yet liberated Rojava has mostly protected itself against such destruction at the hands of IS and others.

Within the Republic of Turkey, the Rojava Revolution and the Syrian war are much on the political agenda. Millions of Kurds live within its borders, most of them close to the Kurdish freedom movement and most of whom strongly support the Rojava Revolution. Revolutionary, socialist, leftist, libertarian, and other groups and individuals in Turkey also increasingly support the revolution, and many have initiated or deepened relations with the Kurdish freedom movement.

But the governing AKP and other reactionary political parties tend to support, either tacitly or directly, Salafist-jihadist groups like IS, Jabhat Al-Nusra, and Ahrar Al-Sham, or nationalist-chauvinist orga- nizations, like the Syrian National Coalition. When supporters of the Rojava Revolution mounted a widespread popular uprising in October 2014, during the Kobanî war, the Turkish state and its counterinsurgency forces reacted harshly.

In June 2015, Turkish elections were held, and citizens who supported a democratic alliance of peoples turned out to the polls in huge numbers, enough to overcome the 10 percent threshold and give the pro-Kurdish and left Peoples' Democratic Party (HDP) many seats in the Turkish Parliament. That summer massacres in Amed (Diyarbakir) and Suruç (at the border to Kobanî), along with hundreds of other attacks, paved the way for a brutal war against Turkey's free Kurdish and leftist-demo- cratic people.

The AKP government, fearing that the growing leftist-democratic opposition and the growing strength of the Rojava Revolution could lead to the collapse of its political power, stirred up a hateful and racist campaign against the HDP and the Kurdish movement, culminating on October 10, 2015, in a massacre by IS of 102 peace protesters. The ruthless campaign contributed to the success of the AKP in a so-called "snap election" on November 1, 2015. The Turkish state went on to system- atically destroy many Kurdish neighborhoods and cities like in Nisêbîn (Nusaybin), Sîlopî, Şırnak, and Sur—a war crime by any standards. In the basements of Cizre alone around 150 civilians were massacred.

Resistance, however, is escalating, and that fact, along with the continued existence of the Rojava Revolution, is impeding the AKP's foreign policy goals. The Turkish state once hoped to play a decisive role in Middle East politics with the "Sunni Axis," its alliance with Saudi Arabia and Qatar, but that has now lost ground. The involvement of Russia in the Syrian war has further obstructed Turkish influence. The attempted military coup of July 15, 2016, in Turkey was the result of the growing conflict among reactionary forces. Strengthening the revolutionary democratic forces in Rojava and Syria could help defeat the Turkish state's war policy in North Kurdistan.

Meanwhile in Syria, the declaration and establishment of the Federal System of Rojava/Northern Syria in March 2016 has the potential, as a "third way," to rupture the broad dominance of the Assad regime and the chauvinist-Islamist forces. The federation has brought the three cantons together with areas newly liberated from IS. More and more people of different religious, ethnic, and social backgrounds are starting to organize their life outside the repressive Syrian state. They take this step mainly on their own initiative, even as reactionary powers—headed by the Turkish state—seek Rojava's destruction.

The role of regional and international powers is crucial. Ever since the defeat of IS at Kobanî in early 2015, the Rojava cantons and the Syrian Democratic Forces have successfully cooperated on a tactical basis with the United States on the battlefield and at the same enjoyed relatively positive relations with Russia. Rojava's challenge will be to maintain its complex relationships with these powers yet still adhere to the principles of the revolution.

In May 2014, the three of us set off on a journey to Rojava to learn first-hand how the people of northern Syria were achieving the third way. We wanted to know how they had liberated Rojava and organized their self-defense. We wanted to know how they had built a society based on direct democracy and how the decision-making processes worked through the people's councils. We wanted to know how a communal economic life was organized despite the embargo imposed by Turkey and the Kurdish Regional Government (KRG). And we especially wanted to know about the crucial role of women in the Rojava Revolution.

All of us had been active around the Kurdish question in Germany for many years. But this opportunity to go to Rojava excited us as nothing before ever had. On behalf of the TATORT Kurdistan campaign, we traveled first to Silemani (Sulaimaniya) in the KRG, then via Mosul (shortly before it was captured by IS) to Til Koçer (Al Yarubiya). There we crossed the border into Cizîrê, the easternmost of Rojava's cantons. Over the course of four weeks we visited all parts of Cizîrê, including Hesekê and Serêkaniyê. (Two of us, in a second visit, in early 2016, also visited Kobanî.) We interviewed some 120 people (30 more in 2016) and participated in countless conversations. We moved around freely; no door was closed to us. We slept in the homes of activists and private citizens. We were privy to conversations about difficult subjects as well as to self-criticisms, such as most journalists and other outsiders normally never hear. We are grateful to everyone who made possible our journey into Democratic Autonomy and most of all to the activists and freedom fighters on the ground, particularly the women, the core of this revolution.

This book reflects our observations about the political atmosphere as we found it in May 2014 and early 2016. We make no claims to "objectivity" as defined by the hegemonic authority of science. Claims to objectivity are actually inextricable from subjectivity and are often used to conceal the investigator's original purpose. Each of us comes from different backgrounds and interest areas, but we share a feminist, internationalist, ecological, and left-libertarian approach. We are open and transparent about our solidarity with the Rojava Revolution, yet our solidarity is not of the kind that ignores problems and difficulties.

The time we spent with the women activists and fighters in Rojava revealed to us that the events of July 2012 and after unquestionably constitute a revolution. The activists' patient encouragement of all members of the society to voluntarily participate in decision-making processes is a rare example of commitment to revolutionary principle. Millions of volunteers are making a great effort to build a polity outside the nation-state, and despite war and embargo, they are wisely shaping a democratic order on the basis of social justice. It is also becoming communalized economically.

The Rojava Revolution has seen several serious cases of human rights violations, but more than most other leftist revolutions in history, this one emphasizes the need to learn from its own mistakes. Activists in Rojava have thoroughly studied world revolutions of the past and early on made a strong internal commitment not to succumb to the dangers of hierarchism and authoritarianism.

Rojava's third way may well be the only solution to the sea of conflicts, massacres, and forcible displacements that are now drowning the Middle

East. At the same time, it has become a beacon of hope for all who resist repression and exploitation and who fight for freedom, equality, and an alternative life. North Kurdistan and Turkey may be the next region where this hope can spread—no, it should be! Political developments in Rojava/Syria and North Kurdistan/Turkey remain as interconnected as they were when the defense of Kobanî began in the autumn of 2014. If the revolution crosses over into Turkey, let us take hold of it!

Michael Knapp
Anja Flach
Ercan Ayboğa
May 2016

Note

1. Before the summer of 2014, IS was named ISIS/ISIL.

Prologue: On the Road to Til Koçer

In May 2014, it was not easy to cross the border from South Kurdistan (in northern Iraq) into Rojava. You could follow smugglers' and guerrillas' routes. Or you could cross at the town of Til Koçer (in Arabic, Al Yarubiya).

The Kurdish Regional Government[1] had installed a pontoon bridge over the Tigris at the small town of Semalka. But its purpose wasn't to allow free travel. It was to induce Rojava's residents to leave, so that those who had enriched themselves in South Kurdistan could gain a foothold in Rojava as well. Later the KRG would open and close the Semalka crossing arbitrarily. It also dug a deep ditch in order to enforce the embargo that was squeezing Rojava from all sides [see 12.3].

On our journey, we were accompanied by two Kurdish exiles from Silemani, Zaher and Sardar. They explained to us that in the KRG, income from its oil—which makes up an extraordinary 17 percent of Iraq's oil income—had produced a nepotistic economy. Much of the population lives on government allotments. Thousands of members of the two ruling parties, the KDP and the PUK, receive a monthly allowance of some 5 million dinars (about $4,200). Peshmerga fighters receive 700,000 dinars (about $588), and police get 900,000 dinars ($756). Anyone tied to one of the two ruling parties is set. People from Bangladesh or the Philippines do the actual work or serve as domestics to former Peshmerga fighters. Often treated practically as slaves, they are poorly paid and even sexually exploited.

The KRG does nothing to develop the local economy, apart from oil, and as a result, nothing much is produced in its lands. Manufactured goods are imported from abroad, mostly from Turkey. The KRG aspires to become a second Dubai, a republic of imports, producing nothing and living entirely off its oil. Even bread and fruit have to be brought in from outside—to the area that was historically known as the Fertile Crescent, the cradle of agriculture.

In Silemani, we met refugees from Rojava who told us that in order to earn a living, they had to submit to the KRG's despotism. Azad and

Derman, ages 15 and 16, came here from Qamişlo (a city in Rojava; in Arabic, Al-Qamishli, in Syriac, Qamishlo), and worked for a year at a construction site for a Turkish firm. Their salary had been contractually set at $2,000, and they intended to send it back to their families in Qamişlo. But to date they had received almost nothing. The KRG had no independent justice system where they could press their claim. So they had recently begun to work for a private builder as floor tilers. When they need support, they go to the local office of TEV-DEM [see 6.2], which represents Kurds from Rojava.

South Kurdistan is transforming itself into a concrete wasteland, channeling its wealth into an out-of-control building boom. In the majority-Kurdish city of Kirkuk, our driver, Mahmoud, told us that the simple people had no security, and they couldn't move up in society. Politicians always promised a lot but delivered nothing. Recent elections in South Kurdistan brought at least a little hope, he said.[2] The new Gorran Party had won the election in Silemani. Mahmoud didn't hope for much from it, but at least it published the state budget. Still, it was opportunistic, and apart from disclosing existing government corruption, it offered no program of its own.

Mahmoud had been much better off under the butcher Saddam Hussein, he told us. Back then the government subsidized basic foodstuffs. His father had been a driver too, and was able to feed ten children, but Mahmoud couldn't provide properly even for his three. Anyone who didn't belong to the KDP or PUK, he said, and anyone who supported the Kurdish freedom movement, wouldn't be able to find work in the all-controlling KRG machine. Our two British co-travelers said it could be worse: in Nigeria, none of the people at all benefit from the oil wealth.

We entered Mosul, which IS was in the process of taking over. The streets were lined with military posts, and there was a checkpoint at every corner. The soldiers, from their uniforms to their tanks, were fitted out with American equipment.

In the 1920s, Mosul was a predominantly Kurdish and Christian city, but the Kurds and Christians had mostly been expelled. A city of 4 million, its appearance shocked us—there was dust and dirt everywhere, and soldiers were stationed on every street corner. Traffic roiled through filthy canyons. Bombed-out houses and loose electrical cables contributed to the apocalyptic picture. *Wear a headscarf when you're traveling near Mosul,* someone had advised us. (Only a week after our return journey, Mosul would be overrun by IS.)

As we left Mosul, soldiers were still visible. The driver said the army held the streets only with great effort. Our companions told us to put our heads down whenever Iraqi military or police came into view, because they were often collaborating with IS.

At Til Koçer, that border point between South Kurdistan and Rojava, we had difficulty obtaining an entry permit. After a long ordeal, we were finally able to cross, and then: we are in free Rojava!

The landscape is very different here. Wheatfields extend to the horizon. Rojava is the breadbasket of Syria, producing 60 percent of the country's wheat. A million tons of wheat are produced here annually, we will later learn, but only 10,000 tons are consumed. As a result of the embargo [*see* 12.3], all Rojava's trade routes are blocked, and it can't export wheat. The street signs, erected after the liberation, bear Kurdish names. Images of martyred fighters abound.

As we pass through the small city of Tirbespî (in Arabic, Al-Qahtaniyah), we see a bombed-out house. Two months earlier the Islamists attacked it, explains our companion Cûdî, martyring a *heval*.[3] But the YPG [*see* 8.1] fended them off, so they are now trying suicide bombs. To prevent attacks, Asayîş and volunteers patrol the streets in

Figure P.1   A house bombed to rubble in Tirbespî

24-hour shifts. They don't earn any salary—they just want to protect their free country.

Despite the bombed-out house, our first impression of Rojava is as a place of peace and beauty. Mud-plastered houses merge into the terrain, and sheep graze peacefully along the roads. What a contrast with the menacing landscapes, the rude cities of concrete, on the Iraqi side. Welcome to the Rojava Revolution!

Notes

1. The Kurdistan Regional Government (Kurdish: Hikûmetî Herêmî Kurdistan) is the official governing body of the predominantly Kurdish region in northern Iraq, referred to as Iraqi Kurdistan or South Kurdistan. The KRG was created by the Iraqi Constitution of 2005 and is governed by the Democratic Party of Kurdistan (KDP).
2. On the KDP, *see* 14.6. The KDP and PUK duopoly had been in power for 19 years in September 2013 when new parliamentary elections were held and the new Gorran Party gained the second most votes, thereby breaking the duopoly.
3. The Kurdish word *heval* means "friend" and is used in the sense of "comrade."

1

Background

The name *Kurdistan* ("Land of the Kurds") first appeared in Arabic historical writing in the twelfth century, referring to the region where the eastern foothills of the Taurus Mountains meet the northern Zagros range.[1] Estimates of the number of Kurds in the world vary considerably, but the most realistic range from 35–40 million; of that number, about 19 million live in Turkey, 10–18 million in Iran, 5.6 million in Iraq, 3 million in Syria, 0.5 million in the former Soviet Union, and about 1 million in Europe.[2]

The Kurds are the third largest ethnic group in the Middle East, after Arabs and Turks. Today, the area of Kurdish settlement, while relatively compact, straddles Turkey, Iraq, Iran, and Syria. The region is of strategic importance due, among other things, to its wealth in water. The Tigris and Euphrates rivers, which supply water for Syria and Iraq, flow through the Turkish part of Kurdistan (Bakûr).

Linguists agree that the Kurdish language belongs to the Iranian branch of the Indo-European family, although Kurdish differs significantly from Persian. There is no common, standard Kurdish language, nor even a standard alphabet or script, owing in part to the division of Kurdistan and to the bans on Kurdish language in the various states. Kurdish can be divided into five main dialects or dialect groups: Kurmancî, the southern dialects (Soranî, Silemanî, Mukrî), the southeastern dialects (Sinei, Kimanşah, Lekî), Zaza (sometimes considered a separate language), and Guranî.[3] These dialects are so different that speakers can't readily understand each other.

As to the Kurdish people, we have no certain knowledge of their origin. Researchers, nationalists (both Kurdish and Turkish), and even the PKK have all offered theories, depending on ideological orientation. Kemalism, the official state ideology of Turkey, upholds the "indivisible unity of the State with its country and its nation."[4] According to Kemalism, all citizens of Turkey are Turks, and any aspiration to recognition of a non-Turkish identity is persecuted as separatism. Turks insist that the Kurds descended from the Turkic peoples.

Many Kurds, for their part, consider the ancient Medes their forebears. The PKK's first program, issued in 1978, states, "Our people first attempted to reside on our land in the first millennium BCE, when the Medes, progenitors of our nation, stepped onto the stage of history."[5] When Kurds try to legitimize their rights as a nation to live in Kurdistan, their arguments tend to rest on territorial settlement rather than consanguineous ancestry.[6] But assumptions about continuous Kurdish settlement and descent from the Medes entered the collective understanding long ago.

1.1 Geography of Rojava

During the Ottoman Empire (1299–1922), nomadic Arabs entered the area that is now northern Syria, where they encountered the local Kurds. A central trade route connected Aleppo with Mosul and today's southern Iraq. Between the two world wars, Kurds and Christians fleeing persecution in Turkey settled here. Together with the region's nomads, they make up the bulk of Rojava's population today.

In 1923, the victors in World War I created the 511-mile (822-kilometer) border dividing Syria and Turkey. This arbitrary line was drawn between Jarabulus and Nisêbîn (in Turkish, Nusaybin) along the route of the Berlin-Baghdad Railway.

Three islands of mostly Kurdish settlement lie just south of that border. The easternmost is Cizîrê, which also abuts Iraq for a short stretch of the Tigris; the middle island is Kobanî, and the westernmost is Afrîn. Due south of Cizîrê, in Iraq, lie the Şengal mountains (also called Sinjar), which are inhabited by Kurdish Ezidis.

In July 2012, during the Syrian war, the Kurdish movement was able to liberate these three majority-Kurdish regions from the Ba'ath regime. In January 2014, these three regions declared themselves cantons and embarked on the task of establishing a Democratic Autonomous Administration.[7] Each canton is currently under the administration of a transitional government. In March 2016, the Federal System of Rojava/Northern Syria was declared [see 6.9], encompassing the three cantons and some ethnically mixed areas that had recently been liberated from IS.

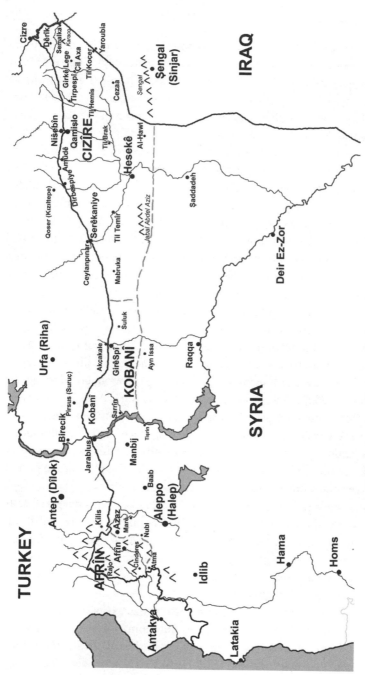

Figure 1.1 Rojava's three cantons: Afrîn, Kobanî, and Cizîrê

Afrîn Canton

Afrîn (in Arabic, Afrin), the westernmost canton, is bounded by the Turkish provinces to the north (Kilis) and west (Hatay). Covering about 800 square miles (2,070 square kilometers), it includes eight towns— Afrîn city in the center, then Şêrawa, Cindirês, Mabata, Reco, Bilbilê, Şiyê, and Şera—and 366 villages. Afrîn canton also encompasses the highland known as Kurd Dagh ("Mountain of the Kurds"; in Kurdish, Çiyayê Kurd or Kurmanc; in Arabic, Jabal al-Akrad), which rises westward to the Turkish border and southward and eastward to the Afrîn River, extending slightly beyond. Kurd Dagh is 4,163 feet (1,269 meters) high.[8]

Afrîn city was founded at a junction of nineteenth-century trade routes. In 1929, its population numbered approximately 800, but by 1968 it had risen to about 7,000 and in 2003 to 36,562.[9] At the onset of the Syrian civil war in 2011, the canton's population was estimated at 400,000, but once the attacks began, many refugees from Aleppo immigrated to Afrîn, boosting the population to 1.2 million.

Most of the inhabitants are Sunni Muslim Kurds. Additionally, about 8,000 Alevi Kurds live in Afrîn, mostly in the northern town of Mabata,[10] where a small number of Turkmens also live. A number of Ezidi Kurd villages contain between 7,500 and 10,000 inhabitants, which are called here Zawaştrî. According to the canton's foreign relations board president, Silêman Ceefer, about 10 percent of the population is Arab. In contrast to the other cantons, aşîret (tribes) no longer play a significant role here.

Afrîn's terrain is mostly upland, having been settled continuously since antiquity and unthreatened by nomads. It differs in this respect from the two other cantons, which came under the plow in the period between the world wars.[11] The climate is Mediterranean with average annual rainfall of 15–20 inches. In the lowlands, Afrîn's deep, red soils are cultivated intensively, using groundwater pumps powered by diesel. Wheat, cotton, citrus fruits, pomegranates, melons, grapes, and figs are harvested, but the main crop is olives; by some estimates, the canton has more than 13 million olive trees. Beyond the region, the olives are renowned for their high quality.[12]

Afrîn, under the Syrian administrative system, is part of the Aleppo Governorate. It declared Democratic Autonomy on January 29, 2014. The assembly elected Hêvî Îbrahîm Mustafa board chair, who in turn appointed Remzi Şêxmus and Ebdil Hemid Mistefa her deputies.[13]

4

Kobanî Canton

Some 61 miles (98 kilometers) east of Afrîn lies Kobanî (in Arabic, Ayn Al-Arab). Situated at about 1,710 feet (520 meters) above sea level, it is economically significant for grain cultivation. The Euphrates, which provides most of Syria's water, marks the canton's western boundary; its waters reach their highest levels in April and May, after the North Kurdistan snowmelt.[14] Due to its border location and its rich freshwater resources, Kobanî canton is of great strategic importance.

Its capital, Kobanî city, was founded in 1892 as a company town during the construction of the Berlin-Baghdad Railway. The name *Kobanî* is thought to be a corruption of the German word *Kompanie* (company). The artificial Syrian-Turkish border, drawn in 1923, divided the city: the Turkish border town Mürşitpinar (in Kurdish, Etmenek), north of the railroad, was formerly a suburb of Syrian Kobanî. Northeast of Mürşitpinar, the nearest town is Suruç (Kurdish Pirsûs), in Urfa province. While Kobanî was under Syrian occupation, it had an Arabic name, Ayn Al-Arab, which means "spring" or "eye of the Arabs."

Kurdish *aşîret* long lived in the Kobanî region. Many of them were nomadic.[15] During the twentieth century, Kurdish refugees fleeing persecution in Turkey made Kobanî their home. Turkmens also live in Kobanî, and Armenian refugees settled here as well, fleeing persecution by the Ottoman Empire, but most left in the 1960s for Aleppo or Armenia. At the time of the 2011 Syrian uprising, an estimated 200,000 people lived in Kobanî region.[16] During the Syrian civil war, the massive migrations within Syria expanded the population to around 400,000. As for Kobanî city, before 2011, it had 54,681 inhabitants, mostly Kurds, but it now has more than 100,000.[17]

On July 19, 2012, Kobanî city was the first in Rojava to expel the Ba'ath regime. Kobanî canton declared autonomy on January 27, 2014. The head of Kobanî's executive council is Enver Muslim, who appointed Bêrîvan Hesen and Xalid Birgil his deputies. Like Afrîn canton, Kobanî canton, under Syrian administration, is part of the Aleppo Governorate.

In late 2013, IS attempted to capture the canton and the city, but the YPG and YPJ [*see* 8.1 and 8.2] repeatedly repulsed its attack. In mid-September 2014, the Islamist militias commenced another major offensive on the city. Isolated from Afrîn and Cizîrê, Kobanî was surrounded by enemies. Most of the population fled, leaving only fighters to mount a defense. The resistance drew much global attention and was supported significantly by people of North Kurdistan and also by the US-led international coalition with air strikes. In January 2015, the YPG/YPJ liberated Kobanî and drove IS from the area.

By the beginning of 2016, even though 80 percent of Kobanî city and villages had been destroyed, two-thirds of the population had returned. Before the war, tribal membership had great meaning for many in Kobanî, but wounded fighters from Rojava, brought to Germany for treatment, reported in November 2015 that since the war, tribal membership had become meaningless, while a close bond with the new political structures of the revolution and the YPG/YPJ has grown.

At the time of our May 2014 visit, the 61 miles (98 kilometers) separating Afrîn and Kobanî were partly controlled by the Free Syrian Army (FSA) [see 14.1] and by Jabhat Al-Akrad (associated with the YPG),[18] but since end of 2014, IS terror militias controlled most of the area. The Turkish Army wanted to establish a "buffer zone" between the two cantons, to prevent the YPG/YPJ from also controlling this stretch, which includes Jarabulus, an important supply route for IS.

In June 2015 the YPG/YPJ and Burkan Al-Firat (an FSA group) liberated Girê Spî (in Arabic, Til Abyad), which lay between Cizîrê and Kobanî cantons. A mixed Kurdish, Arab, and Turkmen self-administration was established there. The liberated area was annexed to Kobanî canton, thus closing the gap between Cizîrê and Kobanî cantons.

Cizîrê Canton

Cizîrê (in Arabic, Jazīrat Ibn 'Umar, and in Aramaic, Canton Gozarto), situated about 30 miles (48 kilometers) east of Kobanî canton, is the largest of the three cantons, stretching 174 miles (280 kilometers) along the Turkish border. It encompasses 8,880 square miles (23,000 square kilometers).

The landscape is dominated by wheatfields interspersed with numerous tells, after which many towns are named: Til Koçer, Til Brak (in Arabic, Tall Brak), Til Temir (in Arabic, Tall Tamir).[19] The only elevation in the canton is Karaçox, between Dêrîka Hemko (in Arabic, Al Mālikiyah, and in Syriac, Dayrik) and Rimelan (in Arabic, Rmelan), but at 2,460 feet (750 meters) above sea level, it is not very high. Southwest of Hesekê (in Arabic, Al-Hasakah) stand the Kezwan (in Arabic, Abd al-Aziz) mountains, about 920 meters high, and east of Hesekê is the Kewkeb, a volcanic cone of about 300 meters. Driving west through Cizîrê, one can see the Cûdî and Bagok mountains, off to the right on Turkish territory, and to the left (that is, to the south), the Şengal range.

Cizîrê is home to 1.377 million inhabitants, averaging 60 people per square kilometer. While most residents of Afrîn and Kobanî cantons are Kurds, Cizîrê's population is ethnically diverse, comprising Kurds, Syriacs, Arabs, and Armenians. Today, in the wake of the revolution, Cizîrê has three official languages: Kurdish (Kurmancî), Aramaic, and Arabic. Many Arab villages have been liberated, and many people from Deir ez-Zor and Raqqa (in Arabic, Ar-Raqqa) have fled to Cizîrê canton, while many Kurds and Christians have emigrated to Europe.

Cizîrê is dotted with 1,717 villages, of which 1,161 are predominantly Arab—the Ba'ath regime settled Arabs here during the 1960s [see 2.2], and Arabs now make up 54 percent of the population. Kurds make up 42 percent of the population, and 453 villages are predominantly Kurdish. Fifty villages are mainly populated by Syriacs, who are 2.9 percent of Cizîrê's population. Forty-eight villages are inhabited equally by Arabs and Kurds, while three have equal populations of Arabs and Syriacs, and two, Syriacs and Kurds.[20]

Most cities have three names: a city in the far northeast is called in Arabic, Al-Malikiya; in Aramaic, Dêrîk; and in Kurdish, Dêrîka Hemko. Qamişlo is its administrative center, but since parts of that city are still under control of the Ba'ath regime, aspects of the administration have been shifted to the city of Amûdê. Under the Syrian administration, Cizîrê canton belongs technically to the Al-Hasakah Governorate.

All four ethnic communities (Kurds, Arabs, Armenians, and Syriacs) are represented in Cizîre's 101-seat Legislative Assembly. The canton's current board president is Ekram Hesso, a Kurd; the deputy board presidents are Hussein Taza Al Azam (an Arab) and Elisabeth Gawriye (a Syriac).[21]

Cizîrê comprises several districts: Dêrîk, Qamişlo, Serêkaniyê, and Hesekê.

Dêrîka Hemko

Dêrîk (the name is often used also by Kurds) is a city of 75,000 in the northeast, near the borders with Turkey and Iraq. In 2004, about 189,634 people were living there. The majority of Dêrîk's inhabitants are Kurds, followed by Syriacs, Armenians, and a few Arabs. The northern part of the city is inhabited by Kurds, the south by Syriacs. Under the Assad regime, numerous Alawites lived in the region, working as government officials, but most have since left Rojava. Other cities in the Dêrîk district are Girkê Legê, Çil Axa, and Til Koçer.

Social organization through *aşîrets* is still important, especially among some parts of the Arab population. Crops grown in the region include wheat, barley, lentils, and cotton. Much of Syria's oil comes from Dêrîk.

Qamişlo

The Qamişlo district includes the city of Qamişlo and the towns of Til Hemîs (in Arabic, Tall Hemis), Amûdê (in Arabic, Amuda), and Tirbespî. The French Army established Qamişlo city in 1926 to serve as an administrative center and military garrison; it also served as a home for Christian refugees from Turkey, and many Syriacs still live there today. The Syrian-Turkish border divides the city—the part located on the Turkish side is called Nisêbîn.

In 2004, Qamişlo city had 184,231 inhabitants; together with its 557 surrounding villages, Qamişlo district had 423,368 inhabitants.[22] Due to the many refugees, these numbers are larger now—in April 2013, some 800,000 people lived in the city and its surroundings.[23]

Serêkaniyê

The city of Serêkaniyê (Kurdish for "At the Source"; in Arabic, Ra's al-'Ain; in Syriac, Res Ayna) was established in 2000 BCE, it is said, under the Mitanni empire. It too is divided by the border: the northern part (today Ceylanpınar) is occupied by Turkey.

The Serêkaniyê district is home to Kurds, Arabs, Syriacs, and Chechens. In 2010, its population was estimated at 55,000; the current population is unknown. Kurds and Arabs are approximately equal in number. The district's 279 villages are mostly Arabic, and a smaller number are Kurdish; there are also Syriac and some Ezidi villages. From January until July 2013, Islamists of Jabhat Al-Nusra as well as FSA units occupied Serêkaniyê [see 8.4].

Hesekê

Hesekê, settled by Syriacs fleeing the Ottoman Empire, was established in the 1920s and 1930s by the French Mandate. In 2011, the city's estimated population was 188,000.[24] Northern Hesekê is predominantly inhabited by Kurds; Syriacs are the second largest population group, followed by Arabs. Among the 595 villages in the region are a number of Syriac villages. The Hesekê district includes the cities of Temir, Hol, and Al-Shaddadî.

Stock farming and village agriculture were traditional here, but in the mid-twentieth century, large-scale land cultivation began, made possible by modern machinery. The Xabur (in Arabic, Al-Khabur; in Syriac, Khabur) River, supplied by several highly fertile karst springs near Serêkaniyê, is an important source of water.[25]

After the Ba'ath regime took power in 1963, it distributed huge fields among the semi-nomadic stock farmers there, who began to cultivate grain and cotton. The Xabur Project built several dams and channels to irrigate 16,000 square kilometers of fields for the future breadbasket of Syria. The growing population and the continuous expansion of the fields into the steppe are contributing to a water shortage today [see 13.2].

1.2   Historical Overview

If Mesopotamia's long history has lasted an hour, then the nation-state has existed for only a second. The region's recent history, which is the focus of this book, can be understood only in the context of its far distant past, which this brief overview will sketch.

Prehistory and Ancient History

Mesopotamia is one of three places on the globe (the others are China and America) where the Neolithic Revolution took place. Starting in 15,000 BCE, for reasons that are still debated, human beings gradually shifted from hunting and gathering ways of life to agricultural settlements.[26]

The oldest known Neolithic edifice is located in North Kurdistan, at Xerawreşk (Göbekli Tepe; in English, Potbelly Hill). Dated at 10,500 BCE, it seems to have been a place of assembly or a temple complex, with massive stone pillars. Cult and religion often became professionalized as a society needed to interpret celestial objects and to determine sowing and harvest seasons. The likely turn to a professional priesthood may have led to the earliest social stratification, in which priests as specialists lived on the farmers' surplus while they interpreted the stars.

Urban society emerged in the fourth millennium BCE with the first large cities such as Tell Brak (in today's Cizîrê canton) and Uruk (in what now is southern Iraq). Innovations such as writing, irrigation, and transportation are deeply intertwined with these settlements. From city-states such as Urkesh (at Girê Mozan, near present-day Amûdê) in present-day Rojava, and elsewhere in upper Mesopotamia, the earliest states arose.

Beginning in the fifth millennium BCE, in mythology, the strong female goddesses typical of the Neolithic age (as found on Tell Halaf, dating to 6000 BCE) gave way to myths of patriarchal domination. The temple became the center of the economy, from where the grain supply was distributed.[27] The surplus produce made possible monumental architecture such as Uruk's five-mile-long city wall.[28]

Patriarchal rule was extended from Uruk to Babylon. While we have evidence of female scribes and rulers in Sumerian and Akkadian times,[29] the development of centralized statehood, especially in the second and the first millennia BCE, seems closely connected to the subjugation and exploitation of women.

Present-day Rojava was thus a highly dynamic place in ancient history. The Assyrians and the Hittites annexed the region, but in the eleventh century BCE, as the Sea Peoples—apparently a melding of peasant rebels and social bandits—arrived from the west, the Hittite kingdom devolved into chaos.[30] Into the resulting power vacuum stepped the Aramaeans, who established small principalities here. These principalities developed cuneiform scripts, creating the alphabetical foundation for written Greek, Latin, Hebrew, and Arabic. In the seventh and eighth centuries BCE, the Assyrians subdued the Aramaean principalities, but the Aramaean language became the lingua franca in western Mesopotamia.[31] Persian rule followed, then the Macedonian conquest (under Alexander the Great), and then the wars of the Diadochi states, at the beginning of the Hellenistic period. In 62 BCE, the region of present-day Syria became part of the *Imperium Romanum*. After the rise of Christianity, the eastern Roman Empire spawned diverse creeds that exist today. Debates over Gnostic mysticism, among other elements, influenced the formation of the Alawite religion in Syria.

At the beginning of the Islamic expansion, Muslim/Arab troops conquered eastern Roman Syria at the Battle of Yarmouk in 636 CE, and the Umayyad caliphs ruled the region from Damascus. In 750 CE, the Abbasids overthrew the Umayyads and moved the caliphate's seat to Baghdad. Thereafter came fragmentation among the principalities, skirmishes with Crusaders, and Egyptian rule. Finally, in 1516, the Ottoman Empire overran Syria. Ottoman rule continued, punctuated by insurrections, until 1918. The Ottoman Empire, a close German ally, collapsed at the end of World War I. Germany, Russia, Britain, and France were the main actors to pursue interests in the remnants of the Ottoman Empire.

Colonialism, Pan-Arabism, and the Ba'ath Party

On May 16, 1916, Britain and France secretly concluded the Sykes-Picot Agreement, which defined their respective spheres of colonial interest— and the political divisions of the Middle East for the next century. Syria was to go to France. The San Remo conference of 1920 divided the Middle East into parts that favored the interests of the colonial powers England and France, and re-drew the region into the mandated territories of Syria and Iraq.

The unstable new states of Syria and Iraq "were cobbled together from various ethnic, religious, and denominational groups," observes the Turkish political scientist Haluk Gerger. "Kurdistan was dismembered, and the Kurdish people stripped of status. Kurdistan's petroleum-rich regions were apportioned to Syria and Iraq—states under the colonial control of France and England—while Turkey received the northern part of Kurdistan."[32]

In Syria, French policies under the Mandate were classically colonialist, attempting to foster a class of compradors—that is, to bind large landholders and other members of the upper class to itself. France privileged members of the Alawite, Christian, and Druze minorities and installed them in military and administrative positions.[33] French banks and corporations gained privileges to plunder resources. Under pressure from Britain, France formed a Syrian state around Damascus and in the Aleppo region, adding more regions in 1937. In the 1930s, Syrian Kurds rebelled against Arab rule from Damascus and agitated for autonomy in Cizîrê. In response, in 1938, the French government placed Cizîrê under its direct control.[34]

During World War II, the Allies repeatedly promised Syrian independence, but was only under pressure of riots and rebellions and British intervention did the last French troops finally depart the region on April 15, 1946.[35] Two days later, the independent Republic of Syria was declared. The old elites remained in power, but more Syrians, through military careers or education, were rising into the middle class. Christian minorities had the advantage of support from abroad and from missionaries, while the Sunni population was socially disadvantaged.[36] In the countryside, a growing challenge to the conservative landowners led to a flowering of socialist and communist movements, but also nationalist and religious ones.[37]

As an antithesis to this, colonial policies had generated a pan-Arabist discourse, influenced by European nationalism and especially German romanticism.[38] The Muslim Brotherhood, founded in Egypt in 1928, was active in Syria by 1945–46, combining Islamic law with a social program. But pan-Arabist identity was built on nationalism, not on religion.[39] Syria's Ba'ath ("Reawakening") Party, founded in 1940, sought to stimulate pan-Arabist consciousness: it was secular and anti-imperialist, offering careers to supporters of Arab nationalism.[40] It offered a limited socialist program that was intended to channel and thus contain the more radical socialist movements. The Ba'ath Party found support among Druze, Alawites, Christians, and the rising middle classes, far more than among Syria's Sunnis.[41] And by definition, pan-Arabism excluded "non-Arab" population groups, notably the Kurdish people in the north. Partly due to this exclusion, many Kurds joined the Communist Party of Syria,[42] while others founded the Kurdish nationalist El Partî in 1957, from which would issue most of the region's later Kurdish parties.

In 1948, Syria participated in the Palestine war (Israeli war of independence), in which the Israelis decisively defeated the Arab states, expelled 750,000 Palestinians, and established the State of Israel (in what is termed in Arabic Al-Nakba, "the catastrophe"). Within Syria, defeat led to destabilization and turmoil. The army took the opportunity to gain the upper hand. A period of military coups and countercoups ensued: between 1949 and 1956, Syria had twenty different governments and four different constitutions.[43] Many sought closer relations with the Soviet Union for help in realizing the anti-imperialist, pan-Arabist model.

On February 1, 1958, Egypt and Syria declared a union known as the United Arab Republic (UAR).[44] Its intention was for all Arab countries to break with local elites and come together into one pan-Arabist nation. Its "Arab socialist" paradigm stood for strong central government control over all sectors of society: the state would act in the interests of all classes, bringing capitalist and socialist ideas together under the banner of nationalism.[45] It offered land reform and the prohibition of labor unions, to quell the Communist opposition, while its pan-Arabism would eradicate Kurdish opposition.[46] All political parties, including the Ba'ath, were to be dismantled.

The UAR's Egypt-centered administration was unacceptable to Syrian elites, while its program of state control led to further disgruntlement. On September 28, 1961, the Syrian military, supported by the upper classes, declared the Syrian Arab Republic, putting an end to the UAR.[47] The old elites resumed their rule, but with minimal influence from the Ba'ath Party.

Then on March 8, 1963, Ba'athist officers carried out a coup against the old elites.[48] Middle-class military careerists asserted themselves and distributed positions of power among themselves and their clients in the Alawite, Druze, Christian, and Ismaili minorities and, in some cases, even the Sunnis.[49] The party enforced its power against the Communist Party and the Muslim Brotherhood using brute force.[50]

On February 23, 1966, a coup overthrew the traditional Ba'ath leadership, with the support of Syrian Air Force General Hafez Al-Assad, who became minister of defense. On November 16, 1970, Assad seized power and threw the entire former political leadership into jail, creating a system that can best be called a presidential monarchy.

The Assad Dynasty

Hafez Al-Assad's regime combined repression and limited state socialism. He trampled on labor unions and the opposition, but he gained popular support by instituting land reforms, socializing the public sector, and appointing members of the middle and working classes to the civil service. He stabilized it all by a sort of "revolution from above," going beyond Alawite circles, integrating the Sunni population, and allying with their elites.

Assad used the ongoing confrontation with Israel to extend the range of Syria's intelligence service and military. In 1975, Lebanon collapsed into civil war. The left-wing Palestinian Liberation Organization (PLO) sought to use Lebanon as a stepping-stone toward the liberation of Palestine.[51] In 1976, Assad invaded Lebanon, wishing to limit the PLO's influence and prevent left-wing ideas from spreading to Syria. Assad's intervention led to massive protests in Syria. He responded with violent repression and crushed the upheaval.[52] Syria would occupy Lebanon until 2005.

In Syria, membership in the Muslim Brotherhood had been punishable by death since 1980. In February 1982, the Muslim Brotherhood rose up against the Assad regime. One of its instigators, Abu Mus' ab-as Suri, said the Brotherhood used thousands of guns and heavy weapons in the uprising. The jihadists started killing Ba'athists,[53] and the regime reacted with a wide-scale massacre at Hama, killing up to 20,000 people. The Hama massacre led to a social trauma, but the regime crushed all further attempts at rebellion, all opposition, be it from the left or from the Muslim Brotherhood. It expanded the security apparatus with units that enjoyed far-reaching immunity.

By repressing all opposition, Assad stabilized his regime—so much so that upon his death on June 10, 2000, power passed seamlessly to his son Bashar. A "Damascus Spring" was anticipated for Bashar Al-Assad's rule, with hopes that he would expand political liberties, but such hopes were disappointed. In fact, the authoritarian system shed its social aspects and shifted to neoliberalism. The state now promoted economic liberalization.[54] State-owned lands were privatized, and public resources were re-distributed based on nepotism. Commercialized agriculture depleted the groundwater, and price controls on pesticides and animal feed were lifted.[55] Assad turned against the unions, even though they were cowed and loyal to the state—he now considered them an obstacle to economic liberalization and cut off their financing. Economic liberalization led to an influx of foreign investment, especially from Kuwait, Qatar, and the Emirates, but plunged the rural population into poverty. Rojava was one of the regions most affected, forcing Kurds to migrate to the cities. As the last remnants of the social state were dismantled, and as the public sector was devastated and capital accumulated in the hands of the few, popular suffering heightened.

In 2010, Bashar al-Assad streamlined the Ba'ath Party's structure so that it could implement decisions without friction. Officialdom came to be represented mainly by corrupt security forces. The distance between state and population widened, and traditional sources of authority were strengthened. A new free-trade zone flooded local markets with cheap goods, devastating small shops and workshops, the economic backbone of Middle Eastern economies. Wages collapsed, so that in 2010, 61 percent of workers earned less than $190 per month.[56] Investment was channeled into the service sector and into tourism and hotels, while only 13 percent went into production.[57] The social question became more pressing, yet repression and corruption intensified, culminating finally, in 2011, in revolt. Many people in Syria welcomed the Arab Spring.

Notes

1. Vladimir Minorsky, "Kurden-Kurdistan," in *Enzyklopädie des Islam, Geographisches, Ethnographisches, und Biographisches Wörterbuch der Mohammedanischen Völker* (Leiden/Leipzig, 1927).

2. *Kurdistan heute* 18 (May–June 1996), http://bit.ly/1Mhzfku.

3. Hüseyin Ağuiçenoğlu, *Genese des türkischen und kurdischen Nationalismus im Vergleich* (Münster, 1997), p. 182; Martin van Bruinessen, *Agha, Scheich und Staat: Politik und Gesellschaft Kurdistans* (Berlin, 1989), p. 37; Minorsky, "Kurden-Kurdistan," p. 1234.

4. Ismail Beşikçi, *Kurdistan: Internationale Kolonie* (Frankfurt a. M., 1991), p. 31. Kemalism originated with the Turkish state's founder Mustafa Kemal, called Atatürk (Father of the Turks).

5. PKK Program (Cologne, 1978/1984).

6. Andrea Fischer-Tahir, *"Wir gaben viele Märtyrer": Widerstand und kollektive Identitätsbildung in Irakisch-Kurdistan* (Münster, 2003), p. 55.

7. "Alle kurdischen Kantone rufen Demokratische Autonomie aus," *Civaka Azad*, January 31, 2014, http://bit.ly/1dUwqHQ.

8. Katharina Lange, "Peripheral Experiences: Everyday Life in Kurd Dagh (Northern Syria) during the Allied Occupation in the Second World War," in Heike Liebau et al., eds., *The World in World Wars: Perspectives, Experiences and Perceptions from Asia and Africa* (Leiden, 2010), pp. 401–28.

9. "Syria," City Population, citypopulation.de/Syria.html.

10. Alevis are not to be confused with Alawites. The name "Alawite" derives from reverence for Ali, the son-in-law of the Prophet Muhammad, and for the line of the twelve Shiite imams descended from Muhammad through his daughter from Fatima. Until the twentieth century, the name "Nusayris" was more common, referring to Ibn Nusayr, a ninth-century Iraqi cleric: Lieselotte Abid, "Die Religion ist für Gott—das Land ist für alle," in Fritz Edlinger and Tyma Kraitt, eds., *Syrien. Hintergründe, Analysen, Berichte* (Vienna, 2013).

11. Eugen Wirth, *Syrien, eine geographische Landeskunde* (Darmstadt, 1971).

12. Mohamed Cheikh Dibes, *Die Wochenmärkte in Nordsyrien*, vol. 13 of *Mainzer Geographische Studien* (Mainz, 1978).

13. "Syrian Kurds Celebrate Auto Administration," *ARA News*, February 15, 2015, http://bit.ly/29DIMDY4.

14. Wirth, *Syrien*.

15. Günter Meyer, *Ländliche Lebens- und Wirtschaftsformen Syriens im Wandel: Sozialgeographische Studien zur Entwicklung im bäuerlichen und nomadischen Lebensraum* (Erlangen: Fränkische Geographische Gesellschaft, 1984).

16. "Course and Development of the Fighting in Kobanî," *Rojava Report*, July 22, 2014, http://bit.ly/1QeiBF9.

17. Harvey Morris, "Kobanî Under Intense ISIS Attack, Excluded from UN Humanitarian Aid," *Rudaw*, July 17, 2014, http://bit.ly/1Qr2Wgr.

18. Jabhat Al-Akrad (Brigade of the Kurdish Front; in Kurdish, Enîya Kurdan) is a predominantly Kurdish rebel group that fights alongside other organizations against the Assad regime and against IS. Al-Akrad was founded as part of the FSA, but after battling ISIS in August 2013, it was excluded from the FSA because of its presumed ties to the PYD.

19. Tell, from Arabic *tall*, or hill; an ancient elevation consisting of the remains of repeated settlements.

20. "Amajeyek ji kantona cizîrê li Rojava re …," Kanton Rojava, June 2, 2015, http://bit.ly/1NMTl5W.

21. Karlos Zurutuza, "Democracy Is 'Radical' In Northern Syria," IPS News Agency, December 21, 2015, http://bit.ly/1Qb3ZWF.

22. "Syria," City Population, http://citypopulation.de/Syria.html.

23. Mako Qocgiri, "Aufbau der demokratischen Autonomie in Qamişlo," *Civaka Azad*, April 1, 2013, http://bit.ly/1HgDc5W.

24. "Syria," City Population, citypopulation.de/Syria.html.

25. Hans Hopfinger, *Öffentliche und private Landwirtschaft in Syrien* (Erlangen, 1991).

26. Klaus Schmidt, *Sie bauten die ersten Tempel: Das rätselhafte Heiligtum der Steinzeitjäger: Die archäolgische Entdeckung am Göbekli Tepe* (Munich, 2006), p. 37.

27. Heather D. Baker, "Wirtschaft und Verwaltung in Babylonien," in Deutsches Archäologisches Institut et al., eds., *Uruk: 5000 Jahre Megacity* (Petersberg, 2013), pp. 275–81.

28. In the Gilgamesh Epic, one of the oldest written epic poems, the hero Gilgamesh is the king of Uruk, the Sumerian city that is said to have had the first city wall.

29. Helga Vogel, "Frauen in Mesopotamien: Lebenswelten sumerischer Stadt-fürstinnen, " *Antike Welt*, February 2015, http://bit.ly/1PoTcLe.

30. Isaac Finkelstein and Neil Asher Silberman, *The Bible Unearthed: Archaeology's New Vision of Ancient Israel and the Origin of Its Sacred Texts* (New York, 2002), p. 105.

31. Marc van de Mieroop, *A History of the Ancient Near East, ca. 3000-323 B.C.* (Hoboken, NJ, 2007), p. 203.

32. Haluk Gerger, "Zerbricht die Ordnung in Mittleren Osten?," *Kurdistan Report*, no. 174 (July–August 2014), http://bit.ly/1It5YyV.

33. John McHugo, *Syria: A Recent History* (London, 2015), e-Book, loc. 1846.

34. Judith Wolf, "Ausländer im eigenen Land—Buchrezension," *Kurdica—die kurdische Enzyklopädie*, http://bit.ly/1H67p7B; David McDowall, *A Modern History of the Kurds*, 3rd edn. (London, 2003), pp. 470f.

35. McHugo, *Syria*, loc. 1956.

36. Ibid., loc. 1971.

37. Tyma Kraitt, "Das Scheitern des Damaszener Frühlings: Baschar al-Assads uneingelöste Versprechen," in Fritz Edlinger and Tyma Kraitt, eds., *Syrien. Hintergründe, Analysen, Berichte* (Vienna, 2013), p. 34.

38. Carsten Wieland, "Syrien und Irak. Panarabische Paradoxien und der Bankrott des Ba'athismus," in Edlinger and Kraitt, *Syrien*, p. 89.

39. Ibid., p. 91.

40. Ibid., p. 92.

41. Albert Hourani, *A History of the Arab Peoples* (Cambridge, MA, 1991), p. 404.

42. Katharina Lange, "Syrien: Ein historischer Überblick," *Bundeszentrale für politische Bildung*, February 14, 2013, http://bit.ly/1EYMfSW.

43. Kraitt, "Das Scheitern des Damaszener Frühlings," p. 33.

44. Ibid., pp. 34f.

45. Hourami, *History of Arab Peoples*, p. 406.

46. McHugo, *Syria*, locs. 2500, 2516.

47. Ibid., locs. 2500, 2561ff.

48. Lange, "Syrien: Ein historischer Überblick."

49. Raymond Hinnebusch, "Syria: From 'Authoritarian Upgrading' to Revolution?" *International Affairs* 88, no. 1 (2012): 95, and McHugo, *Syria*, loc. 2595.

50. Patrick Seale, *Asad: The Struggle for the Middle East* (London, 1988), p. 83.

51. Manus I. Midlarsky, *The Internationalization of Communal Strife* (London, 1992), p. 112.

52. Kraitt, "Das Scheitern des Damaszener Frühlings," p. 41.

53. McHugo, *Syria*, loc. 3450.

54. Hinnebusch, "From 'Authoritarian Upgrading' to Revolution?" p. 95.

55. Kraitt, "Das Scheitern des Damaszener Frühlings," p. 50.

56. Samir Seifan, cited ibid., p. 51.

57. Hinnebusch, "From 'Authoritarian Upgrading' to Revolution?" p. 98.

2

Rojava's Diverse Cultures

In pursuit of freedom and out of respect for faiths, we as Kurds, Arabs, Syriacs (Assyrians, Chaldeans, Aramaeans), Turkmens, and Chechens declare and establish this charter ... The regions governed by the Democratic Autonomous administration are open to the participation of all ethnic, social, cultural, and national groups through their associations and in constructive understanding, democracy, and pluralism.

Social Contract of Rojava

Of the three cantons, as we have seen, the most ethnically diverse is Cizîrê. "Kurds, Syriacs, and Arabs all live here together—our society is very diverse," we were told when we visited the Dêrîk office of TEV-DEM [see 6.2] in May 2014. "We want friendship, not hostility. We are building the new society together. Everybody can celebrate their own festivals—there are no restrictions."

"Relations among the different groups are very good," the TEV-DEM representative continued: "TEV-DEM itself has Arab, Armenian, and Syriac members. The good relations don't extend to intermarriage—the religious barriers are too high for that. Traditionally Kurds and Christians enjoyed very good relations, but the state created divisions between them. In the schools, teaching is still done in Arabic, but Kurdish and other languages are also available supplementally. About 70 percent of the people in Dêrîk are organized in the council system. We offer our services, of course, to everyone."

At our request, the office arranged for us to visit institutions representing the different groups.

2.1 Kurds

Kurds have a long history in Syria. During Ottoman times, semi-nomadic and nomadic Kurdish *aşîret* (tribes) resided here; some even formed confederations with Arab *aşîret*. "Even in pre-Islamic times," writes Ismet Chérif Vanly, "Kurdish tribes descended from the mountain ranges near Mosul, Mardin, and Cizre, to winter in the milder climate of the steppes of present-day Syrian Cizîre ... Today ... the same tribes still live in Cizîrê in the same places, albeit with the difference that since then the Kurds have become sedentary farmers or urban dwellers, while the members of the [Arab *aşîret*] Tai remained nomads."[1]

Today, most Syrian Kurds are assimilated and have forgotten their language and heritage.[2] Those who identify as Kurds now live mainly in the three autonomous cantons of Rojava. Before the Syrian civil war began, about 600,000 Kurds lived in Damascus and half a million in Aleppo, especially in the Sêx Maqsud neighborhood, but now their numbers are down to about 60,000, as a women's movement activist, Rojîn, told us in November 2014 [*see* 6.4].[3] In all, some three million Kurds live in Rojava.

After World War I, when the Syrian-Turkish border was drawn, many Kurdish nomads abruptly found themselves on one side or the other and were forced to settle down. In the 1920s, the Turkish military carried out pogroms in the territory of the French Mandate, with the result that some Kurdish *aşîret* fled. The French encouraged the Kurds to farm in northern Syria.

The Syrian Arab Republic, since its founding, has always identified itself as an ethnically homogeneous Arab nation-state.[4] The Assad regime therefore pressured the Kurds to assimilate, considering them, as the country's largest ethnic minority, more of a threat than Syriacs and Armenians.

Some Kurds living in Syria had fled there from Turkey, seeking to escape repression. But in 1962, the regime carried out a census of the residents of Hesekê province that required Kurds to prove that they had lived in the region before 1945. Those who could not produce such documents were declared *ajanib* (Arabic for "foreigners"). Even those who had immigrated to Syria in the 1920s and 1930s were now designated *ajanib*. Stripped of their Syrian citizenship, they were considered stateless and could not own property and hence were condemned to poverty.

Other Kurds in Hesekê had been missed by the census altogether—for example, they weren't at home while the census took place. They were categorized as *maktoumeen* (Arabic for "hidden").[5] Not permitted to officially register, and having no identification papers, they encountered even more discrimination than the *ajanib*. They could not apply for passports, work in the public sector, participate in the health or social system, travel internationally, or even stay in a hotel. In some instances, their access to higher education was limited.

In all, some 120,000 to 150,000 Kurds were stripped of their citizenship, leaving them with no legal standing whatever. This condition would be passed down to their descendants.[6] By 2004, there were in Rojava approximately 200,000 *ajanib* and 80,000 to 100,000 *maktoumeen*.[7]

After the 1963 coup that brought the Ba'ath Party to power, it became official ideology that Kurds in Syria were recent immigrants from Turkey. The head of internal security for Heseke province, Muhammad Talab Hilal, developed a twelve-point plan for the Arabization of northern Syria, which he introduced this way: "The bells of Jazira sound the alarm and call on the Arab conscience to save this region, to purify it of all this scum, the dregs of history until, as befits its geographical situation, it can offer up its revenues and riches, along with those of the other provinces of this Arab territory ... The Kurdish question, now that the Kurds are organizing themselves, is a malignant tumor which has developed and been developed in a part of the body of the Arab nation. The only remedy which we can properly apply thereto is excision."[8]

This passage summarizes the way the Syrian government would handle the Kurdish population over the next decades. Hilal's plan included removal of the Kurds from their land, denial of education for Kurds, extradition of "wanted" Kurds to Turkey, denial of job opportunities for Kurds, a divide-and-conquer policy within the Kurdish population, the replacement of Kurdish clerics with Arabs, a propaganda campaign against the Kurds, the settlement of Arabs in Kurdish areas, the establishment of an Arab cordon sanitaire along the Turkish border, the creation of cooperative farms with Arab settlers, denial of the right of non-Arabs to vote or hold office, and denial of Syrian citizenship to non-Arabs who immigrated.[9]

Several of these points had already been implemented with the deprivation of citizenship in 1962; the rest were carried out from 1966 onward. Kurdish landowners who were critical of the system were expropriated. Arabs were forced to settle in the region. The regime "Arabized" the region through the "Arab Belt" policy [*see* 2.2], expropriating Kurdish-owned lands and installing tens of thousands of Arab settlers on the "socialized" acreage. When Hilal's plan became publicly known in 1968, the Ba'ath government denied that it reflected official policy toward the Kurds, but the implementation of its measures belies that denial.

Through the 1990s, life expectancy would increase in Syria, and the number of homes served by electrical power, for example, would soar from a mere 3 percent (in 1963) to 92.11 percent (in 2011).[10] But the Kurdish region would not experience these improvements. The regime excluded, denied, and persecuted the Kurdish people, reducing their region to a domestic colony for internal economic exploitation.

Ezidis

The Ezidis are a community of 800,000 to one million Kurds who speak Kurmancî. They live in South Kurdistan (Başur), North Kurdistan (Bakûr), and Rojava. They have suffered religious persecution for centuries. "Under the Ottoman Empire, there are presumed to have been at least 72 pogroms," says a document of the Federation of Ezidi Associations. In the twentieth century, almost every Islamic country of the Middle East has persecuted them politically and ethnically for their Kurdish identity. Fanatical Muslims insist that by Sharia criteria, Ezidis do not belong to an Abrahamic religion and therefore must be forcibly converted or killed.

The Kurdish community increasingly regards Ezidis as the preservers of ancient Kurdish culture and language. According to the Federation of Ezidi Associations: "The Ezidi religion is monotheistic, originating particularly in Kurdistan. All Ezidis are Kurdish ... [In their religion] the highest angel is the Peacock Angel, the representative of God. Woman plays a particularly important role in Ezidi society, as she gives life alongside God and is therefore sacred. Ezidis believe in reincarnation. Their religion is far older than present-day religions of the book. Their religion being peaceful, the Ezidis do not seek conversion."

The center of Ezidism is Şengal (also known as Sinjar), in northern Iraq, near the border with Rojava. At the Mala Ezîdiyan (House of Ezidis), in Amûdê, the chairman, Şêx Seid Cindo, told us that only 10,000–15,000 Ezidis live in Rojava today. They are concentrated in Afrîn, in some 25 villages, as well as a few villages near Tirbespî. Under the Assad regime, Ezidis in Afrîn and Azaz were well integrated and enjoyed good economic conditions, but in Cizîrê the regime considered them foreigners. "We were very oppressed under the Ba'ath regime," Şêx Seid Cindo explained. "Marriages were Islamized, and children were forced into the Islamic religion. We couldn't celebrate our religious festivals. The regime never appointed Ezidi officials, and its bureaucracy, and its police, repeatedly subjected us to extortion."

But things have changed since the revolution. "Today we are free," he continued. "We are no longer oppressed. In mid-April we celebrated a festival that would have been banned under the regime. TEV-DEM even encouraged us to celebrate it." The Ezidis have organized themselves in the council system, he stressed. Only the YPG/YPJ will protect the Ezidis, he insisted. In Serêkaniyê, jihadists attacked three Ezidi villages and murdered its inhabitants, and they have threatened Ezidis in Afrîn as well.

Ezidis often complain that Europeans encourage them to emigrate rather than help them live safely in their homeland. About 100,000 Ezidis from North Kurdistan now live in Germany,[11] yet when Turkey razed Ezidi villages in the 1990s, the Federal Republic turned a blind eye. In summer 2014, the Ezidis of Şengal were attacked by IS [see 8.9]. Given the current exterminationist policies of IS, international assistance is needed urgently.

2.2   Arabs

In 1921–22, at the outset of the French Mandate, Syria's Arabs were nomads. The first Arab village in Cizîrê was not founded until 1933. During the 1920s, the Kurds and the Arab Şammar tribe clashed repeatedly, as the powers-that-be portrayed the Kurds as recent immigrants from Turkey. In 1945, war broke out between Kurds and the Arab tribes, during which 150 Kurdish villages were looted.

In 1965, the Ba'ath Party decided to establish an Arab Belt along the Turkish border, 200 miles (322 kilometers) long and 6–10 miles wide. The purpose was to shift the area's demography from Kurdish to Arab. The Arab Belt would stretch from Serêkaniyê eastward to the Iraqi border. In 1973, after Hafez al-Assad became head of state, Syria began to implement the Arabization project, under the name "Plan to Build State Model Farms in the Jazirah Region."[12] Forty-one Arab villages were constructed along the Turkish border, and all Kurdish place names there were Arabized. An Arab village was settled next to every Kurdish village. In addition to the residents of the newly built villages, about four thousand Arab families from Raqqa and Aleppo provinces were settled there; they had previously lost their homes due to the construction of the Tabqa Dam, on the Euphrates near Raqqa, and its associated reservoirs. Hence they are referred to as *machmurin*, "victims of the flood."

Under the Arabization program, about 2 million hectares of Kurdish lands were expropriated and handed over to resettled Arabs. The original plan was to deport around 140,000 Kurds, from 332 villages, to the southern desert area of Al-Raad. But the Kurdish farmers refused to abandon their homes. Those who had been declared foreigners (*ajanib*) were not allowed to own property or to build new houses or repair old ones.[13] It was a phased system of privilege and disadvantage in which the Kurds were on the lowest level.

"Many Kurds back then had no identification," the longtime movement activist Heval Amer told us. Those who had been stripped of their citizenship "... couldn't register a child or record a marriage. They could attend school only up to twelfth grade ... My father had two hundred *dunams* of land.[14] Our village, Kaniya Nevî, had fifty households. But all the land was taken from us—only two Kurdish houses remained there. From then on, my father had to find work as an unskilled laborer. I have seven siblings, including five girls. We were very poor."

But in those areas the only possible livelihood was from agriculture, so those whose land was expropriated had to leave. "They went to Damascus," a TEV-DEM representative explained to us. "The children had to leave school and became cheap labor in the Syrian cities." But "to get work in civil service" as a teacher, clerk, etc., Heval Amer told us, "Kurds first had to deny their own Kurdishness. Half of the population became agents of the state, because if you wanted to work, you became an agent."

If economic factors estranged Arabs and Kurds, the nadir of Kurdish-Arab relations was the *serhildan* (uprising) in Qamişlo in 2004 [*see* 4.1], in which several Arab tribes allied with the Ba'ath regime to attack Kurds, and Kurds fought back.

Even in the wake of the 2012 revolution, Heval Amer explained, "some Arab tribal leaders see the Kurds as foreigners in Syria who should have no rights. They consider Syria an Arab-Muslim state." They fear that the Kurds will reclaim their former lands and villages. "If Arabs want to sell some of the land now," Heval Amer continues, "the Kurdish movement says, 'Why should people buy land that actually belongs to us? In the future, the state should compensate the Arabs and return the land to the original owners.'" The land question in Cizîrê is a sensitive issue that awaits a solution.

Figure 2.1   Members of an Arab unit at Til Koçer

Some Arab and Kurdish *aşîret* distrust each other, and reducing that tension will require much diplomatic work on the part of TEV-DEM. Sometimes conflicts break out between Arab *aşîret*, because some of them side with the jihadists and some with the Kurds. The Şarabia and Zubeyd, two of the largest Arab tribes, have many members within the YPG, and one of the most important tribes, the Şammar, supports the Kurds.[15]

But one of the largest *aşîret*, the Şarabia, who had settled in Til Hemîs in 1970, traditionally clash with the Şammar. They participated in the attacks on the Kurds in 2004.[16] Early in the war, jihadists overran Til Hemîs. When the YPG was trying to liberate it, some of the *aşîret* supported the jihadists. This led to the YPG's biggest military defeat, in January 2014, when dozens of fighters lost their lives.[17] Not until February 2015 did the YPG/YPJ liberate Til Hemîs, and nearby Til Barak a month later—in a joint Kurdish-Arab operation.[18]

Most of the Arab tribes prefer not to take sides—they prefer to stay aloof from the conflict, but it's not easy. "The Arab tribes in the area usually support whatever force is strongest at that moment," Heval Amer told us. "Sometimes it's the IS, sometimes the state, and sometimes the YPG." As the Kurdish saying has it: *Whichever way the wind blows*. Since IS's cruelty is fearsome, Arabs must always fear that the jihadists will come back. But most of the Arabs in Rojava did not sympathize with the Islamists who attacked in 2013.

In March 2013, when jihadists overran the Til Koçer region [*see* 8.5], most of the Arab residents fled to the nearby Kurdish villages, where they were graciously accepted. About ninety representatives of the *aşiret* asked the YPG for help. The following October, the YPG liberated Til Koçer, which won the hearts of the Arab and Christian residents, who proceeded to join the YPG in large numbers and even YPJ.

With every victory achieved by the YPG/YPJ and their allies—at Kobanî (January 2015), at Til Hemîs (February 2015), at Girê Spî (June 2015), and at Şengal und Hol (November 2015)—Arab support for the YPG grows stronger. Anti-Kurdish resentments are being tossed overboard. In Cizîrê canton, where Arabs are the majority, the YPG/YPJ have convinced many of them that they are ready to protect them and to provide services like water and electricity. The municipalities' practice of nondiscrimination in ethnically mixed cities is a result of that approach.

After Til Hemîs and Til Barak were liberated, TEV-DEM began to establish the commune system of Democratic Autonomy there. TEV-DEM is making an enormous effort to involve the Arabs, sometimes with great success. Leadership is apportioned according to the composition of the local population, among Arabs, Syriacs, Armenians, and Circassians. The co-chairs of Cizîrê's executive council, for example, are Sheikh Hamedi Daham, head of the Şammar tribe, and Hediye Yusîv, a Kurdish woman who was previously in the YPG leadership.[19]

Today Arab women are seeking support at the facilities offered by Yekîtiya Star, the women's organization [*see* 5.3]. Many have joined YPJ and the Asayîş.

Rojava and especially Cizîrê canton are a splendid example of equitable coexistence in a multi-ethnic and multi-religious region. Here, cultural diversity has been reconceived as an indispensable element of common life and democracy. After the transitional administration was established, its co-chair Ekram Hesso explained, "With the experience that we will gain in the autonomous administration of Gozarto/Cizîrê, we want to serve as a model for a future Syria."

2.3 Armenians and Syriacs

In 1915, to enforce Islamization, the Ottoman Empire issued a call for jihad against all non-Muslim populations within its domains: all non-Turkish populations were to be destroyed. The deportations and massacres that followed cost the lives of 1.5 million Armenians, 750,000 Syriacs, and 500,000 Pontic Greeks, as well as other Christian groups and Ezidis. Syriacs call this dark chapter in their history Seyfo (Aramaic for "Sword"). The Armenians call it Aghet, "Catastrophe." Numerous historical studies have classified the events between 1896 and 1914–18 as genocide.

In carrying it out, Kurdish *aşîret* partly collaborated with the Ottoman Army. In 2013, the Kurdish movement in North Kurdistan accepted historical responsibility and apologized for the Kurdish Hamidiye militia's collaboration with the genocide. It is the only force within Turkey to have done so. The Turkish state still denies these crimes and does not recognize them as genocide. All efforts to persuade it to acknowledge the genocide fall on deaf ears.

The survivors and descendants of the affected peoples have had to live with the lie ever since. For these now-small ethnic minorities, recognition of the genocide is of utmost importance to their collective memory—if not by Turkey, then at least by other states.[20] In October 2014, at the Frankfurt Book Fair, the Kurdish lawyer Mahmut Şakar asserted that the genocide of the Armenians and Syriacs in Turkey continues today. In November 2015, a report from Nîsebîn, in Turkish-occupied Kurdistan, by the Syriac chairman Yûhanna Aktaş, confirmed that attacks on Syriac churches and other significant sites continued, with the intention of driving the Syriacs out.[21] To this day, the Turkish government adheres to its policy of expelling the Christian population.

Armenians

We arrived here barefooted, we will leave barefooted.[22]

Armenians have lived in Syria for two thousand years. The Armenian community in Aleppo is very old. But most of those in Rojava today arrived as refugees from the Ottoman-perpetrated genocide. Concentration camps were created in the Syrian desert, and in 1915, the camp at Deir ez-Zor became the final destination of the death marches. Native Syrian Arabs did not hesitate to give the persecuted Armenians shelter and support.

In 1989–90, the Armenian Apostolic Church opened a complex in Deir ez-Zor to memorialize this tragedy. Every year on April 24, the remembrance day for the Armenian genocide, tens of thousands of Armenians from around the world visited the memorial. But on September 21, 2014, IS destroyed it.[23]

Syria's Armenian population today is estimated at 100,000. A significant proportion live in Rojava, approximately 12,000 in Qamişlo, some 80 families in Dêrîk, 80 in Hesekê, and about 30 in Serêkaniyê. The majority speak Syrian Arabic as well as Western Armenian. The most widespread religions are the Armenian Apostolic, the Armenian Catholic, and the Armenian Evangelical Church.

The community in Dêrîk was founded after the 1915 genocide. The Armenian language is still spoken there and is taught at school through the sixth grade. In Dêrîk, the Armenian pastor Dajad Akobian told us that 80 Armenian families, or about 440 people, live in that city; a few individuals have left. Armenians in Dêrîk, he continued, farm, or make handicrafts, or are clerks. "We cooperate with TEV-DEM," he explained. "The Armenians participate in the Asayîş and the YPG. We have Armenian YPG fighters." As a minority, he pointed out, Armenians have perpetually been forced to come to terms with whoever was in power, but they are grateful to the YPG for defending the country against the Islamists.

Even before the Syrian war began in 2011, Syria's Armenian population had declined after twenty years of the Arabization policy. According to the Syriac National Council, once the war began, many Armenians fled to Hesekê province and then to Armenia.[24] We could see that the shrinking of the community was painful to Akobian.

Syriacs

We are Aramaean—don't you dare take our dreams from us. We are fire and light simultaneously; you can illuminate your path with us, but we may burn your fingers![25]

Syriacs are Aramaic Christians who adhere to several different faiths of the East and West Syriac traditions.[26] They claim to be indigenous to Mesopotamia and to descend from the Assyrians, appearing in the archaeological record around 2000 BCE. Their native language is Aramaic, the language of Jesus.[27] Since the Islamization of the Middle East, Syriacs have been subjected to persecution, so now only a few hundred thousand people speak their language. They call their home Bethnahrin, the land between the Tigris and the Euphrates.

In Syria, Syriacs make up 10–12 percent of the Syrian population or, depending on the source, 900,000–2.6 million.[28] Around 1 million live outside Syria, mostly in Europe, Australia, the United States, and South America.[29] Some 400,000 Syriacs are said to have fled the country in the last two years.[30] Most of those still in Syria are assimilated into the Arab population and speak Arabic, rather than Aramaic, as their first language.

Syriacs consider Cizîrê to be one of their historic areas of settlement, and they have another name for it: Gozarto, in Aramaic. By their own account, they make up 10 percent of the population, or about 200,000 people. Before the civil war, they numbered approximately 300,000.[31] In July 2013, when the Al-Nusra Front and Al-Qaeda in Syria were attacking Rojava, Syriacs were living in the southern part of Hesekê province and in Serêkaniyê. Businesspeople, nuns, bishops, and well-known personalities were kidnapped and murdered, which resulted in a mass exodus to Turkey and Europe. Most of the Syriacs who remained joined TEV-DEM. The Syriac National Council emphasizes that many of those who fled will return should the situation improve.[32]

According to Ishan Gawriye, the head of the Syriac Union Party, the Syriacs see themselves as a nation, not as a religious community, and like the Kurds they have encountered much repression. Gawriye himself had been imprisoned; his predecessor as party chief was murdered by the regime while in prison. He expressly thanked the Kurdish movement: "We can live with Chechens, Kurds, Arabs; we have been living together for two thousand years. The Ba'ath regime and all previous governments oppressed us. We would wholeheartedly like to participate in the project of our friends in the PYD, to finally put an end to chauvinistic thinking. We participate in the YPG and all other institutions, although we are a small community and can't contribute much."

He also said that in Iraq a genocide against Syriacs was under way: "In Iraq, there were previously 14.5 million Christians before the 2003 Iraq War. Now there are only 400,000, and none live in Baghdad anymore."[33]

Dêrîk city's northern neighborhood is inhabited largely by Muslim Kurds and the southern by Syriac Christians, with about five hundred households; the Aramaic language is spoken and is taught in schools. Murad Murad, a priest of the Syriac Orthodox Church, told us that the name "Dêrîk" refers to an original monastery. "We're all here together and stand together," he explained as we sat in his church. "We are all one here. We want our connections to grow even stronger. If love and compassion exist, then we are all together, we're like brothers, and we will defend this part of Dêrîk."

Echoing the Armenians we spoke to, Murad told us that the attacks by Islamist terrorists were making life difficult for Syriacs. Christian refugees had arrived in Dêrîk from other parts of Syria and were renting houses there now, but other Christians had left—about seven hundred households, by his estimate. Many families had gone to Sweden and Germany, for economic reasons but also out of fear of terrorism. But life in Rojava was much better than in the neighboring regions, he said.

The community was at one with TEV-DEM, he emphasized, and they defend the region together. Part of the city is being protected by the Sutoro, the Syriac security forces. David Vergili, member of the Brussels-based European Syriac Union, said in January 2014 that "Democratic Autonomy in Rojava recognizes the commonalities and equal status of the peoples of the region and represents them democratically and equitably. The Syriacs are fighting to ensure that in a reconstructed Syria and in a reorganized Middle East, their rights are and positions will be guaranteed. That's why Rojava is a project suited to the Syriacs' interests."[34]

Chaldeans

The Chaldean Catholic Church (Syriac-Aramaic) is an Eastern church united with the Roman Catholic Church but with East Syrian rites. Its members are also called Syriacs. Starting in the seventeenth century, Catholic missionaries worked among the East Syriac Christians; their influence led to splits in large parts of the church.

When we visited the Chaldean community in Dêrîk, their spokes-woman told us that about 240 Chaldean families, some 1,200 people, lived there; 15–20 families had left. In contrast to Orthodox Syriacs, they participate directly in TEV-DEM organizing, and they also have a representative, Kayser Moger, in the Dêrîk district council. She praised the great safety in the city and the many kinds of help that the Chaldean community has received from TEV-DEM. "Even at four o'clock in the morning, girls can walk safely on the streets," she said. "Our economic situation has improved. We support the election of the new government. Many of us participate in the Asayîş and the YPG. We oppose Syriacs having their own security forces; we want Syriacs to be part of the Asayîş, like the Kurds." Only 60 percent of the Chaldeans speak their own language, she said, which differs a little from that of other Aramaeans. The communities live mainly by farming, and the economic situation is currently good, because the prices of many products have increased.

The Chaldeans support the system of Democratic Autonomy in Dêrîk, she tells us. Every 15 days a meeting takes place to evaluate the joint work and to determine the tasks for the next two weeks. The Chaldeans set up a health commission and a commission on language. Some of the Chaldean women participate in the Peace Mothers. A commission for arts and culture has been set up, as well as a folklore group.

* * *

The Syriacs have their own security force, the Sutoro (Aramaic for "defense").[35] And on January 8, 2013, the Syriac Military Council (Mawtbo Fulhoyo Suryoyo, or MFS) was founded. It operates mainly in areas where Syriacs live, especially in Hesekê province. The day it was formed, the MFS joined forces with the YPG to fight IS.

In October 2014, all the Syriac parties convened in Cizîrê and agreed on close cooperation. They all wanted to support the Sutoro and the Syriac Military Council—even the Chaldeans, who didn't approve of independent security forces.

In September 2015, the Bethnahrin Women Protection Forces was formed. "Along with the MFS and Sutoro, we needed a women's force," said a spokesperson. They aim to "improve the values of Syriac people, fight for women's rights, act in solidarity with women of other nations, and struggle against the forces of reaction." In the war zone, she noted, the YPJ served as a model.[36]

In Dêrîk, Sutoro's head of security, Melke Rabo, assured us that relations between Sutoro and the Asayîş were very good, that they share security tasks both within and without the city: "We work with the general Asayîş whenever the situation requires it. We are responsible for the security of the Syriac population." Following the example of the Asayîş, they also train women: "The Syriac community has no unified position—some work for the system, and some work for the Kurds." In Qamişlo, there is a Syriac community that supports the Assad regime. They have their own security force, called Sootoro.

Melke's tone turned regretful. "The peoples in this region have a long shared history and tradition," he told us. "We've lived here in peace for many years. But we're very upset that so few Syriacs live in the region today. Many have fled because of the war." He criticized the European refugee policy that entices Syriacs with financial incentives to give up on their homeland for Europe instead of defending it. This makes Europe a supporter of those who want to expel the Syriacs from Gozarto [Cizîre], he said. "People should come back here—they shouldn't give up their old homeland so easily. We're doing well economically. And in the history of our people in Syria, we've never had as many rights as we have now."

He continued, "The Syriacs and Armenians know well that without the YPG/YPJ, our homelands would have been lost and that the Democratic

Figure 2.2 A Syriac priest blesses MFS fighters, Christmas 2014 in Dêrîk (Source: Mark Mulhouse/attenzione)

Autonomy system grants them an equitable place. For the first time in recent history, our languages are officially recognized."

2.4 Smaller Population Groups

In addition to these groups, smaller populations of Turkmens, Chechens, Circassians, and Nawar live in Rojava.

Between 100,000 and 200,000 Turkmens live in Syria, mainly in Aleppo, Damascus, Homs, Hama, and Latakya. They are remnants of the Ottoman Turkish population who remained in Syria after the collapse of the Ottoman Empire. Despite their name, they have no direct connection to Turkmenistan. In Rojava, their numbers are few—the exact number is unknown. Most Turkmens in Syria are strongly Arabized and no longer speak Turkish or the language of South Azerbaijan.

In the Syrian war, they formed their own combat forces, including the Suriye Türkmen Ordusu (Syrian Turkmen Army), which is financed and supported by Turkey. On November 24, 2015, the Turkish Army shot down a Russian Suchkhoi-24 jet. One of the pilots, Oleg Peschkow, parachuted and was shot dead while in the air. The killer was Alparslan Çelik, a Turk from Elazığ who comes from the milieu of the fascistic Grey Wolves. He was a member of a Syrian Turkmen unit, backed by the Turkish state.[37]

After the YPG/YPJ liberated Girê Spî in June 2015 [see 8.9], Amnesty International reported that the YPG had expelled Turkmens and local Arabs from that area. The Syrian Kurdish Human Rights Association (DAD) rebutted the accusation.[38] At Girê Spî, there were five Turkmen villages. When the Syrian Democratic Forces (SDF) were founded in October 2015 [see 8.10], the Turkmen Lîwa Al-Selcuki participated.[39] The SDF's official spokesman, the Turkmen Talal Ali Silo, explained that the Turkmens have lived amicably alongside the Kurds and Arabs for centuries and affirmed that they would all liberate Syria together.[40]

Chechens arrived in northern Syria after fleeing Russia's colonization of the Caucasus, while others had immigrated during Ottoman times.

Circassians have been in the area since 1878. Some resettled from the Balkans, while others traveled from the Caucasus to the Turkish port city of Samsun, thence to Kayseri and subsequently to Syrian territory. In 1920, after Syria became part of the French Mandate, the Syrian Circassians repeatedly sided against rebellious Arabs, which seriously damaged relations between the two groups. Like the Kurds, they were targeted by the Arabization policy. A small number of Circassians live in Cizîrê; they are Sunni Muslims.

The Nawar are itinerant Dom people who speak Domari, an Indo-Aryan language that is the Middle Eastern variant of Romani. In Rojava, they are called Qerecî (gypsies).

Across Syria, there are about 37,000 Dom. Before the war, there was a large community in Aleppo.[41]

About a hundred Nawar families live in precarious circumstances near Qamişlo city. "We offered them houses," Heval Amer,[42] a longtime Kurdish activist, explained to us, "but they prefer to continue in their tents and huts." We were told that the Nawar are famous as musicians. Their social status is very low, and there is prejudice against them.

Notes

1. Ismet Chérif Vanly, *Kurdistan und die Kurden*, 3 vols. (Göttingen, 1988), p. 12.
2. Stefan Winter, "Die Kurden Syriens im Spiegel osmanischer Archivquellen," unpublished paper, University of Quebec at Montreal, 2010, http://bit. ly/1KEQIzz.
3. "Die Revolution in Westkurdistan—Teil 1," *Civaka Azad*, n.d., http://bit. ly/1QcsYpm.
4. Judith Wolf, "Ausländer im eigenen Land—Buchrezension," *Kurdica—die kurdische Enzyklopädie*, http://bit.ly/1H67p7B.
5. John McHugo, *Syria: A Recent History* (London, 2015), e-book, loc. 4609.
6. David McDowall, *A Modern History of the Kurds*, 3rd edn. (London, 2003), p. 475. The variation in numbers resulted in part from the different counting methods: some counted individuals while others, as is common in Syria, counted households.
7. Robert Lowe, "The Syrian Kurds: A People Discovered," Chatham House, January 2006, http://bit.ly/1cafjAZ.
8. McDowall, *Modern History of Kurds*, pp. 474–5.
9. Ibid.
10. "Syrian Arab Republic," UN Development Programme, *Human Development Report 2014*, http://bit.ly/1KWqqcW; and "Syria Access to Electricity," *TheGlobalEconomy.com*, http://bit.ly/1DD94lm.
11. Telim Tolan, "Yezidentum: Eine Kurzübersicht," Dengê Êzîdiyan, http://bit. ly/1KXCKfR.
12. The Jazirah region meant here is northern Mesopotamia.
13. Between July 2012, when the Assad regime left Rojava, and the summer of 2013, when the radical Islamists' war on Rojava began, Cizîrê saw a building

boom. During our May 2014 visit, we could see unfinished buildings everywhere.

14. A *dunam* is 1,000 square meters or about a quarter of an acre.

15. Carl Drott, "Arab Tribes Split Between Kurds and Jihadists," Carnegie Endowment for International Peace, May 15, 2014, http://ceip.org/1DWrs3a.

16. Til Hemîs is 20 percent Kurdish and 80 percent Arab; 20 percent of the Arabs are Şammar, and most of the inhabitants are Şarabia.

17. In addition to the Islamic front, IS, Jabhat al-Nusra, and units of the FSA, Lîwa Hamza, were also involved in the attacks. Source: Interviews with representatives of the Democratic-Autonomous Administration, May 2014.

18. "Til Hemîs Liberated by Joint Operation of YPG/YPJ, Syriac Units and Local Arab Tribes," *Rojava Report*, February 28, 2015, http://bit.ly/24ZFIoV; "Kurds: Til Hemîs—Til Barak Operation Ended Successfully," *Kurdish Daily News*, March 10, 2015, http://bit.ly/1tvGTRi.

19. "Kurdish Canton Led by an Arab Sheikh," *BasNews*, July 10, 2014, http://bit.ly/1JqMOJJ.

20. "Seyfo 1915—Ein Verbrechen gegen die Menschheit," *Bethnahrin*, http://bit.ly/1FIKRcl.

21. Ferhat Arslan, "Li Nisêbînê dêr û mizgeft hatin bombekirin," *ANF News*, November 25, 2016, http://bit.ly/1ILZsqU.

22. Jürg Bischoff, "Syriens Armenier fürchten um ihre Zukunft," *Neue Zürcher Zeitung*, April 14, 2014, http://bit.ly/1DWqJPl.

23. "ISIS-Kämpfer zerstören armenische Genozidgedenkstätte in Der ez-Zor," *HayPress: Armenische Nachrichten*, September 22, 2014, http://bit.ly/1GSccrp.

24. Syriac National Council, "Syriac Christians After Three Years of Civil War," Christian Coalition for Syria, January 7, 2014, http://bit.ly/1HeUJXW.

25. "United Suryoye," Suryoye.com.

26. The West Syriac tradition, or the Ancient Church of Antioch Patriarchy, includes the Syriac Orthodox Church of Antioch, the Syriac Catholic Church, and the Syriac Maronite Church of Antioch. The East Syriac tradition, or Ancient Church of Seleucia-Ctesiphon Catholicate, includes the Assyrian Church of the East, Ancient Church of the East, Chaldean Catholic Church.

27. All Aramaic tongues belong to the Semitic language family. Ancient Aramaic is documented to the beginning of the first millennium BCE. From that tongue, new Aramaic languages developed over the centuries. Today, some 550,000 people, mostly Christians, speak about 15 of these neo-Aramaic languages.

28. "Syria Population 2014," *World Population Review*, http://bit.ly/1Pg9LAR; Syriac National Council to authors, n.d.

29. Bassam Ishak, president of the Assyrian National Council of Syria, interview by Michael Knapp, June 4, 2014, http://bit.ly/1zGjgb2.

30. Syriac National Council, "Syriac Christians After Three Years of Civil War," Christian Coalition for Syria, January 7, 2014, http://bit.ly/1HeUJXW.
31. Syriac National Council, "Syriac People in Syria," Christian Coalition for Syria, n.d., http://bit.ly/1dhKgUm.
32. Ibid.
33. Ishan Gawriye, interview by Michael Knapp, Qamişlo, October 2013.
34. "3 Sprachen, 1 Land," BasNews, February 13, 2014, http://bit.ly/1S7xI1v.
35. Karlos Zurutuza, "Syrian Split Divides Christians," IPS, May 4, 2014, http://bit.ly/1GmEcVQ.
36. "Bethnahrin Women Protection Forces Founded Against ISIS," English Bianet, September 2, 2015, http://bit.ly/1IM0IKO.
37. "Syrian Turkmen Commander Who 'Killed' Russian Pilot Turns Out to Be Turkish Ultranationalist," RT, November 27, 2015, http://bit.ly/1Z6AmHj.
38. "Statements of Arabs and Turkmens from Giri Spi Reversed in Istanbul," ANF News, July 12, 2015, http://bit.ly/1Uiahm6.
39. "Declaration of Establishment by Syrian Democratic Forces," ANF News, October 15, 2015, http://bit.ly/1Z5mTQb.
40. "QSD Turkmen Comander: 'Turkmens Are Syrians, not Turks,'" Ronahi TV English, December 3, 2015, http://bit.ly/1UiaooM.
41. "Domari," Ethnologue.com, http://www.ethnologue.com/language/rmt.
42. Heval Amer is a longtime supporter of the Kurdish movement. His brother, Diyar Dêrîk, a courier, was killed in 1997 in a war with the KDP in Gare (in South Kurdistan, in the Medya Defense Zones). Another brother, Mehrdin, is head of the council in Dêrîk. His son serves with the Asayîş in Til Koçer, and his wife is with the PYD. He has seven children.

3

Democratic Confederalism

3.1 The PKK and its Paradigm Shift

In 1978, Kurdish and Turkish revolutionaries, among them Abdullah Öcalan and Sakine Cansız, founded the Kurdistan Workers Party (PKK) in North Kurdistan as a Marxist-Leninist liberation movement.[1] In those years, the revolutionary left in Turkey was relatively strong, and a socialist revolution seemed possible. But much of the Turkish left was steeped in the neocolonial chauvinism and anti-Kurdish racism propagated by Kemalism, the Turkish state ideology, and as a result, many revolutionary-left Kurds concluded that a movement like the PKK was necessary.

On November 12, 1980, the military seized power in Turkey for the third time. The coup, the most brutal in Turkish history, and carried out in consultation with the United States, would traumatize Turkish society for years to come. Some 650,000 people were soon arrested, while thousands disappeared into the prisons.

The Ba'ath regime permitted the PKK to resettle in Syria, knowing it could use the group as a lever against Turkey, Syria's traditional enemy. In Cold War politics, Turkey was a NATO member, while Syria was supported by the Soviet Union. The PKK set up camp in Damascus and in Syrian-occupied Lebanon, where a group of about four hundred fighters began training. The PKK's ideological and political base was established in Damascus. Domestically, the Ba'ath regime was repressing the Kurdish movement, detaining many activists as political prisoners. But the main goal of the Kurdish freedom movement was to liberate North Kurdistan; only later would revolutionary organizing get under way in Syria and in Iran as well. Until then, the PKK had to be careful not to jeopardize its safe haven, which was crucial for its survival.

On August 15, 1984, the PKK initiated a guerrilla war against the Turkish state in Turkish-occupied North Kurdistan. Thousands of young Kurds from Syria left to join the PKK guerrilla army, men and women alike. Women participated even in these first armed actions.[2] During the Cold War, the PKK struggled as a Marxist-Leninist-oriented liberation movement, with the goal of establishing a socialist, democratic-centralist Kurdistan, although it maintained a critical distance from Real Socialism (the Soviet Bloc). It regarded the Kurdish question not solely as a national or ethnic issue but as a matter of the liberation of society, of gender, and of all people.

In 1990–91, with the collapse of the Soviet Union, Real Socialism came to an end. Liberation movements around the world disintegrated. The end of Real Socialism led to a searching critique of statism, and in the early 1990s, the PKK began pondering other models.[3]

In Damascus, the PKK ran a Party Academy where ultimately more than ten thousand cadres and supporters would be schooled. (Cadres are people who adhere to a movement as militants. They live for the liberation struggle, which entails that they give up their private life. They have no home or property; they renounce family and even romantic relationships. They are ready to fight wherever they are needed, be it in the military or any other social sphere.) The PKK analyzed political and social dynamics and developed programs toward a liberated society. And where they could, they would discuss with Abdullah Öcalan himself as well as other figures. During these years, the PKK developed close contact with Kurdish civilians in Syria.

In 1993, the PKK created a women's army known as YAJK (the Union of Free Women of Kurdistan), with its own headquarters. Women who became guerrillas rejected women's traditional patriarchal role and slipped into the new role of freedom fighter, because they had so much to win and so little to lose. One of YAJK's goals was to overcome the traditional socialization of feudal society that was reproduced in the guerrilla army. There in the mountains, the YAJK developed principles of autonomous women's organizing, dual leadership, and the minimum 40 percent participation of women in all areas—principles that now apply to the movement in all four parts of Kurdistan. In the mid-1990s, one of this volume's authors spent several months in the Kurdish areas of Syria.[4]

By the mid-1990s, the military conflict between the PKK and the Turkish military seemed to be at a stalemate. The PKK issued several unilateral ceasefires with the aim of achieving a civil society solution within Turkey. But the Turkish state and elements of the Deep State repeatedly sabotaged the PKK's efforts.[5]

In the late 1990s, Turkey, controlling the water supply to Syria, threatened to go to war in Syria unless it expelled the PKK. On October 20, 1998, Turkish and Syrian officials secretly met in the Turkish city of Ceyhan. Syria promised to break up the PKK camps and expel them, and as a result, Assad shut down all the PKK camps and forced Öcalan to leave Syria.

The PKK might have reacted by escalating the guerrilla struggle and taking it into Turkish cities, but the leadership, including Öcalan, decided to seek a nonviolent solution instead. On February 15, 1999, Öcalan was arrested and abducted. The CIA—and probably indirectly the Mossad—abducted him from the Greek consulate in Nairobi, Kenya, and brought him to Turkey.[6] In northern Syria "everyone cried," Heval Amer told us. "In Dêrîk there was a rotating hunger strike. A friend called Beyram set himself on fire in protest." The PKK was on the brink of rising up and starting a civil war.

In Istanbul, Öcalan was tried, convicted, and initially sentenced to death. He used the legal process to present his peace initiative and to demand negotiations. As a gesture of goodwill, he called on the PKK to withdraw from North Kurdistan into South Kurdistan. Turkey took military advantage of this retreat and murdered more than five hundred guerrilla fighters.

Öcalan was re-sentenced to solitary confinement and imprisoned on the island of Imralı, in the Sea of Marmara, as its sole inmate. During this time, he critically engaged Marxist theory and practice and intensively studied the writings of the libertarian theorist Murray Bookchin and the historians Immanuel Wallerstein and Michel Foucault. He carried out an intensive study of the history of the Middle East, of Neolithic society and ancient Sumer, of Attic democracy and contemporary tribal organization. He studied works on Sumerian mythology, religion, philosophy, archeology, physics, and much more. From all these sources, he developed the models of Democratic Confederalism and Democratic Autonomy that the PKK would adopt as a paradigm shift, and that would become foundational for the revolution in Rojava.

3.2   Democratic Confederalism

Peaceful coexistence between the nation-state and Democratic Confederalism is possible as long as the state does not interfere in central matters of self-administration. Any such intervention would require the civil society to defend itself.[7]

Drawing on communalist traditions of primitive society, Öcalan oriented himself toward "natural society," which he thought existed some ten thousand years ago. It had a communal, egalitarian social organization. It was matricentric or matriarchal, and was marked by gender equality. "During the Neolithic period," he wrote, "a complete communal social order, so called 'primitive socialism,' was created around woman, a social order that 'saw none of the enforcement practices of the state order.'"[8] This idea of "natural society" clearly resembles the concept of "primitive communism" developed by Lewis Henry Morgan, Friedrich Engels, V. Gordon Childe, and others.[9]

From the point of view of historical materialism, primitive communism had necessarily to be overcome by statist society on the journey through stages of economic development, from primitive communism through slave society, feudalism, capitalism, socialism, and finally communism. This succession of stages is teleological, deterministic. Society moves inexorably.

But in Öcalan's view, the emergence of hierarchy, class rule, and statism was not inevitable but forced: "Hierarchy and the subsequent rise of the state was enforced by the widespread use of violence and fraud. The essential forces of natural society, on the other hand, tirelessly resisted and had to be continually pushed back."[10] Against the Marxist principle of a necessary passage through stages of development, Öcalan posed the concept of building up radical democracy in the here-and-now.

A matricentric, communal society ultimately gave way to a statist, patriarchal society. Patriarchy, in his view, was the basis for the emergence of hierarchy (in Greek, "holy rule," or divinely sanctioned dominance) and state repression. State centralism, capitalism, and nationalism, in Öcalan's view, are all consequences of patriarchy.[11]

To study this transition, Öcalan used discourse analysis to examine mythology, as well as sociological methods. From Sumerian myths, he gleaned information on how hierarchy, patriarchy, and the enslavement of men and women came about. They tell of the oppression of women, the lowering of their prestige, and the destruction of the female elements in life and society. They tell of the ordering of society into female and male identities in the form of hegemonic man and "his wife."

The decline of society, in this analysis, began with the fall of woman. The *Epic of Gilgamesh* presents male identity as a tool of hegemony. Masculinity becomes an ideology, a ruling ideology such that Gilgamesh sees women not as human beings but as objects that men can use for pleasure. At the same time, the epic separates the individual from a nature-based tribal society. It contrasts the patriarchal city-state culture with nature. The nature-man Enkidu is "urbanized," using female sexuality and prostitution, and destroys individuals' subsistence, rendering them dependent, and hence their freedom. Thus the *Epic of Gilgamesh* is a narrative of expulsion from, and forced abandonment of, villages. Other mythologies, such as the Babylonian *Enuma Elish*, define the emergence of the social status quo as a violent process of patriarchal self-empowerment. Together they correspond to an archeologically ascertainable ancient economy controlled by the state-temple with mass production and by the Sumerians' statist model of domination.

Today in the statist societies of capitalist modernity, Öcalan implies, commodification and assimilation wreak destruction on people, isolating them from one another and defining them as amorphous masses to be ruled under the tutelage of elites in nation-states. But linking people together in councils and creating an active and activist citizenship is a base on which the alternative to nation-state and capitalist modernity can—and should—be built.[12]

For Öcalan, the concept of "democratic civilization" is a permanent sub-tradition of resistance to statist civilization. It opens new possibilities beyond classical historical materialism. Indeed, it criticizes historical materialism as Euro- and androcentric for requiring colonized societies to develop an industrial proletariat; moreover, it is subject to ecological critique, as capitalist industrialization is not sustainable for this planet and its inhabitants.[13] By contrast, the Kurdish freedom movement's approach proposes to strengthen democratic civilization and develop a democratic modernity.

The modernist ideology of Kemalism agrees with classical Marxism in regarding the Middle East as an underdeveloped region and disparages the Kurdish areas as "less advanced." But if capitalism has not yet totally absorbed the social fabric of the Middle East, that is an advantage. The Kurdish areas in particular are not a feudal society that must be overcome by capitalism in order to reach socialism and communism. On the contrary, the Kurdish democratic approach regards it as positive that the Middle East has not yet been fully submerged by the alienation and atomization of capitalist modernity, since it means opportunities for development beyond modernist lines remain—that is, a different approach to tradition and society. So the area in which Kurds live now is a relatively fertile ground for development along nonmodernist lines.

We thus have two traditions: the tradition of democratic civilization and the tradition of statist civilization, which in political and social terms we can express as "Democratic Modernity" and "Capitalist Modernity." These traditions are classified according to their emancipatory content. Those that have established themselves by statism and patriarchy are to be criticized, while traditions of collectivity, that embrace the social role of women, that solve social conflicts through compromise, and that further the coexistence of diverse social singularities are to be strengthened. Power is not to be conquered; rather, an alternative is to be constructed at this historical moment.[14] By connecting people to each other in councils and by empowering people through self-administration, the Kurdish approach resists Capitalist Modernity and the nation-state and constructs a practical alternative.

3.3   Council Democracy

> The creation of an operational level where all kinds of social and political groups, religious communities, or intellectual tendencies can express themselves directly in all local decision-making processes can also be called participatory democracy.[15]
>
> Abdullah Öcalan

Ever since the Paris Commune of 1871, organization by councils has been an integral part of the European and Russian socialist movements. Councils were the main institutions in the Paris Commune, in the Russian Revolution of 1917, and in the German uprisings of 1918, when workers' and soldiers' councils were established. But in all cases, the council movement was neutralized, either because the revolution consolidated (in the case of the Soviet Union), or because the counter-revolution defeated it (in the Paris Commune and the German council movement). Hannah Arendt called the council movement the "lost treasure of democracy."[16] Councils, she argued, allow for political participation by the people, whereas representative systems structurally exclude people from power. Council movements have been a spontaneous part of every revolution and an alternative to representative systems.[17] The revolutionary process of spontaneous council formation, in her view, stemmed from the heterogeneity of society. After the American Revolution, she reminds us, Thomas Jefferson criticized the US constitution-making process, saying the revolution had brought the people freedom but had created no place where they could exercise it.[18]

But Arendt condemned the inclusion of the social question in self-administration. On this point, Jürgen Habermas accused her of failing to understand revolution as the emancipation of oppressed social classes.[19] Rosa Luxemburg, by contrast, saw revolutionary councils as attempts to endow the producing classes with legislative power. They were institutions of the working class that should also represent the "totality" (that is, the whole of society). Luxemburgian thinking can be considered a counterweight to authoritarian tendencies in socialist movements.[20] In her view, a socialist revolution should be carried out not through the conquest of power by political actors but by the masses organizing radical democratic self-governance.[21]

In the tradition of Luxemburg, Democratic Confederalism extends the concept of democracy to economic conditions—that is, the economy, as part of society, is to be democratized. Democratization or socialization of the economy must be distinguished from nationalization. Socialization means the administration of free economic resources by the councils and communities and the establishment of affiliated cooperatives—that is, it is communal rather than statist or private.

But Luxemburg's notion did not include women, families, or unemployed people.[22] In the 1970s, discussions began aimed at developing a politics beyond government, political organization, and party, and a political subjectivity that went beyond class.[23] In the West, an alternative to liberal democracy evolved that inspired international liberation movements and the anti-globalization movement. Michael Hardt and Antonio Negri proposed overcoming representative systems by means of direct participation, in which each "singularity" among the "multitude" would be represented through a process of radical democratization.[24]

Democratic Confederalism is a concept for the radical democratization of society. "In contrast to centralized administrations and bureaucratic exercise of power," Öcalan writes:

> ... confederalism proposes political self-administration, in which all groups of the society and all cultural identities express themselves in local meetings, general conventions, and councils. Such a democracy opens political space for all social strata and allows diverse political groups to express themselves. In this way it advances the political integration of society as a whole. Politics becomes part of everyday life.[25]

In order to achieve a radical democracy, Öcalan writes, the role of women is of primary importance: "the reality of the woman determines social reality to a large extent ... Therefore, no movement has a chance of creating a real and lasting, free society unless women's liberation is an essential part of its practice."[26] Gender equality is thus a central pillar of Democratic Confederalism. For the Kurdish freedom movement, the main social contradiction lies within gender relations. This idea is now deeply rooted in the Kurdish freedom movement. If we are to build a stateless society, he argues, we must overcome patriarchy. This idea is being implemented, in Democratic Autonomy, at all levels of local government, through both the autonomous women's institutions and mixed-gender institutions [see Chapter 5].

3.4 Democratic Concepts

How can a progressive system based on self-determination be designed and implemented? Öcalan's ideas on democracy take several forms.

Democratic Autonomy

Democratic Autonomy means the autonomy of the commune, the community, as an anti-centrist, bottom-up approach; the commune is the political center of self-government, the unit that integrates the neighborhoods: "While the Democratic Nation is the spirit, Democratic Autonomy represents the body."

Democratic Confederalism

Democratic Confederalism aims at achieving the autonomy of society, that is, a society that administers itself through small, self-governing decentralized units. It entails a permanent social revolution, reflected in every aspect of the social structure. All institutions are self-organized and self-administered.

Neither state nor territorial boundaries play a role in Democratic Confederalism, since the self-management of society renders the state and the nation-state superfluous.

The nation-state has left a trail of blood throughout world history, notably in the Arabization of Syria and the Turkification of Turkey. It relies on social homogenization through identity formation and its inevitably violent enforcement. By contrast, Democratic Confederalism is grounded in diversity.

Democratic Confederalism also differs from federalism because federalism presupposes quasi-statism.

Democratic Republic

Democratic Republic is the remnant of the nation-state that has the role of guaranteeing the rights that make possible Democratic Autonomy and Democratic Confederalism.[27] It presupposes a radical democratization of the existing states of Turkey, Syria, and others.

Democratic Modernity

Democratic Modernity is the alternative to Capitalist Modernity, the disempowering, homogenizing consumer society. Against this stalled model, Öcalan proposes a "moral and political society" that self-governs through grass-roots democracy.

Democratic Nation

The concept of the nation is distinct from the nation-state. The nation may be transformed through the common moral, democratic and emancipatory institutions of Democratic Autonomy.

Notes

1. Sakine Cansız, detained a political prisoner from 1979 to 1992, subsequently became a leading figure of the PKK women's movement and cofounded the women's army YAJK. On January 10, 2013, she and two other women's movement activists, Fidan Doğan and Leyla Şaylemez, were murdered in Paris.

2. Anja Flach, *Frauen in der kurdischen Guerilla: Motivation, Identität und Geschlechterverhältnis* (Cologne, 2007).

3. Abdullah Öcalan, *Democratic Confederalism* (Cologne, 2011), p. 6, http://bit.ly/1AUntIO.

4. Flach, *Frauen in der kurdischen Guerilla.* Today the YAJK is known as YJA Star, the Ishtar Unit of Free Women.

5. "Deep State" (in Turkish, Derin Devlet) refers to Turkey's decades-old state-within-a-state, involving interconnections among the military, the intelligence agencies, the political, judicial, and administrative systems, right-wing extremism, and organized crime.

6. "With Abdullah Öcalan from Athens to Nairobi," interview with Savvas Kalenteridis, Ekurd, May 7, 2013, http://bit.ly/28KQi1u; Helena Smith, "Athens in Crisis over CIA Links to Öcalan Capture," Guardian, December 21, 1999, http://bit.ly/28Jmkal; Murithi Muriga, "11 Years Ago: How Israel's Mossad Captured Kurdish Fugitive Abdullah Öcalan in Kenya," Afro Articles, March 1, 2010, http://bit.ly/28Jma2y; "Die PKK und die Kurdenfrage," *N-TV*, July 10, 2008, http://bit.ly/28Kcasm.

7. Abdullah Öcalan, *Jenseits von Staat, Macht und Gewalt* (Neuss, 2010), p. 32.

8. Abdullah Öcalan, "Women's Revolution: Neolithic Era," http://bit.ly/296Nihg.

9. Lewis H. Morgan, *Ancient Society* (1877); Friedrich Engels, *The Origin of the Family, Private Property, and the State* (1894), and V. Gordon Childe, *Man Makes Himself* (1941).

10. Öcalan, *Jenseits von Staat, Macht und Gewalt*, p. 11.

11. Ibid., pp. 21ff.

12. Joost Jongerden and Michael Knapp, "Communal Democracy: The Social Contract and Confederalism in Rojava," unpublished.

13. Murray Bookchin, *The Rise of Urbanization and the Decline of Citizenship* (San Francisco, CA, 1986).

14. Abdullah Öcalan, "Demokratik Konfederal Örgütleme ve Demokratik Özerklik," in Fırat Sezgin, ed., *Demokratik Ulus Çözümü* (Neuss, 2012) p. 32.

15. Öcalan, *Democratic Confederalism*, p. 26.

16. Hannah Arendt, *On Revolution* (New York, 1963), chap. 6.

17. Hannah Arendt, *Crises of the Republic: Lying in Politics; Civil Disobedience; On Violence; Thoughts on Politics and Revolution* (New York, 1969), p. 89.

18. Arendt, *On Revolution.*

19. Jürgen Habermas, *Philosophical-Political Profiles*, trans. F.G. Lawrence (Cambridge, MA, 1983), pp. 171ff.

20. Gustav Auernheimer, "Revolution und Räte bei Hannah Arendt und Rosa Luxemburg," in *UTOPIEKreativ*, nos. 201–2 (July–August 2007), p. 700.

21. Rosa Luxemburg, "Rede der Gründungsparteitag der KPD," *Gesammelte Werke* (Berlin, 1974), p. 4:512.

22. Michael Hardt and Antonio Negri, *Declaration* (2012), http://bit.ly/1gxKMPn.

23. Alain Badiou, *Ethics: An Essay on the Understanding of Evil* (London, 2002), pp. 95–100.

24. Hardt and Negri, *Declaration*; Joost Jongerden and Ahmet Hamdi Akkaya, "Democratic Confederalism as Kurdish Spring: The PKK and the Quest for Radical Democracy," in Mohammed M. A. Ahmed and Michael M. Gunter, *The Kurdish Spring: Geopolitical Changes and the Kurds* (Costa Mesa, CA, 2013).

25. Öcalan, *Democratic Confederalism*, p. 26.

26. Öcalan, *Jenseits von Staat*, pp. 266ff.

27. Jongerdern and Akkaya, "Democratic Confederalism as a Kurdish Spring," p. 171.

4

The Liberation

4.1 Organizing Begins

After Abdulah Öcalan was expelled from Syria, the Assad regime's repression of the PKK movement was intense, so much so that it could no longer function. "When Serok left Rojava, it got much harder," said Silvan Afrîn, a Yekîtiya Star representative in Dêrîk: "The repression was extreme. The regime arrested many people in Rojava. We continued, but underground ... There could be only a few protests, and all the organizing had to be done covertly. We did actions for our martyrs and demonstrations for International Women's Day, but about five hundred women would come, and a thousand soldiers."

"Meanwhile in 2005 the Lebanese politician Rafiq Al-Hariri was murdered, and high-ranking Syrian functionaries were blamed," said Hanife Hisên, a member of the TEV-DEM leadership.[1] "Syria was isolated internationally—it was surrounded by enemies, Lebanon and Iraq. Turkey became its only friend in the region. Turkey and Syria held talks in Adana and agreed on the goal of isolating the Kurds. In fact, they secretly decided on a plan to annihilate the Kurds. So for us, the years from 2004 to 2011 were a period of decline and betrayal."

On March 12, 2004, in Qamişlo, a soccer game was to be held between the Kurdish team Al-Cihad from Qamişlo and the Al-Fatwa team from Deir ez-Zor. According to Pro Asyl, armed Arab Ba'athists were bused in, with the approval of the provincial governor, the Syrian intelligence service, and the local councils. At the stadium, before the game began, the armed Arabs chanted pro-Saddam and anti-Kurdish slogans, to provoke the Kurds. The Kurds, in turn, reacted with anti-Saddam and pro-Kurdish cries. Then in an organized mob, the Arabs attacked the Kurds with iron chains and weapons.

The security forces in the stadium, instead of trying to restore peace and calm to the crowd, supported the armed Ba'athists and shot at the Kurdish fans. Panic surged among the fans, and eight Kurds and four Arabs died. In the following days, the protests spread to other cities in a spontaneous uprising, which the state crushed with devastating violence. By one estimate, 70 people died and 300 were wounded.[2] Afterward, explained Hisên, "the Assad regime used [that] soccer game as an opportunity to arrest hundreds of Kurds and to ban the parties."

The leftist Democratic Union Party (PYD) had already been founded. But the South Kurdish KDP went all out to try to suppress it, and so did the Syrian and the Turkish states, and so did opportunists from the ranks of the PKK itself, including Nizamettin Taş and Osman Öcalan.[3] "Turkey, the Syrian state, the KDP, and the traitor Osman Öcalan all wanted to destroy it," said Hisên. For example, on November 29, 2004, Şîlan Kobanî and three other leading cadres of the PYD were killed near Mosul: "Şîlan Kobanî [Meysa Bakî] was in the party leadership and in the leadership of the Kurdish People's Congress [Kongra Gel]. She was determined not to let them and to keep the project going. But ... she was murdered. So were Zekerya Îbrahîm [Zekerya Toros], a member of the PYD board; Hîkmet Tokmak [Fuat]; and PYD members Haci Cumalî [Cîvan Kobanî] and Nebû Alî [Cemîl Kobanî]."

A climate of fear and repression prevailed, said Hisên. "At this stage, the state tortured some friends to death. The people withdrew into private life. In one week in February 2011 a hundred people were arrested in Aleppo." People were terrified, various TEV-DEM representatives told us—they didn't dare come out and support the movement openly.

But the organizations continued between 2004 and 2011 on a clandestine basis, underground. Sympathizers supported them financially. "At one time we had around 15 members in a neighborhood," said Silvan Afrîn, a Yekîtiya Star activist. "We were committed to building a substantial confrontation, and the people were very much aligned with the movement's ideals."

In 2008, recalled an Arab woman, Aysa Afendi, "I was arrested because of my political work and taken to Aleppo. There I was imprisoned for a year and tortured repeatedly." But she kept working: "We women in the Arab culture were nearly slaves. So we had the most to gain from this revolution—but also the most to lose. And overturning the clan structures and the various ethnic boundaries takes time."[4]

Despite the severe repression, the organizing not only continued but gained momentum. "In 2005 women founded Yekîtiya Star," said Hisên. "They conducted educational sessions, held meetings, and did grassroots work. But it was all very precarious. The men who were arrested suffered brutal punishments. That's why the women did all the organizing. Only the women could move around openly."

4.2 The Arab Spring in Syria

In late 2010 and early 2011, popular uprisings challenged the ruling dictatorships in Tunisia and Egypt, as opposition groups campaigned for a democratic transformation. Their actions inspired opposition groups in neighboring countries, opening the door for change across the region, in what became known as the "Arab Spring."[5]

The first Syrian protests were held in February 2011 in several cities, but they were small and had limited impact. Then in mid-March in Dara'a, in the south, two youths had allegedly sprayed slogans on a wall. Syrian police arrested them, and some sources report that while in custody, one youth was fatally tortured.[6] Strong protests and demonstrations broke out, demanding not only the release of the youths but also political reform and an end to corruption. Police attacked the demonstrators, opening fire and killing several. The next day's funeral was accompanied by an even larger demonstration, and protests then spread to other parts of the country.

The regime tried to calm the situation, but the protest wave could not be contained. People from all strata of Syrian society, even from within the Ba'ath Party, took to the streets to express their outrage at what had occurred in Dara'a. The shootings by the security forces finally drove people in most Syrian towns to armed revolt.

In the spring of 2011, the protesters won several concessions. In June, the state of emergency that had been in place since 1963 was ended. And in April, a Syrian ministry announced that the stateless Kurds would finally receive Syrian citizenship, and the next month they were told they had the right to work. But this policy affected only those who were registered as "foreigners," the *ajanib*. The "hidden," the unregistered *maktoumeen*, would not. Many Kurdish activists interpreted this sudden concession as an attempt to induce Kurds to support the regime.

But repression by the intelligence service and the security forces continued. A new constitution was written, from which the words "socialism" and "pan-Arabism" were scrubbed.[7] Gradually in the spring and summer of 2011, the Muslim Brotherhood became central to the mobilizations. Despite the Hama massacre, it had a still working underground organization and solid ties to the Gulf States and to Turkey.[8]

In July, former soldiers, including onetime Colonel Riad Al-Asaad, founded the Free Syrian Army (FSA) as the armed wing of the Syrian opposition. It comprised mainly Sunnis, who were Syria's majority. The Gulf States backed the FSA financially.[9] The FSA was also backed by Turkey [see 14.2], which meant it would not be an acceptable ally for the Kurdish movement.

The Kurdish freedom movement, especially the youth organization and the PYD, supported resistance to the Assad regime as a matter of democratic change; it did not want the conflict to be militarized. But gradually the political conflict turned into civil war, the opposition to Assad became Islamized to a large extent, its democratic character became marginalized, and foreign regional and international forces began to dominate these Islamized parts and the Ba'ath regime. Neither the regime nor the opposition were responsive to Kurdish demands for recognition, so Rojava's Kurdish movement opted for a third path: it would side neither with the regime nor with the opposition. Would it defend itself? Yes. Would it participate in the civil war? No.

"We positioned ourselves as a third force" between the regime and the opposition, said Hisên: "Our declared goals within the Syrian rebellion were (1) to permit no attack on Syria from the outside, (2) to avoid armed struggle, (3) to find solutions through dialogue and ally with other opposition forces. But once we established ourselves, people started attacking us. They accused us of collaborating with the regime. It's a lie—the regime had always oppressed the Kurds. Even as you and I are speaking today, there are still people in prison from the old days. We don't collaborate with the regime ... And most of the Syrian opposition was Islamist, and we couldn't ally with them—a revolution can't come from the mosque.

"Abdullah Öcalan had said only a few sentences about Rojava," Hisên recalled, "but those became our program. 'I know the people of Rojava,' he said. 'They should organize themselves, build a party, and create self-defense forces. Politically, they should organize themselves independently from both the regime and the opposition.' We took these sentences as the basis of our work."

4.3 Illegal Councils

"In the spring of 2011, we expected that the protest movement would spread," Silvan Afrîn told us. "We talked about how to get ready for it, and what we would do. We were very watchful. That spring we began to build people's organizations. The question arose as to how we would protect ourselves. So in July or August we established the YXG [predecessor of the YPG]," the Self Protection Units. "At first we were few in number, as most people were still so intimidated by the state. We invited all the minorities to a founding congress, but because the war was going on, only a handful had the courage to show up.

"The only party that supported us was the PYD. We were always criticized for that, but the PYD had worked every day at the grass-roots, and our numbers grew. We built the armed units illicitly. Many people in Kurdistan had weapons hidden away: shotguns, pistols, Kalashnikovs. Within six or seven months we organized the self-defense committees of the YXG clandestinely."

"The first to join," Heval Amer told us, "were young people from the streets, with no strong [political] views. As soon as the first martyrs fell, more people joined. Almost every family already had members who were martyrs," meaning PKK guerrillas. "At first our work was very dangerous. Regime agents were everywhere, all around us. In all of Dêrîk there was only one friend [heval]. But gradually we visited all the families of martyrs and prisoners, and everyone was ready to do something. The state left us in peace, and we established a few strong points."

During the PKK's two-decades-long presence in Syria, many Kurds had had a close relationship with Abdullah Öcalan. That contact and the presence of the Kurdish freedom movement in Syria altered Rojava's feudally dominated society, as women who had been working to liberate Kurdish women for more than twenty years emphasized to us in May 2014. During the 1990s, many Syrian Kurds had left to join the PKK and fight in the guerrilla army in North Kurdistan. Tens of thousands of activists from Rojava participated in all levels of that struggle, and many had given their lives. That experience accounts for the strength of popular organizing in the wake of the 2011 uprising.

Once the protests in Syria started on March 15, 2011, people of diverse identities encouraged Democratic Autonomy in Rojava, as a way to create a society together without a nation-state. Öcalan's models of Democratic Confederalism and Democratic Autonomy were widely known, driving forward the radical democratic organizing. The construction of multiethnic councils, courts, security forces, military units, women's organizations, and economic cooperatives spread all over Rojava in the following months.[10]

"Before the revolution began," recalled the current PYD co-chair Asya Abdullah, "both as a party and as a movement, we had stayed away from people's assemblies and instead hashed out our differences in ideas at congresses. But then at people's assemblies we listened to the views of the people. Projects were proposed, decisions were made, and a road map was created. Subsequently, we published our project for Democratic Autonomy. We think it's the best solution not only for West Kurdistan but also for all of Syria."[11]

"We decided to hold a regular anti-regime demonstration every Friday," Hanife Hisên said. "But we saw that if we were going to send people out into the streets, we had to be able to protect them. Otherwise, all it would take was one attack, and they wouldn't go out anymore." Councils had already been created illegally, but in August 2011, the PYD established the People's Council of West Kurdistan (MGRK) to continue and advance the councils [see 6.2]: "Throughout Rojava we held elections, and three hundred people were elected to the People's Council, to shape the politics of Rojava."

As part of the third path, the MGRK proposed a peaceful democratic solution to Syria's political problems, leading to the creation of the National Coordination Committee for Democratic Change (NCC) in 2011 in Damascus. The NCC advocated nonviolent protest and opposed intervention from abroad; it also advocated a new political system for Syria that was neither religious nor ethnic in orientation. It pointed out that should the anti-Assad protests become militarized, the result would be an endless civil war, and the parties would become enmeshed in the bloc conflict between the West and China, Russia, and Iran.

Countering the NCC was the Syrian National Council (SNC), founded in August 2011 in Istanbul, to oppose the Assad regime; sponsored by Turkey and Gulf States, it was dominated by the Muslim Brotherhood. It did not seek the formation of a decentralized and multi-ethnic Syria as a priority. (Although it accepted different cultures, the Arabic element was considered superior; it said that the discussion of a future Syria should be postponed until after the Ba'ath regime was no more.) It sought the immediate overthrow of Assad rather than a democratic transition, and it opened the country to the influence of external powers. The fact that one Kurdish or Syriac party joined the SNC did not change its character. The MGRK met several times with the SNC but found no basis for collaboration because of the latter's close ties to the Turkish state.

4.4 The Hewlêr Agreement

As the MGRK grew stronger, other Kurdish parties were watching, and in October 2011 about 16 small, fractious groups formed a coalition called the Kurdish National Council in Syria (ENKS, Encûmena Niştimanî ya Kurdî li Sûriyê).[12] In the summer of 2012, the MGRK and the ENKS were the two influential political blocs in the Kurdish region of Syria.

In July, they sat down in Hewlêr (in Arabic, Erbil) under the auspices of KRG president Massoud Barzanî (who is also head of the KDP), to hammer out an agreement. "We knew the Kurds could never unite ideologically," Ilham Ahmed, a TEV-DEM councilor, told us, "but under the circumstances, we thought political unity was necessary." The civil war was intensifying, and the fighting was nearing Rojava. While the PYD and the ENKS shared a few common "national" interests, each side had its own reasons for seeking an agreement. The PYD/MGRK wanted to prevent the Kurds from splitting and preying on one another; the ENKS, seeing that political developments since 2011 had increasingly eroded its power in Rojava, wanted to stop that process and win back its lost influence. "So we decided to work together," said Ilham Ahmed.

On July 11, mediated by their host, Barzanî, the blocs came to an agreement. This Hewlêr Agreement stipulated that the two groups would share power during a transitional phase, and to this end it established the Supreme Kurdish Council (SKC). The SKC comprised ten members: five from the MGRK/PYD and five from the ENKS. It was, from that point on, to be the highest authority in Rojava.

That agreement, said Ilham Ahmed, "made the Kurdish people very happy ... The world has to understand how things are for the Kurds in Syria. We're not trying to seize power and subjugate the Turks, Arabs, or Persians. We only want to protect our own existence, to govern ourselves, and to freely enjoy our culture."[13] Hanife Hisên agreed: "The creation of the Supreme Kurdish Council was an attempt to bring both sides together and to include all Kurdish voices. It was a very good development for the Kurds."

At the same time, the Hewlêr Agreement underscored Barzanî's pragmatism—it showed that he recognized that compared to the ENKS, the PYD-led MGRK was relatively strong, and that any possible military confrontation with the MGRK would risk failure. So he took steps to strengthen his own military position as well, announcing that the KRG was building its own military force for Rojava, setting up camps to train Kurdish defectors from the Syrian Army: "There are 10,000 to 15,000 Kurdish refugees from Syria in Kurdistan, many of them young men. A few of them have gone through training, not for attack but for defense. They've got to be ready to prevent chaos there."

4.5 The Revolution Begins in Kobanî

At 1 a.m. on the night of July 18–19, 2012, the YPG took control of the roads leading in and out of Kobanî city. Inside the city, the majority of the people, who supported the MGRK, occupied the state institutions. "We had marked which buildings we should take over," recalled Pelda Kobanî, who participated that night, "which ones were useful for the people, even bakeries."[14] The people then assembled at the regime army's strongpoint in Kobanî, and a delegation informed the regime soldiers, "If you give up your weapons, your security will be guaranteed." The soldiers looked out over the mass of people, and seeing that they had no alternative, they agreed; some returned to their families in the Arab cities, while others preferred to remain in Kobanî because they had lived there for forty years.[15]

"The state had no substantial military force," said Hanife Hisên. "We surrounded them … and they surrendered. The regime couldn't send them any reinforcements. We didn't turn a single soldier over to the regime—we just talked to them and called their families to come pick them up. The ones who wanted to join the FSA, we let them go to Turkey." Heval Amer points out that when the regime troops left, "we didn't let them take their weapons. So they left behind many, even heavy weapons." Because the liberation was bloodless, Hisên recalled, "people said the regime had turned the weapons over to us. But it's a lie." "When the people awoke the next morning," Pelda Kobanî recalled, "and saw our flags flying over the roofs instead of the regime's, they were stunned. Even months later many were still worried that the regime would return." People had so internalized their fear of the regime, she recalled, that the actions of July 19 were initially incomprehensible to them.

After the abduction of Abdullah Öcalan in 1999, PKK institutions in Syria had collapsed, but now many fighters with a Rojava background came back and joined the YPG (as the defense force had been renamed). Over the next days, as the revolution spread from Kobanî to other cities and villages of West Kurdistan, they were welcomed joyously, and the people threw rice at them.

A week after the Kobanî liberation, a team of American journalists from *Vice News* who tried to enter encountered YPG checkpoints. Kobanî "is surrounded by Kurdish checkpoints," they recounted. "Heavily armed fighters inspect every car that tries to enter. 'We're trying to prevent the forces of the FSA from entering, but also statist saboteurs,' reports one of the masked men. He proudly displays his pump-action shotgun, which he'd found at a police station. 'We don't want our cities to be dragged into a bloodbath like Homs or Idlib.'"[16]

4.6   The Liberation of Dêrîk and Afrîn

The liberation quickly spread to other cities and towns. "As the action unfolded," Heval Amer told us, "the people had no more fear—everyone joined in, many with only wooden clubs in their hands." "In Dêrîk we tried to hold the people back," Hanife Hisên told us, "but they pushed out ahead of us. We set up control points. The people said, 'Give us the weapons,' and we distributed them.

"There were many military outposts in Dêrîk, especially in the Kurdish neighborhoods," she continued. "We went to the state security forces and surrounded them and told them to go. They got their things and left." Reported the *Vice* team, "Several Arab guards at the municipal court were detained and disarmed, and posters of Assad were ripped from the walls. The compound of the military news service was overrun quickly … Hundreds of inhabitants, stepping into the gaudily furnished rooms, stood astonished with tears of joy."[17]

Only in Dêrîk did fighting break out, resulting in several deaths. "In the town of Girziro we surrounded an army battalion for twelve days," Amer said. "One soldier and an officer, an Alawite, were killed, but then the rest gave up. Military helicopters arrived, and as in 2004, we were bombed." Hisên explains that the "high-ranking officer was killed with a sniper rifle—he'd refused to give up. Afterward his unit surrendered. The friends [*hevals*] surrounded them. We didn't want any fighting, but we did tell them that if they didn't surrender, we would kill them."

Far away, at the opposite end of Rojava, Afrîn canton was also liberated. "On Sunday armed Kurds surrounded all the institutions of the regime still in Afrîn," reported the *Frankfurter Rundschau*, "and demanded that the staff give themselves up. Only some military intelligence agents resisted. They fought for two hours but finally surrendered. 'That's how we liberated Afrîn,' says Ghareb Heso, with the trace of a smile. The intelligence agents sat in the prison; there were only three wounded. In response a bomber destroyed ... a beloved Kurdish restaurant in Afrîn. Two people lost their lives. That was terrible, said the Kurdish leader, but now we hold the balance."[18]

In town after town, the pattern continued. The people surrounded the military bases and gave the scant regime troops the option to withdraw. The popular self-organization prevented anyone from committing acts of vengeful destruction. "We weren't trying to grab some weapons and point them at the regime," said Ilham Ahmed. "We wanted to achieve a democratic Syria by peaceful means. Because we made that choice, we were criticized: 'Why aren't you fighting? You're not resisting.' We tried to explain that we thought our course was the better one. The Middle East is known for spilling blood. As Kurds, we wanted to show that things can be different, that people can also stand up for their rights using peaceful means."

Finally, recalled Heval Amer, "only Qamişlo remained in regime hands. The situation was critical. Many tribes live there, and they have federations. We liberated the predominantly Kurdish neighborhoods, but the center of Qamişlo remained under the control of the regime, and also the road to the airport. We had no intention of fighting a war against the Syrian state—we're a defense force. If we had started a war, the regime would have bombed our cities. We preferred to solve things at the level of dialogue."

4.7   After the Liberation

After the liberation, buildings that had belonged to the regime, on streets that the people hadn't been allowed to enter, were transformed into people's houses, cultural centers, and educational institutions. In Kobanî, "the police building was stripped of emblems of the old regime, and important files were confiscated. For the first time civilians could enter the torture chamber in the basement. Traces of blood are still visible on the walls. How many regime opponents were killed here, no one knows."[19] The office of the district governor of Dêrîk is now the headquarters of the women's freedom movement.

In Kobanî, the *Vice* team reported, "life seemed to return to normal. People are shopping, students hurry to their next classes, and women buy bread for the traditional fast-breaking in the evening. In one café I [the *Vice* reporter] have a conversation with an older Christian Arab woman, Maryam. 'We know that the war could reach our region, especially if, after the fall of the Assad regime, a new government doesn't allow us religious freedom.' But she feels safer now than she did under Assad. 'Here in Kobanî we've been fighting Assad since 1990. We've supported our Kurdish neighbors, of course. We surely aren't going to give up now.'"

"In Kobanî alone around 250 şehîd [martyrs] are counted. Most had joined the PKK to fight for Kurdish rights; others vanished into Syrian prisons because of their political work. These martyrs, who represent every religious and ethnic group, unite the community now, as Kurds, Arabs, Christians, Armenians, and Turkmens try to shape their newly won freedom together."[20]

In Qamişlo, regime supporters—around 20 percent of the city's population—still live in a section of the city, and the airport is still in regime hands, but this is tolerated. In the following months and years in the cities of Hesekê and Qamişlo, the regime has attacked the liberated areas several times, but the YPG/YPJ respond proportionately. One attack occurred just a few days before our visit to Qamişlo in May 2014, when Syrian soldiers wanted to capture some strategic points in the city, and another during our visit in Hesekê.[21] In mid-April 2016, the Ba'ath regime mounted a large attack that led to the deaths of several dozen Syrian soldiers and YPG/YPJ/Asayîş members. The regime force was defeated.[22]

Heval Amer told us that after the liberation, many of the Kurds who had emigrated to other parts of Syria for work—Damascus, Raqqa, and Hama—returned to Rojava. "Everyone was accepted back into the movement, even those who worked as agents," he told us. "We had to proceed carefully ... Regime troops were still in Qamişlo and Hesekê, and a few stayed here [in Dêrîk and Rimelan] ... But some of their children joined the Asayîş. Every place we liberated, we celebrated. After so many years of repression, that's no small matter. We never thought we'd see this in a hundred years. The friends said, 'We're doing it,' but we couldn't believe it.

"I think about 40 percent of Dêrîk supports us," he continued. "Many lived for so long in degradation, they still don't believe we're independent ... The regime had intimidated the population so much, they're afraid it'll come back ... We try to persuade them that we've built the councils ourselves, and the organizations for youth, art, and culture. But they still don't believe it.

"Every place we liberated, we set up protection, and we ensured that nothing would be destroyed ... The people celebrated. Arabs came here from other parts of Syria because we had no war ... The Revolution of Rojava is like a newborn child—we don't know how it will grow up."

Remziye Mihemed, co-leader of the Qamişlo People's Council, recalled the moment when the people finally got the right to determine their own future: "It's a great honor for me, a Kurdish woman, to be elected to head the Qamişlo People's Council. And it's remarkable for the people of Qamişlo to finally be able to choose their own representatives. We as Kurds are gradually demanding our rights, and that sparks ever more enthusiasm. In this revolutionary phase we've established councils in all the neighborhoods. People now have a chance to see to their own needs and wishes and get their own projects under way. Of course we have many challenges, especially with water and electricity. We're trying to work them all out. But if you try to tell us we can't function without the state, or that the people can't provide water and power for the city themselves, we will object. Yes, the war is causing economic problems, but I'm optimistic we'll solve every one of them. We're in the middle of a revolution, and we're working day and night to see to people's needs. It's very helpful that people are acting with great solidarity and mutual support. Yes, some have fears about the new institutions—especially men have difficulties with the women's commissions and councils. But we'll persuade them that the liberation of society can proceed only with the liberation of women."

Notes

1. In the early 1990s, as a young woman, Hîsen joined the YAJK, the women's army of the PKK. When the Rojava Revolution began, she returned to help build Democratic Autonomy.
2. Abubeker Saydam, "Massaker gegen kurdische Bevölkerung in Syrien— Mehr als 70 Tote und Hunderte von Schwerverletzten in den kurdischen Regionen," *Pro Asyl*, March 16, 2004. http://bit.ly/1HV6t6F.
3. Osman Öcalan, a younger brother of Abdullah Öcalan, was a PKK member. In 2004, he participated in an attempt to split the organization. During the ideological transformation, Osman Öcalan tried to reorient it along nationalistic-neoliberal lines. When he failed, he left, taking many members with him.
4. Benjamin Hiller, "Die vergessene Front in Syrien," *Vice News*, http://bit.ly/1Hqh9b9.
5. Aldar Xelîl, interview by Devriş Çimen, "Laßt uns die Einheit Syriens gemeinsam stärken," *Kurdistan Report* 163 (September–October 2012), pp. 29–31, http://bit.ly/1RvdMYD.
6. Werner Ruf, "Revolution und Konterrevolution in Nahost," in Fritz Edlinger and Tyma Kraitt, eds., *Syrien: Hintergründe, Analysen, Berichte* (Vienna, 2013), p. 163.
7. Carsten Wieland, "Syrien und Irak. Panarabische Paradoxien und der Bankrott des Ba'athismus," in Edlinger and Kraitt, eds., *Syrien*, p. 92.
8. Ibid.
9. "Bürgerkrieg in Syrien: Assad-Gegner erwarten 100 Millionen Dollar aus den Golf-Staaten," *Spiegel*, April 2, 2012, http://bit.ly/1dhO6gk.
10. Mako Qocgirî, "Aus der Kraft der eigenen Bevölkerung—Die Revolution in Rojava schreitet voran," *Kurdistan Report*, no. 172 (2014), http://bit.ly/1Gj9bS4.
11. Asya Abdullah, interview by Perwer Yas, "Die Demokratische Autonomie ist massgebend für ein demokratisches Syrien," *Civaka Azad*, October 18, 2012, http://bit.ly/1ET2TrV.
12. Three of those parties dominate: the Azadî Party (led by Mustafa Cuma), El Partî (led by Abdulhakim Bashar), und Yekîtî. Together these three parties make up the KDP-S, the Syrian branch of the South Kurdish KDP (also led by Bashar), founded in 1957. Because of the dominance of the KDP-S, the ENKS very often functions as the KPD-S itself.
13. "Die Revolution in West Kurdistan—Teil 3," *Civaka Azad*, n.d., http://bit.ly/1cfpVi7.

14. Pelda Kobanî, unpublished interview. Pelda is a Kurd who grew up in Europe and later joined the YPG.
15. "The Revolution in Westkurdistan—Teil 1," *Civaka Azad*, http://bit.ly/1QcsYpm.
16. Hiller, "Die vergessene Front in Syrien."
17. Ibid.
18. Frank Nordhausen, "Zwischen den Fronten," *Frankfurter Rundschau*, September 15, 2012, http://bit.ly/1QkDvyX.
19. Hiller, "Die vergessene Front in Syrien."
20. Ibid.
21. "20 Regime Soldiers Killed in Clashes in Hassake," *Syriac International News Agency*, May 22, 2014, http://bit.ly/28MxHio.
22. "Rojava Public Security Forces Declare Ceasefire in Qamişlo," *ANHA*, April 23, 2016, http://bit.ly/28JMkUL.

5

A Women's Revolution

"This may be the first time in history that women have played such an active role in organizing a revolution. They fight on the fronts, they serve as commanders, and they participate in production. There's no place in Rojava where women are not to be seen. They're everywhere and part of everything."[1]

In the latter half of 2014, the battles for Şengal [see 8.9] and Kobanî [see 14.2] shined a spotlight on something the West had thought impossible: a Middle Eastern society with women at its center. The region is otherwise universally considered to be patriarchal and regressive, but the resistance in Kobanî in particular has radically transformed the image of Kurdish women.

Now Kurdish women—like Meysa Abdo, the commander of the Kobanî front, and Asya Abdullah, the PYD co-chief—are lauded for behaving with determination and self-confidence. Even the bourgeois newspaper *Die Welt* observed that "the Kurds, men and women equally, have become an earnest secular actor in the Middle East, and as a result, enormous progress in civil society has become possible."[2] Women's magazines like *Elle* and *Marie Claire* run multi-page reports on the YPJ,[3] while a well-known Australian TV network broadcasts a documentary called *Female State*;[4] chain stores like H&M and the fashion magazine *Madame* display models in clothing adapted from the uniforms of armed fighters in the PKK and the YPJ. A 40-year-long conflict has all at once become conspicuous on the world stage and even appears to be chic. But what lies behind those images?

Women participated in the social uprisings of the recent Arab Spring, but in most of the countries that achieved a regime or government change, women did not go on to have a share in the new order: indeed, as Islamist organizations gained partial or full political power, women were plunged into situations even more hopeless than before. A 2013 study of the role of women in the Arab Spring in Egypt, Morocco, Yemen, and the Palestinian areas found that the political groups that held power after the uprisings surpassed the previous ones in conservatism and patriarchalism.[5] Only Tunisia had a development that varied from this pattern.

5.1 Rojava Women

Kurdish women in Rojava were and still are oppressed in multifarious ways. As Kurds, they were denied basic rights, in many cases even citizenship; and as women they were trapped in patriarchal domination. In traditional society, a man's "honor" in relation to his family manifested itself in the "purity" of his wife. As in much of the Middle East, Kurdish women and girls were usually not permitted to learn a trade or become economically independent. Since jobs were few in the Kurdish north of Syria, the men often went to work in Arab cities, but for women that was out of the question. Marriage was the only life open to them, and they married young, even becoming the second or third wives of much older men. Even girls who attended university usually grew up to be economically dependent on husbands or fathers; only a few found work in health or education. Domestic violence was and still is widespread. And women were excluded from public life.

A 49-year-old representative of TEV-DEM told us that her parents had coerced her into marriage because they were afraid she would join the PKK guerrilla force. In 2007, she was one of the first women in Syrian-occupied Kurdistan to obtain a divorce. "Of course patriarchy prevailed here as well," Evîn, a Kurdish woman fighter, recalled to an interviewer, "and gender equality was something that could not even be whispered about."

In the Middle East, women who have been raped are commonly abandoned by their families, sometimes even murdered in "honor" killings. Men who experience economic, political, and sexual oppression soon learn to compensate for it psychologically by committing acts of violence on their family members. Taking out one's resentments on one's family is less risky than challenging oppressors. Additionally, society reinforces men's assumption that their "honor" depends on their ability to control women and children. This phenomenon is widespread, not only in the Islamic world.[6]

Even though Syrian Kurdish women were socially disadvantaged in relation to men, however, thousands of them participated in grass-roots organizing in the 1980s and 1990s. PKK ideology holds that the liberation of society is impossible without the liberation of women, so the movement offered them a valued place and an education. "You mustn't forget, the head of the PKK lived here for twenty years," we were often told on our May 2014 visit. "His work shaped the way we think." In retrospect, 15 years after the departure of Abdullah Öcalan, his philosophy and methods, and especially his efforts to empower women, seem foundational for the new society and the mainspring of the revolution. Öcalan's influence "was immense," said Evîn. "In Rojava at that time, it was mainly the women who supported the movement."[7]

The Kurdish women's movement seeks to overcome the alienation of Kurdish women—that is, the colonialist disparagement of their own culture. It seeks to ensure that they take responsibility for their own lives and become capable of making their own decisions. They discuss ways the patriarchal system of domination maintains its power by dividing and isolating women from one another. These women become determined to carry out a struggle for their liberation and that of all women. A further principle is to create a new aesthetic, to define ideal values that contrast with the materialistic culture of patriarchy, to find women's own forms of expression, and to reconfigure art and culture from a women's perspective.[8]

In the 1990s, the PKK encouraged and educated thousands of women in this way, creating spaces where women could participate. Women went from house to house, knocking on doors, to try to convince the women at home to join the movement. They did regular educational work and held women's assemblies. And many women from Rojava, like Evîn, went to North Kurdistan to join the PKK women's army, the YAJK [see 3.1].

5.2 Women in the Revolution

In Rojava, the idea gained acceptance that women would be the spearhead of the revolution. They played a prominent role in the preliminary organizing. Between 2004 and 2012, as Hanife Hisên explains, "only women could function politically ... They organized at the grass-roots, did educational work, and held congresses. The men who organized would get arrested, so the organizing work fell to the women."

"There were 60-year-old women who had been active in the freedom struggle for 30 years," says Ilham Ahmed. "Even if they couldn't read or write, they knew the philosophy of the movement and could share it as well as their own knowledge." But most *could* read and write. In Syria, as of 2011, more than 90 percent of children attended elementary school, and more than two-thirds continued their education further. And the fact that women's organizing was considered strategic was also decisive. According to PKK ideology, patriarchy, a system that justifies the exploitation of nature and society, can be overthrown only by creating a new society that rests on non-patriarchal principles of communality, ecological economy, and grass-roots democracy.

Once the revolution began, women arrived from other parts of Kurdistan to support it, including many who had spent decades fighting with YJA Star. They brought their fighting and organizing skills, as well as their theoretical and practical experience with Democratic Autonomy. Öcalan "described the organizing model in detail, and we were very familiar with the books," said Amara, a women's movement activist in Dêrîk. "Now we just had to implement it."

5.3   Kongreya Star—Kongreya Star a Rojavaye Kurdistanê

Yekîtiya Star (the Star Union), Rojava's umbrella women's movement, was founded in 2005. *Star* refers to the ancient Mesopotamian goddess Ishtar, and nowadays the name also refers to celestial stars. In February 2016 at its Sixth Congress, it was renamed Kongreya (Congress) Star, in accordance with the Kurdish women's movement as a whole, which changed its name in February 2015 to Kongreya Jinen Azad (Congress of Free Women).

Under the Ba'ath regime, Yekîtiya Star activists were arrested and tortured. Today, all women in West Kurdistan who are involved in TEV-DEM's social, political, and military work are also members of Kongreya Star. It's basic to the Kurdish women's movement to build women's institutions in every area, so that women can disengage intellectually, emotionally, and spiritually from the authority and violence of patriarchal domination.

Kongreya Star in the Communes

Hilelî is a relatively poor neighborhood in Qamişlo, but support for the council system is very strong there. Şirîn Ibrahim Ömer, a 45-year-old

Figure 5.1   A Kongreya Star assembly, Dêrîk

woman in Hilelî, told us about the women's work. "We are sixty active women in the commune. Once a week we do educational work, we read books together and discuss them."

In building Yekîtiya Star, explains Şirîn, the primary goal was to educate the whole society politically. Political education is still the core of their work: "Twice a month we visit women in the neighborhood and explain the agenda of the revolution." Their goal is to visit every woman in Hilelî at home, regardless of whether she is part of the Kurdish movement. "We even go to [women of] the KDP," she says. "Many women still have the mentality of the state—they don't see themselves as people who can function politically. They have lots of kids, and they have conflicts at home.

"Before the revolution," Şirîn says, "many women married young, in girlhood. Now they see that education can give them a better life." And "once it was normal here for people to have the television on 24 hours a day," she told us, "with lots of Turkish programs in Arabic. But then the electricity was shut off, and that left people's minds free to think about something else." As a result of the grass-roots work, she says, "we know everyone in the neighborhood."

They offer the women a ten-day training on the subject of communes and councils. Once women are connected, they take part in a weekly two-hour educational session. One of the authors had a chance to participate in educational work when Zelal Ceger, of the Yekîtiya Star board, spoke to representatives of the women's councils in Dêrîk. She made a comprehensive assessment of the current situation, then emphasized the necessity of visiting every family in a commune, not just the families that TEV-DEM had already recruited. That way perhaps the family could be brought into the commune system. "If you aren't knowledgeable, you can't work," says Zelal Ceger. "Women have to educate themselves in order to participate."

"We want women to become self-reliant," says Adile, of the Dêrîk women's center. "We go to the villages too and talk to women there. Many of them don't dare to speak to us, but afterward, secretly, they make their way to us. We collect a little money, but it's symbolic, a token amount. And we distribute a newspaper"—*Ronahî*—"which appears once a week, in both Arabic and Kurdish. It's cheap, so everyone can get a copy. When we get together now, we don't gossip and chitchat the way we used to. Instead we talk about the political developments and women's organizing."

The women's movement also publishes a newspaper called *Dengê Jiyan*, which carries articles on women's history and analyses of, say, "the democratic family"; it also publishes news about, for instance, the family law recently passed by the council. Women proposed that law to the Supreme Constitutional Committee; after it was passed, it became binding on everyone in Rojava. As a result, childhood marriage and forced marriage are now forbidden, as is *berdel* and polygamy.[9]

The women's movement's values have had a great impact on the new society, as people try to live by them.[10] Legislation and the administration of justice represent only a transitional phase—the goal is an ethical society in which a justice system is superfluous.

For now, the peace committees [*see* 9.2] solve family problems. "If a man hits a woman," says Adile, "he gets at least a month in jail. Previously women had no rights. But now we even have women's courts. The *mala jinan* [women's houses], the Asayîşa Jin [*see* 9.4], and the courts all mutually assist one another. When there are problems between men and women, we document the problems, and we talk to the men. Many times they've left their wives. If we can't solve the problem, such as when a man pays no alimony or child support, then we go to court. And we investigate underage marriages. There is a real marriage market in Turkey. Girls are sold over the Internet."

The Sara women's center in Qamişlo investigates and documents cases of domestic violence.[11] Asayîşa Jin can be called in to help the women. And in Hilelî, any man who beats his wife is now socially ostracized, says Şirîn, so wife beating has all but vanished.

Almost every day the media in Rojava report on the creation of new women's communes, not only in the Kurdish neighborhoods but also in the Arab neighborhoods and villages.[12] These communes send representatives to the assembly of the women's councils (Meclîs). Remziye Mihemed, the co-chair of the Qamişlo People's Council, explains that "a society that can't maximize women's potential has a great weakness. We're struggling to make people aware of this fact. Because like it or not, over the years, the regime and the Arab mentality have strongly shaped the thinking of our men. We now have to use everything we've got to try to shake that mentality off. We're trying to ensure that women play a leading role in Qamişlo. Our work is already bearing fruit in the cities. Many families are already encouraging their daughters to get socially involved."[13]

In addition to the communes, the Rojava Revolution has created a system of councils, in villages and districts and neighborhoods [see 6.3]. And alongside the mixed councils are women-only councils, established first in Kurdish cities, then in Damascus, Aleppo, Raqqa, and Hesekê, and other cities and villages: "Yekîtiya Star established a women's council in every district in the cantons and also in the Syrian cities with large Kurdish populations, in order to advance the interests of women and to promote a democratic, ecological, gender-liberated society. They are the interconnecting decision-making bodies for all women."[14] Nûha Mahmud, a 35-year-old activist in Qamişlo, explains that innumerable victims of sexual violence have made contact with the women's councils.

5.4 Women in the Three Cantons

Because of Turkey's embargo against Rojava [see 12.3], we could not travel to Afrîn or Kobanî. But women's organizing differs among the three cantons, we were told.

In Afrîn, the westernmost canton, women are very self-aware, Ilham Ahmed told us, and "men's influence within the society is very weak.

Both within the family and in the society, women have organized a coexistence with men. Children flock to the women. The idea that women should stay home and run the household is very rarely heard in Afrîn." Afrîn women perform heavy agricultural work alongside men and are equally represented in the institutions. They have laid a good foundation for educating and organizing themselves. Many take part in Democratic Autonomy organizations and in the women's councils. One reason for Afrîn's gender equality is the fact that "the clan structures play no special role" there, the fighter Evîn told us, "and society has more petit-bourgeois features."

As a result of the Syrian war, Ahmed told us, people have fled the embattled areas and poured into Afrîn. Among them were organized crime groups, people with no personal connection to Afrîn, who committed attacks on women. Violence against women and prostitution, said Ahmed, "became serious problems. The leadership in Afrîn's democratic self-government tried to raise awareness through education, seminars, projects, and workshops, and do something about these problems."

In Kobanî canton, the influence of the tribes is more persistent, along with their feudal clan structures. As a result, Ilham Ahmed told us, the movement in Kobanî was weak before the revolution. "The tribes are more important than the political parties," she said. "They hold the society together. But unlike other political parties, they were not against the revolution." During the revolution, Kobanî's tribes became more open. Most people sympathized with the liberation. The PYD is popular here—other parties are present, but they have little influence and insignificant support. "The revolution had the biggest influence" in Kobanî, Ahmed told us in May 2014.

Before the revolution, she told us, "it was impossible for women and girls to walk alone in the city. State-employed teachers and officials would sexually assault girls, and the regime tolerated these attacks, so women and girls couldn't move around freely, or organize, or go to work. But the revolution put an end to the sexual attacks, and those responsible were punished, which allowed a positive social climate to emerge. Women in Kobanî could then participate more freely in revolutionary work. And because of their formerly acute oppression, they had enormous revolutionary potential."

Kobanî canton has "communal values that have not been destroyed as in capitalist society," the fighter Evîn pointed out. But the movement's pre-revolutionary weakness in Kobanî meant that it encountered many problems in building Democratic Autonomy. The women, however, brought all their energy to it. At first, the women were active only in the nine mixed councils in the Kobanî neighborhoods. Then a women's house (*mala jinan*) in Kobanî created the women's council, so that women would be able to make decisions autonomously. In the spring of 2013, 135 women participated in the Kobanî women's council to address local women's issues. All councils observe the 40 percent gender quota and the dual leadership principle [*see* 5.5].[15]

The 2014–15 attack by IS destroyed much that was built in Kobanî. But on October 27, 2015, Kobanî passed a set of women's laws that are binding on everyone in the canton, banning childhood marriage among other things.[16]

5.5   Dual Leadership and the 40 Percent Quota

The principle of dual leadership (*hevserok*) applies everywhere in Rojava. Whether it's in a commune or in a court, everywhere leadership is vested in two people, and one of them must be a woman. As Asya Abdullah, one of the two co-chairs of the PYD, states, "Look at the purported opposition in Syria. You won't find a single woman among them. Ask yourself, what kind of a revolution do they want, in which some parts of society aren't represented? How can they talk about freedom and democracy yet overlook the equality of men and women? How can a society be free when its women aren't free?"[17]

For all mixed-gender institutions, a gender quota applies. That is, in every council, every commission, every leadership position, every court, women must make up at least 40 percent. A hefty proportion of women are participating in Rojava's revolutionary work: in Afrîn, 65 percent of the civil society, political, and military institutions now consist of self-organized women. That includes communal administration, councils, and commissions. In the 44 municipal institutions, 55 percent of the workers are women. In the agricultural sector, it's 56 percent, and in the Kurdish-language institutes and the teachers' union, the proportion of women is 70 percent.[18] In the education sector, the proportion of women among the teachers is even larger: in Kobanî, it's about 80 percent, and in Tirbespî almost 90 percent.[19] Women are founding their own radio stations to address women's issues—in Kobanî ten young women are running such a station.[20]

"We're still a long way from achieving our goals," says Asya Abdullah, co-chair of the PYD. "But we've learned from the failed revolutions in the past. They always said, 'Let's carry the revolution to success, and then we'll give women their rights.' But after the revolution, of course, it didn't happen. We're not repeating that old story in our revolution."[21]

Figure 5.2   Dual leadership: The co-mayors of Serêkaniyê

5.6   Women's Organizations

Women's Education and Research Centers—Navenda Perwerde û Zanist Jinê

In Rojava women have established Women's Education and Research Centers not only in Kurdish cities and villages but also in Arab cities with large Kurdish populations. Since 2011, two women's academies have opened, as well as 26 educational centers.[22] Women bring their family and social dilemmas to these centers and find solutions by talking with other women. The centers also offer courses on computer use, language, sewing, first aid, and on children's health, and culture and art. The women decide for themselves what they need. "We are laying the foundation so that in the future women can decide about women's subjects," says Ilham Ahmed. "A new consciousness and self-awareness is emerging."

The Women's Education and Research Centers double as meeting places for other women's organizations. A representative of the center in Serêkaniyê told us that "through the commune system we get to know every family. We know their economic situations, we know who beats his wife and children." While we were visiting the women's center in Serêkaniyê, we witnessed such an inquiry. Two older Arab women came and asked for help. After marital separations, they were demanding compensation.

The primary task of the Women's Centers is to educate women politically, to encourage them "to investigate reality, then to change reality with new knowledge and new learning, to reconfigure it to achieve a more beautiful life and a free society," says CENÎ, the Kurdish women's office for peace.[23]

Since 2011, Yekîtiya Star has been building academies whose purpose is to strengthen women ideologically. Women in the PKK guerrilla army have developed Jineolojî, or "women's science." (The Kurdish word *jin* means "woman" and *ologî* derives from the Greek for "knowledge." The word *jin* is also related to the Kurdish concept *jiyan*, which means "life.") According to Jineolojî, knowledge and science are disconnected from society—they are a monopoly controlled by dominant groups, used as a foundation for their power. The goal of Jineolojî is to give women and society access to science and knowledge and to strengthen the connections of science and knowledge to society. Jineolojî also wants to develop the vision of a good life, and the councils are putting it into practice; theory and practice are always in communication.

Dorşîn Akîf, the head of a women's academy in Rimelan, reports that Kurdish women regard Jineolojî as "the culmination of that decades-long experience" of fighting in the guerrilla army. It represents "the kind of knowledge that was stolen from women" and that can be recovered. At the women's academy in Rimelan, she says, students of Jineolojî "are trying to overcome women's nonexistence in history. We try to understand how concepts are produced and reproduced within existing social relations, then we come up with our own understanding. We want to establish a true interpretation of history by looking at the role of women and making women visible in history."[24]

The women's question is no longer limited to legal and political issues—it is empowering women to consider all social problems as their own and as part of their struggle. For example, some women in the Kurdish movement want to find a new aesthetic, to reinvent art and culture from women's perspective, using their own forms of expression.

Young Women's Movement—Tevgera Jinên Ciwan

Doz Kobanî, of the Youth Confederation, says that "the most important part of our work is the women's work. Our chief [Abdullah Öcalan] says correctly that without the freedom of women, society cannot be free. So we especially address young women and do educational work. First we explore the history of civilization and the 5,000-year history of patriarchy. We explain the position of woman in society before patriarchy and what man has done to her in all the eras since. These discussions are very important for us."

On May 16, 2014, one of the authors attended the third conference of Young Revolutionary Women in Cizîrê, held in Rimelan. Around 230 young women from all parts of the canton converged here to assess the work of the previous year and to set new goals for the coming year. They analyzed the role of women in the Middle East in general and rejected traditional role models. They discussed Capitalist Modernity, rejecting its commodification of women's bodies. "As Kurdish women in the Middle East," declared Hanife Hisên in her opening speech, "we oppose these images. If we want to build a democratic, egalitarian society, we have to solve the woman question first. The basis of all oppression is women's subordination, which as a system is tied to Capitalist Modernity."

One of the principal themes of the conference was youth: "We started [the revolution] with young people, and with young people we will achieve success." The women all spoke with great determination and composure. They evaluated the obstacles to their organizing work, such as the persistent attempts of families to prevent young women from political engagement. The attendees resolved to do more work within families. They valued educational work highly. A few pointed to the underage marriages that many girls are still forced to enter. The discussions were frank and animated. The young women elected a 15-member board and resolved to strengthen their ideological and political struggle for women's liberation.

Figure 5.3   Conference of Young Revolutionary Women, May 2014 in Rimelan

Syrian Women's Association—Însyatîfa Jinên Sûriyeyê

Yekîtiya Star laid the foundation in Rojava for collaborations among women of different ethnic groups. In March 2013, the Syrian Women's Association was founded, by women who were Kurds, Arabs, Ezidis, and Syriacs. The association is not part of the council system, but Kurdish, Arab, and Syriac women are working together to write a new democratic constitution for Syria, one that will guarantee the rights of all women and all the peoples.[25] The association has crafted laws and conducted numerous forums on the subject of women's liberation.

At the Dêrîk women's center, Zîhan Davut, head of the Syrian Women's Association, explained that "when the revolution began, we didn't want to have the same negative experiences as in the Arab Spring. We wanted the rights of women to be established legally. Up to that point, individual women here had no rights here at all. We wanted to change that not only in Rojava but in all of Syria. Here it's mostly the women who work and organize ... Here in Rojava it's difficult to reach the Arab women, because they don't know their rights. Just to go to a meeting, they have to get permission from their husbands. But we're gradually building contacts with them. Meanwhile we already have lots of Arab women in our organization."

Syriac Women's Association—Huyodo da Nesge Suryoye b'Suria

Later, Zîhan Davut accompanied us to the Syriac Women's Association. "We're beginning to organize," a young Syriac woman there told us, "and our social position has already improved. Some of us were inspired by Yekîtiya Star and decided to organize an association. Since then more women have joined, especially in Qamişlo."

Domestic violence has long existed in Syriac families just as in Kurdish ones, although it was more taboo. In Syriac society, Zîhan Davut explained to us, a few women worked as doctors and lawyers and led economically independent lives. And once upon a time, another woman explained, Syriac women thought of themselves as more progressive than Kurdish women. Now they realize that Kurdish women, through organizing and discussions, have attained more freedom. Syriac women have been inspired by their example to adopt entirely new roles, such as by joining the Asayîşa Jin.

The revolution, a Syriac woman explained, has led women to exchange ideas and mutually expand each other's understanding. Many Syriacs live in Hesekê, so on October 13, 2013, the first Syriac women's center was opened there. Still, "our society is unfortunately very fragmented, and there are many parties and organizations that compete with one another," lamented one of the women.

Kurdish Women's Press Association (RAJIN)

"To overcome patriarchal hegemony"

"Women should become visible and write their own history": the Rojava's women's movement takes this principle very seriously. In the cantons, women have above-average representation in all media, from radio and TV to news agencies. But they consider it important to also be organized into a union of journalists.

The Kurdish Women's Press Association (RAJIN) was founded in the Qandil Mountains in 2013. In May 2014, the Kurdish women journalists of Rojava held their first conference in Qamişlo, where they founded the Kurdish Women's Press Association of Rojava (RAJIN Rojava). The conference was organized as part of the YJA campaign "Free Woman for the Democratic Nation" and organized around the slogan "A free women's press and a free society, in honor of Gurbetelli Ersöz."

(Ersöz was editor-in-chief of the Kurdish newspaper *Özgür Gündem* in Turkey in the early 1990s. She was arrested on December 10, 1993, and the paper was banned. After six months, she was released, but the proceedings against her continued, and she could no longer find work as a journalist. In 1995, she joined the PKK guerrilla army. On October 7, 1997, she lost her life in an ambush by the KDP.)[26]

At RAJIN Rojava's founding conference in Qamişlo, 70 delegates participated, as well as Yekîtiya Star board members Ilham Ahmed, Zelal Ceger, and Medya Mihemed, not to mention the YPJ press office. The conference agreed that October 7 would be the annual day commemorating women journalists in Kurdistan.

"We're fighting to recover our identity," Medya Mihemed said in the opening speech, "which was historically free but was stolen from us. Kurdish women in the PKK have chosen to struggle for freedom, for a free way of life. We have now taken decisive steps toward creating a free society. Today the press is tied to a patriarchal mentality, because masculine hegemony dominates in all media. But the struggle is slowly breaking that down … The struggle waged by women of the press will become the basis for the free press."

The conference resolved that RAJIN members would take part in a political and organizational educational effort to enlighten the male members of the press union (Azad-YRA) about gender consciousness and everyday use of language. It further resolved that women should be integrated into the technical and professional aspects of the media, that a women's radio station in Rojava would be set up to broadcast, and that a women's media academy should be opened.

Foundation of Free Women in Rojava—Weqfa Jina Azad a Rojava

In 2014, the Foundation of Free Women was founded in Qamişlo, with the goal of improving women's lives and supporting women's organizing. As a first step, they circulated a questionnaire among women in Qamişlo. Their findings: 73 percent of those surveyed live in small families. Ninety-two percent said they needed education to improve their economic situation. Sixty percent wished they had childcare. The results made it clear that even before the war and the embargo, institutional violence against women was widespread in Qamişlo.

The foundation develops projects like women's health centers and pre-schools, and it supports the creation of women's cooperatives [*see* 12.5] and women's parks. A women's village is even planned. "Because of the preexisting violence and its increase due to the ongoing war," says the foundation, "women and children in Syria experience traumatic events every day. Such deep-seated social problems require long-term and broad solutions. For all our important projects, money is urgently needed."[27]

5.7   Gender Equality is Also a Men's Issue

Women who attempt to emancipate themselves face considerable difficulties. "A woman who wants to play a part in the revolution," observes Ilham Ahmed, "has to overcome obstacles. Her family will give her trouble, especially the men. When a man comes home from work, he expects to see everything ready for him. His wife is considered his property, so she is to be there for him, to see to his comfort. She's not supposed to leave the house. All the social rules and conventions support a husband in this privileged position, by which he exploits his wife. And many men beat their wives. In many cases, when women tried to become politically active, their husbands gave them a choice: political work, or me.

"Many women, faced with the choice, decide against their husbands. They leave home to become politically active. Once they get to know freedom, they never want to give it up. Many women who reach this point are rethinking their relationships with their husbands, because of their newfound economic independence." In December 2015, a women's delegation from Hamburg was told that 30 of 58 women in the Asayîşa Jin in Dêrîk were divorced in one year: "That forces the men to accept reality, to face the facts, and change themselves. They see that women are getting recognition for their work in the society, and they recognize that they should support them instead of subjugating them."

Osman Kobanî, a member of the people's court of Kobanî, emphasizes the role of the new justice system: "Some men have several wives. Often these men value the wives who bear sons more than those who bear daughters, and they treat [the latter] like second-class people. But the people's court is breaking up that mentality. Most of the cases in which women are involved are divorce suits."[28]

Their many long years of struggle have given Kurdish women self-awareness. They reject women's traditional patriarchal role and adapt to the new role of freedom fighter because they have so much to win and so little to lose. Women by the thousands have become active in urban and village councils.

The rapid transformation of women's role has come to many men almost as a shock. We often heard, "The women here have taken over everything!" But much educational work has also taken place in the mixed institutions, which helps the men come to grips with changing gender roles. Young men too are experiencing new roles: in their military units, they have to perform the same tasks as women, they have to learn to cook, to bake bread and do laundry. Fighting sexism and creating gender equality will be a long and protracted process.

5.8   Radical Islam Versus Women's Emancipation

"'These women are defending not only themselves but all Syrian women."

Asya Abdullah

When radical Islamic forces attack in Rojava and South Kurdistan, they are also attacking women—it is femicide. When jihadists take over cities, they announce it over loudspeakers from the mosques, reports Axîn Amed, a human rights worker.[29] Women abducted by IS are either "given" to IS members or "sold" in markets like commodities. Eyewitnesses have reported cases of women who refused to submit whose breasts were cut off and their bodies mutilated.[30]

IS considers it *halal*, permitted, to rape women who don't share their ideology, even girls. On June 18, 2014, in Mosul, the ISIS mufti decreed: "Wives and daughters of soldiers and politicians who work on behalf of Maliki are *halal* for members."[31] Rape and sexual violence are a deliberate, long-standing tool of warfare that expresses absolute contempt for women and disdain for their physical and personal integrity. A rape purports to demonstrate that the woman's male family members have not fulfilled their patriarchal duty to protect her, since in most Middle Eastern societies, a rape destroys the family's "honor" (*namûs*) and a raped woman is considered shameful. The threat of rape is a conscious instrument of war with the goal of provoking revenge and forcing emigration.

According to Asya Abdullah, in the summer of 2013 in Hesekê province, IS "abducted, raped, and murdered a large number of Armenian women. In this region Kurds, Arabs, Christians, Druze, Sunnis, and Alawites had all lived amicably with one another. Peaceful coexistence is itself an object of attack by the [radical Islamic] groups. Today they attack Kurds, but their goal is to eradicate the coexistence of peoples. They have set their sights especially on Kurdish women, because Kurdish women are playing such an active part in the fighting, defending not only themselves but all Syrian women."[32]

In August 2014, IS attacked Ezidi and Christian villages and cities and captured more than 7,000 women. They repeatedly raped them, then sold them at slave markets as chattels; they gave them over to jihadists as war booty or forced them to marry. They sold the children as sex slaves. They pressed cell phones into the hands of enslaved women, so they could call their families and tell them about the atrocities. Some women implored their families to tell the armies to bomb the places where they were being held, because they preferred death to the repeated rapes. "I've been raped thirty times today and it's not even lunchtime," said one woman. "I can't go to the toilet. Please bomb us," she said. "I'm going to kill myself anyway."[33]

The Kurdish women's movement characterizes capitalist patriarchy as "rape culture."[34] The IS is one of the most extreme forms of this supremely exploitative culture. As author Dilar Dirik writes, "Many of the methods and mechanisms of the IS are copies of the dominant nation state-oriented, capitalist, patriarchal world order which reigns everywhere in 2014 in the world. In many ways, the IS is a more extreme version of violence against women all over the world, the world that is considered progressive."[35]

Here are a few of the laws that ISIS decreed on June 26, 2014, in Turkmen villages:

- Women must veil their faces completely.
- Women may not leave their homes without a male escort.
- Women may not go to the markets at all, not even with a male escort.
- If a family has two daughters, one must be given over to IS. A woman whose "husband" dies at the front is "given" to another IS fighter.

- If a woman lives at home for longer than three months without a husband, she must marry a man chosen by IS fighters.

Rojava's woman-centered society is thus the antithesis of IS. Many politically active women in Rojava told us that they wished women would organize everywhere and defend themselves against the horrors committed by the Islamists and struggle for a new role for women.[36]

5.9 Outlook

Not all women participate in Rojava's women's organizations. Women in many places remain economically dependent on their husbands and families. Many have not yet achieved the ability and mentality to determine their own fate. Female students, initially eager to get involved, withdrew in disappointment since they couldn't fulfill their individual dreams; due to the war situation, many aspirations have had to be renounced. Women and men who were privileged under the regime yearn to return to pre-revolutionary times. The system of self-government requires a great deal

Figure 5.4   A women's demonstration in Qamişlo

of work, and it is unpaid. After sixty years of dictatorship and Ba'athism, many people expected that a new state would eventually reemerge and that they would be able to withdraw into private life. But Democratic Autonomy demands much engagement.

Still, women have taken many steps forward in the liberation of women. The most important has been to organize. When women create strong organizations, they clarify for themselves and each other how to imagine another life, and when they use the organization's force to put their imaginings into practice, they have a lever to wield against any future structural oppression. And as Ilham Ahmed points out, now that they have made such considerable sacrifices, they are not going to back down.

The revolution in Rojava has rendered Abdullah Öcalan's paradigm of a women-liberated society—beyond state, power, and violence—more tangible for the Kurdish community. An activist on the women's council in Cologne explains, "For thirty years I've been in the PKK movement, and I've read all of Öcalan's books, but deep inside I always thought, 'We should struggle for a Kurdish state.' Only with the Rojava Revolution, with the women's communes with Arabs and Syriacs, have I really understood what it means to create a woman-centered society without the state."

The Rojava Revolution, with its vanguard of women activists, could catalyze a new image of woman in the entire Middle East. Ezidi women in Şengal and Arab women are already starting to organize according to this model. In Europe, too, these developments have unleashed great enthusiasm. Emulating the academy system in Rojava, feminists in Germany are beginning to discover this educational work.[37]

The Kurdish women's movement in Rojava is not organizationally part of the Komalên Jinên Kurdistan (KJK) system, but it's ideologically related—that is, it shares the KJK's goals.[38] Among those goals are "to fulfill the women's revolution that began in Kurdistan and to extend it into the Middle East as a whole, and to strive for a worldwide women's revolution." These are no small goals. Back in 1993, when Kurdish women decided to establish a women's army, only a few really believed such a thing was possible. Today, as a regular army, they are successfully doing battle with IS.

Notes

1. Zübeyde Sarı, "Women of Rojava," Özgür Gündem, September 8, 2013.
2. "Der kurdische Widerstand verkörpert das Gute," *Die Welt*, October 18, 2014.
3. Elizabeth Griffin, "These Remarkable Women Are Fighting ISIS, and It's Time You Know Who They Are," *Marie Claire*, September 30, 2014, http://bit.ly/1kiDf8c.
4. "Women of the YPJ/Female State," *60 Minutes Australia*, September 28, 2014, http://bit.ly/1IsUpvK.
5. Care Deutschland-Luxemburg E.V., *Arabischer Frühling oder arabischer Herbst für Frauen? CARE-Bericht zur Rolle von Frauen nach den Aufständen im Mittleren Osten und Nordafrika*, September 12, 2013, http://bit.ly/1MSa4k5.
6. Fatima Mernissi, *Beyond the Veil: Male-Female Dynamics in Modern Muslim Society* (Cambridge, MA, 1975).
7. Evîn was interviewed by a German internationalist in the summer of 2013 in South Kurdistan. Her interview is unpublished.
8. Ceni Fokus Nr. 1, *Der Hohe Frauenrat Koma Jinên Bilind* (Düsseldorf, 2011).
9. *Berdel* is a traditional marriage practice in which a family gives a woman to another family either in exchange for another woman or as a settlement for a family feud. The patriarchal family and feudal institutions of property and tribe facilitate *berdel*.
10. "Malbata Demokratik û hevratiya azad" [The Democratic Family and the Free Life Together], in *Xweseriyademokratik a jin* [Democratic Autonomy of Women] (Dengê Jiyan, 2013).
11. "Li Rojava civak bi rengê jinan të avakirin," Azadiya Welat, n.d., http://bit.ly/1OZq6fl.
12. "Yekîtiya Star Establishes All-Women Commune in Til Temir," *ANHA Hawar News*, June 26, 2015, http://bit.ly/1Rh70EM; "Women Establish Commune Center in Efrîn," *ANHA Hawar News*, June 29, 2015, http://bit.ly/1Ni7w1n.
13. Quoted in "Die Revolution in Westkurdistan—Teil 8," *Civaka Azad*, n.d., http://bit.ly/1PpKLr3.
14. Rosa Zilan, "Frauen als treibende Kraft," *Civaka Azad*, n.d., http://bit.ly/1Fs5ER8.
15. Karlos Zurutuza, "For Kurdish Women, It's a Double Revolution" Inter Press Service, November 5, 2013, http://bit.ly/1KjBSoA.
16. "Kobanî Canton Declares Women's Laws," *Besta Nûce*, October 29, 2015, http://bit.ly/1mh9Ddg.
17. Asya Abdullah, interview by Pinar Öğünç, "Ohne die Freiheit der Frau keine Demokratie," *Radikal*, August 22, 2013, http://bit.ly/1QovIQD.
18. "Women in Efrin," *Ajansa Nûçeyan a Firatê* (hereafter *ANF*), September 25, 2013, http://bit.ly/1KjMLzi.

19. *Hawar News*, October 3 and 26, 2013.

20. *Hawar News*, September 21, 2013.

21. Asya Abdullah, interview by Pinar Öğünç, "Ohne die Freiheit der Frau keine Demokratie," *Radikal*, August 22, 2013, http://bit.ly/1QovIQD.

22. "Die Revolution in Westkurdistan—Teil 8," *Civaka Azad*, n.d., http://bit.ly/1PpKLr3.

23. "Aufruf zur Unterstützung der Frauenakademie in Amed und zur Frauendelegation im Sommer 2012 nach Kurdistan," CENÎ, n.d., http://bit.ly/1EYDFbx.

24. Janet Biehl, "Two Academies in Rojava," Biehlonbookchin.com, 2015, http://bit.ly/1xKAhcp.

25. "Information Dossier: Zu den Massakern in Westkurdistan (Rojava)," CENÎ, ca. 2013, http://bit.ly/1Ajhooy.

26. "Gurbetelli Ersöz—Ein Leben für Gerechtigkeit," http://bit.ly/1EiQclf.

27. Jina Azad Bingeha Civaka Azade, http://bit.ly/28Rp9co.

28. "Revolution in Westkurdistan—Teil 5," *Civaka Azad*, n.d., http://bit.ly/1JslHhp.

29. Axîn Amed, of Komela Mafen Mirovan (Human Rights Association), conversation with Michael Knapp, October 11, 2013.

30. CENÎ, Informationsdossier zum IS.

31. *Halal* (Arabic) in the sense of "permitted" by Islamic law.

32. Abdullah, interview by Öğünç.

33. "'I've been raped 30 times and it's not even lunchtime': Desperate Plight of Yazidi Woman Who Begged West to Bomb Her Brothel After ISIS Miltiants Sold Her into Slavery," *Daily Mail Online*, October 21, 2014, http://dailym.ai/1RKHMhx.

34. The Kurdish women's movement considers land grabs, the deployment of armies, and the exploitation of soil and people to be part of rape culture. See Anja Flach, "Jineolojî—Radikales Denken aus Frauensicht: Bericht von der ersten europäischen Jineolojî-Konferenz in Köln," *Kurdistan Report*, no. 173 (May–June 2014): 43–50, http://bit.ly/1URHYfJ.

35. Dilar Dirik, "Die kurdische Frauenbewegung und der Islamische Staat: Zwei gegensätzliche System in Kobanê," *Kurdistan Report*, no. 176 (November–December 2014): 20–21, http://bit.ly/1M4ES5d.

36. "How Refugees Resist and Why They Don't Need Your Help," *Karawane*, June 22, 2016, http://bit.ly/28TCSeR.

37. Anja Flach, "Ansätze für eine feministische Neuorganisierung in der BRD, Feministische Akademien," *Kurdistan Report*, no. 182 (December 2015), http://bit.ly/1NN6r37.

38. "About Us," Komalên Jinên Kurdistan, http://bit.ly/1lWFI9y. The KJK is the umbrella organization of all women's organizations that support the Democratic Confederalism and women's liberation ideology. The KJK was founded in 2014 as the successor organization of the KJB (Koma Jinên Bilind, or Supreme Women's Council). On ideological, organizational, and

political questions and question of the legitimate self-defense of the women's movement that are of strategic importance, the KJK makes decisions and implements them collectively. Each component organization works directly with its statutory identity and in coordination with the other component organizations. See Gönül Kaya, "Eine neue Etappe in der Kurdistan-Frauenfreiheitsbewegung," *Kurdistan Report*, no. 179 (May-June 2015), http://bit.ly/1NP7nTt.

6

Democratic Autonomy in Rojava

6.1 The Democratic Union Party (PYD)

Even before the Party of Democratic Unity (PYD) was founded in 2003, Kurdish movement activists in Rojava were creating committees and working groups clandestinely. On the initiative of the PKK, they established committees to organize and discuss political developments, teach small-group Kurdish-language courses, administer local justice, and address women's issues. After 2003, the PYD sought to bring in as many people as it could, both party and nonparty.

Once the Syrian uprising began in March 2011, the PYD foresaw that a long and brutal conflict could develop. So it made a conscious decision to create a set of people's councils, both in Rojava and in other parts of Syria where it had strong, supportive Kurdish populations. The councils, as institutions of self-rule, would be independent of party structures. By organizing such a council democracy, the movement could begin to implement Democratic Autonomy.

For a practical model, the PYD looked across the border to the achievements of the Kurdish freedom movement in North Kurdistan. Since 2007, the Democratic Society Congress (DTK) had been setting up people's councils in the mainly Kurdish areas. Although the DTK's organizing was hampered by the repression of the Turkish state, the PYD in Syria could benefit from observing its experiences.

Once its own organizing got under way, the PYD was able to create people's councils sooner than expected. Within a matter of months, a functioning council system was in place in Rojava's cities, large and small, and in Aleppo. Not every urban neighborhood had a council, especially those with majority Arab, Syriac, and other non-Kurdish populations and those with Kurdish populations that favored the ENKS. Many rural areas, too, lacked councils—while some self-organization existed at village level, but the structures were weak.

Nonetheless, in 2011, the council system was sufficient to constitute a vibrant structure parallel to the state without being in direct conflict with it. Most Kurds had no interest in an armed confrontation with the state, and as we have seen, they chose to side neither with the state nor with the nationalistic-Islamist opposition but to carve out a "third way" [see 4.2]. The regime, for its part, chose not to attack the council movement and instead concentrated on subduing the uprising in non-Kurdish areas.

6.2 The People's Council of West Kurdistan (MGRK)— Meclîsa Gela Rojavayê Kurdistan

By August 2011, perhaps almost half of Rojava's Kurds were organized in councils. That month, about three hundred delegates from Rojava and other organized parts of Syria met to establish the People's Council of West Kurdistan (MGRK) to further develop people's councils, commissions, and coordinating bodies. They elected a coordinating body of 33 people called TEV-DEM (Democratic Society Movement— Tevgera Civaka Demokratik). The system would be open to all peoples and all democratic parties; no single party or rigid ideology would dominate. The MGRK invited diverse parties, groups, and individuals to join. By the end of 2013, the following parties had joined the MGRK:

- Democratic Union Party (Partiya Yekitîya Demokrat, PYD), which had no special status even though it was the driving force
- Kurdish Leftist Party (Partiya Çepa Kurdî li Surîyê, PÇKS)
- Liberal Unity Party (Partiya Yekîtiya Lîberal)
- National Community Party of Syrian Kurds (Partiya Civaken Niştimanen Kurdî li Suriyê)
- Kurdish Unity Party in Syria (Partiya Yekîtiya Demokrata Kurdî li Suriyê)
- Peace and Democracy Party of Syrian Kurds (Partiya Aşitî u Demokrasî ya Kurdî li Suriyê)

In the summer and fall of 2011, the state was still running—although poorly—the economy and public services. Beleaguered by the war, it could not handle everything. So the MGRK gradually filled in the gaps, and the neighborhood councils took on more tasks. The neighborhood councils were in no position to organize a neighborhood's whole social and economic life, and they had no experience upon which to rely after a certain point, not even in North Kurdistan. But the people increasingly turned to them for solutions, as they gradually became a real alternative to the state, especially in matters of justice, infrastructure, and security.

By the spring of 2012, hundreds of thousands of people were flocking to the neighborhood meetings, eager to participate, in numbers far greater than the venues could accommodate. The revolution unleashed enormous social energy that had been repressed for decades. Clearly, the neighborhood unit was just too large. So to allow all residents to represent and organize themselves, the MGRK created a new level in the cities' council structure: the commune, at the level of the residential street. Mamoste Abdulselam, of TEV-DEM in Hesekê, told us that "there was a gap between the councils and the people—that's why we developed the commune system."

This opened the door to activism on the part of many more people. In 2013, after the communes proved to be a very positive development, the MGRK would initiate a broad campaign to spread them to rural areas.

But in the spring of 2012, the state maintained its grip on power only in the city centers, in public buildings, and in neighborhoods where it had political support (particularly Arab and Syriac). It still provided a few basic services like trash removal, but inadequately. Some predominantly Kurdish neighborhoods, like Hilelî in Qamişlo, were cut off from public services entirely.

On July 18, 2012, armed Syrian opposition forces launched an offensive on Damascus and Aleppo. The MGRK and YPG expected that the FSA and others would enter Rojava soon, to attack the state there. The next day, the revolution started in Kobanî. In just over a year, from March 2011 to July 19, 2012, Rojava had established its new direct-democratic social order. This lead time was very short, but on July 19 it was ready. The revolution succeeded because the people in cities and villages had organized themselves in advance.

After the revolution of July 19, the MGRK became the politically responsible entity in the liberated areas. It had to prove that the people's councils and communes were not simply an emergency administration, as the ENKS claimed; rather, they were a conscious, ongoing project. So they were obliged to come up with solutions for all social problems, even as important sectors of the population remained uninvolved, especially in Cizîrê.

6.3 The MGRK System

Based on our delegation's visits in May 2014 and October 2015 and our subsequent interviews with activists, we developed this description of the MGRK system. Readers should be aware that it has evolved over time and will surely continue to do so.

The Four Levels of Councils

The MGRK councils exist at four levels, organized like a pyramid stepwise from the bottom up.

1. The Commune

The base level is the commune. In the cities, a commune usually encompasses 30–200 households in a residential street, and in the countryside a whole village. In the large cities of Hesekê and Qamişlo, a commune may consist of up to 500 households. Note that it is not individuals but households that determine the size of a commune.

In Hesekê, Mamoste Abdulselam told us, "About fifty houses constitute a commune. We have a lot of communes—each neighborhood has ten to thirty, with fifteen to thirty people each. The Mifte neighborhood has twenty-nine communes, while the next one over has eleven. Each neighborhood has about twenty communes per thousand people." Çinar Sali of TEV-DEM explained to us, "The commune is the smallest unit and the basis of the system of Democratic Autonomy. It is concerned with meeting the needs of the people. Let's say you need something for your street. In the old system, you'd have to file a petition, which would be forwarded to Damascus. It could take years till someone finally took notice and addressed it. Our system is far more effective."

At the end of 2015, the number of communes in Cizîre canton exceeded 1,600. Many villages and residential streets still do not have communes, so efforts continue to establish them. The number of communes grows with every liberated area in Rojava. In Afrîn, all the streets and villages are now organized in communes, approaching five hundred in all. For

Kobanî canton, the level of self-organization is difficult to determine due to the destruction by the IS occupation and siege. But with every week, new communes are (re)founded in Kobanî.

Every neighborhood and every village community in Rojava has a people's house (*mala gel*), where the commissions and the coordinating boards meet to discuss political activities. It is also a contact point for the people on all political and social issues. The people's house is open 24 hours a day. If communes do not have their own spaces, they may also use these people's houses.

Most of the second-level women's councils operate a women's house (*mala jinan*), which is the focus of women's self-government and can assist on all issues. The people's houses are buildings that were socialized after the regime abandoned them. Sometimes they rent out a building. Sometimes the activists build an entirely new building. The people's councils pay attention to whether a house makes sense from an energy standpoint— mud houses are preferred. Çinar Sali adds, "If there's a women-specific problem in the street, a conflict in the family, the commune tries to solve it. If the problem exceeds the capability of the commune, it goes to the next level up, to the neighborhood council, and so on."

Every one or two months, the people living in each residential street can go to an assembly meeting. Silvan Afrîn, a women's economist from Yekîtiya Star in Dêrîk, explained, "Initially communes were established only in the Kurdish neighborhoods, but now we're setting them up in the Arab neighborhoods as well. Anyone can go to a commune assembly— you don't have to be a member of TEV-DEM or the PYD. It's an open meeting, where people in the neighborhood talk about their problems, and everyone comes, Arabs, Kurds, Syrians, everyone."

A commune's coordinating board consists of its two co-chairs (one woman and one man) and one representative (sometimes two, one woman and one man) from each of the commissions at the base level. The two co-chairs and the commission representatives are elected usually biannually, but sometimes annually. Those elected to the coordinating board have an obligatory mandate, meaning they are subject to recall if they do not meet the wishes of the majority. We asked how many had been recalled and were told there had been several cases in Cizîrê, but not many. The coordinating board meets weekly, on a regular basis. Every resident can take part in these meetings, whether it is to listen, to raise a criticism, or to make a suggestion. Citizen participation is much appreciated, activists told us, especially when there's an urgent question that needs addressing.

2. The Neighborhood

The next level up is the neighborhood, usually comprising seven to thirty communes. In the countryside, the second level is the village community, which usually consists of seven to ten villages. The communes are represented at this level through the coordinating board, which makes up the plenum of the neighborhood council. "Hesekê has sixteen neighborhood councils now," Mamoste Abdulselam of TEV-DEM told us. "Every council is made up of fifteen to thirty people."

Delegates from the communes to the councils are subject to imperative mandate. At the neighborhood councils' meeting, members elect its coordinating board and its male co-chair. The women's council at the neighborhood/village community level chooses the female co-chair. As at the commune level, the coordinating board meets often, usually weekly.

The meeting also forms commissions in the eight areas (see below), which will meet separately. Activists who are not members of the people's council can also join the commissions at this level.

Figure 6.1   A meeting of a neighborhood people's council in Dêrîk

Parties, NGOs, and social movements are not usually involved in the lower levels, since in these, people participate broadly, outside the context of political parties.

3. The District

The third level up is the district, which encompasses a city and the villages in that city's surrounding areas, usually seven to twenty.[1] The boards of the neighborhood and village communities' people's councils represent their councils at the district level. Usually 100–200 activists come together in a district people's council. Here once again, the area commissions are formed and co-chiefs are elected.

The coordinating body of a district council, representing many communes and neighborhoods, is known as the TEV-DEM. It consists of 20–30 people.

The political parties and NGOs and social movements usually enter the council system at the district level, since its area of representation is much broader than that of the neighborhoods. Parties actively involved in the MGRK are represented in the TEV-DEM by five persons each. No distinction is made between the PYD and the other parties. "One hundred and one people sit on Heseke's district council," Abdulselam

Figure 6.2 A meeting of the people's council of Qamişlo district

told us. "The PYD has five representatives, as do five other parties. Families of the martyrs have five, Yekîtiya Star has five, the Revolutionary Youth have five, and the Liberals have five."

4. The MGRK

The highest level is the People's Council of West Kurdistan (MGRK), made up of all the district councils. When the MGRK met in August 2011 for the first time, it elected the TEV-DEM for all of Rojava, consisting of 33 people (not including Aleppo). These 33 people plus more activists become members of the eight commissions for all of Rojava. At this level, the commissions have fewer members than at the lower levels. At the second congress of the MGRK, Abdulselam Ahmed and Sinem Muhammed were elected as the co-chairs.

In the summer of 2013, attacks by IS, Al-Nusra Front, and other Islamist organizations made it difficult for MGRK activists to move among the three cantons. In August, movement between Cizîrê and Kobanî was cut off, while movement between Kobanî and Afrîn remained possible until June 2014. Thereafter, the three cantons plus Aleppo were left on their own. Since then, the MGRK, the TEV-DEM, and the eight commissions for each canton have existed separately.

Each cantonal TEV-DEM initially consisted of eleven people. In June 2015, the YPG/YPJ forces liberated Girê Spî (Til Abyad) and its surroundings, which geographically connected Kobanî and Cizîre cantons. Girê Spî is a culturally mixed city of Arabs, Kurds, and Syriacs, while its surroundings, particularly to the east and south, are populated mostly by Arabs, with a strong Kurdish minority. After several months of discussion, a council in Girê Spî was established with the participation of all parts of society. This council discussed forming its own canton, but at the end of 2015 it chose to become part of Kobanî canton. Connecting Kobanî and Cizîrê has strengthened the coordination of the Rojava cantons.

The Eight Areas

Each of the four levels has eight areas (in Kurdish, qada or saha) in which commissions (also called committees) function. Most of the activity of self-administration takes place in these commissions. In some places, the council structure lacks commissions in some of the eight areas, especially

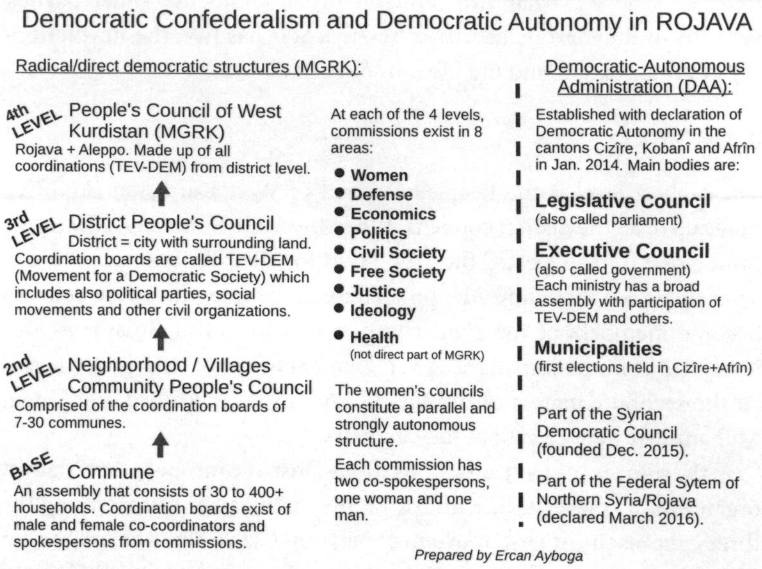

Democratic Confederalism and Democratic Autonomy in ROJAVA

Radical/direct democratic structures (MGRK):

4th LEVEL People's Council of West Kurdistan (MGRK)
Rojava + Aleppo. Made up of all coordinations (TEV-DEM) from district level.

↑

3rd LEVEL District People's Council
District = city with surrounding land. Coordination boards are called TEV-DEM (Movement for a Democratic Society) which includes also political parties, social movements and other civil organizations.

↑

2nd LEVEL Neighborhood / Villages Community People's Council
Comprised of the coordination boards of 7-30 communes.

↑

BASE Commune
An assembly that consists of 30 to 400+ households. Coordination boards exist of male and female co-coordinators and spokespersons from commissions.

At each of the 4 levels, commissions exist in 8 areas:
● **Women**
● **Defense**
● **Economics**
● **Politics**
● **Civil Society**
● **Free Society**
● **Justice**
● **Ideology**

● **Health**
(not direct part of MGRK)

The women's councils constitute a parallel and strongly autonomous structure.

Each commission has two co-spokespersons, one woman and one man.

Democratic-Autonomous Administration (DAA):

Established with declaration of Democratic Autonomy in the cantons Cizîre, Kobanî and Afrîn in Jan. 2014. Main bodies are:

Legislative Council
(also called parliament)

Executive Council
(also called government)
Each ministry has a broad assembly with participation of TEV-DEM and others.

Municipalities
(first elections held in Cizîre+Afrîn)

Part of the Syrian Democratic Council (founded Dec. 2015).

Part of the Federal Sytem of Northern Syria/Rojava (declared March 2016).

Prepared by Ercan Ayboga

Figure 6.3   The MGRK council system

at the lower two levels. The number of commission members is usually not limited. At the communal level, a commission may have five to ten people, but when interest is greater, it can rise to twenty. We should note that health care is organized independently of the MGRK system [*see* Chapter 11].

Below are listed the eight areas in the MGRK system.

Women (Jin)

The women's commissions have a special status among the commissions, since they are organized as councils. Formed by Yekîtiya Star [*see* 5.3], women's councils exist in all four levels of the MGRK system, from the bottom (communes) to the top (canton/Rojava level) The women's council (at the commune level, they are called women's communes) alone chooses the female co-chair: men may not contribute to the decision. Members of the women's communes visit local women in their homes in hopes of engaging them in social and political activities [*see* 5.2]. The women's councils also work to create women's cooperatives. In the other seven areas, women are represented with a 40 percent gender quota.

Defense (Parastin)

The defense commissions work at all four levels to ensure security. The defense commission, Çinar Sali explained to us, is the smallest unit of the security system. In every commune, three people are elected for the defense commission. "They talk to the young people and get them ready," said Silvan Afrîn, "and organize the defense of the district. We have a lot of situations in which the general population, not only the YPG and YPJ, have to fight."

After the IS attack on Kobanî in September 2014, local people systematically formed defense committees called HPC (Hêzên Parastina Cewherî—Society Defense Forces). If a neighborhood is attacked, the local HPC will constitute its first line of defense, independently of the YPG/YPJ and Asayîş. The HPCs also go after drug dealers and criminals who take advantage of wartime instability. The YPG/YPJ turn to the HPCs only in exceptional circumstances; the Asayîş have much closer and more regular ties to them [see 9.4].

Economics (Aborî)

Through the economics commissions, the council system ensures that all adults have a livelihood and can support themselves and their dependents, as well as contribute to the revolution. Economics commissions are responsible for construction, agriculture and other production, shops, the supply of oil, gas, and foodstuffs, and the administration of public enterprises. During their first two years (2011–13), the economics commissions were occupied mainly with the food supply. They also create cooperatives as part of the aim to develop an alternative communal economy. People with low incomes, women, and other disadvantaged groups tend to be engaged in the cooperatives. At all four levels, the commissions collect donations and create long-term incomes for the maintenance and development of the MGRK system.

Politics (Siyasî)

Politics commissions exist in all levels but are most important at the district and canton levels. They include all political parties that support the MGRK system. They conduct diplomacy and maintain contact with parties, civil society organizations, and political groups outside the MGRK. They are also responsible for the work of municipal administrations.

Civil Society (Civakî)

Civil society commissions organize occupational groups, small tradespeople, cooperatives, and workshops and represent them in the MGRK system. Employers and wage-earners collaborate on the commissions [see 7.1].

Free Society (Civaka Azad)

Free society commissions address the needs of families of martyrs, young people, and others. They correspond to the NGOs common in statist parts of the world.

Justice (Adalet)

The justice commissions comprise the peace committees, which are the base of the new justice system [see Chapter 9]. Each peace committee has around ten members, with gender parity. They administer justice in their respective areas, attempting to resolve conflicts through consensus. The women's peace committees are separate, applying conflict-resolution strategies in cases of domestic violence and other violence against women. In Rojava, conflicts arising from patriarchal violence are not to be judged by men.

Ideology (Ideolojî)

Ideology commissions are responsible for all educational activities. In Rojava, as in the Middle East generally, the word "ideology" has fewer negative connotations than it does in Western states. The revolution has taken over the education system of the Ba'ath regime and transformed it. The ideology commissions also open and maintain academies for all eight areas of the MGRK system, using innovative teaching approaches [see 10.4]. Sub-commissions of the ideology commissions are concerned with press, with culture and art [see 7.2], and with language. Academies fill the wide social need for education in all fields. They organize seminars and meetings for the people's councils and communes, and members conduct seminars and discussions in the neighborhoods upon request.

* * *

Commissions exist at all four levels of the MGRK, but they are also cross-connected. Commissions in adjacent communes or neighborhoods, for example, often cooperate, especially in the economics area. All the economics commissions come together in a TEV-DEM economics movement and thus form their own political movement. Several sub-commissions are organized separately from the MGRK system, such as the culture and art sub-commission, which is part of the ideology commission.

Each of the women's communes and councils at the neighborhood and village community level have, parallel to the general peace committees, a women's peace committee, a judicial board consisting entirely of women. It has the right to determine whether a case significantly affects women and thus whether to take the case. The commissions of the women's councils work together with the general commissions—say, in economics, to create cooperatives for women. When the women's councils consider it necessary, they can establish commissions in each area and sub-area.

The council system has distant roots in the councils of elders in traditional society, which were widespread until the 1960s and 1970s. The MGRK system has infused these traditional institutions with the values of council democracy, gender liberation, cultural diversity and human rights. The continuity provides a bridge of understanding between tradition and revolution.

By 2014, the MGRK system had achieved support of more than 70 percent of the population of Rojava. It also gained the support of seven Kurdish parties. At first, almost all the participants in the councils were Kurds, due to the historical legacy of animosity. But with the 2012 revolution, bringing in the diverse ethnicities and cultures became one of the MGRK's leading imperatives. It carried out an active policy, with the result that some Arabs and Chaldeans join the MGRK structures. What is happening now is a lengthy process of trust building between Kurds and non-Kurds.

6.4 The Commune of Aleppo

Before the civil war, Aleppo, with more than 2 million inhabitants, was Syria's second largest city. It was also Syria's economic center, home to people from all cultures and social strata. Aleppo's northern neighborhoods were heavily Kurdish, and starting in 2011 the Kurds of Aleppo established distinctive democratic people's councils and assemblies. As expressions of the radical council democracy, they soon achieved a sophisticated level and were exemplary for the rest of Rojava and Syria. But due to the intensive bombardment by the Syrian state and the FSA and other military groups that started in 2013, they have mostly been suppressed.

At the moment of the 2011 Syrian uprising, just over half a million Kurds lived in Aleppo. In preceding decades, they had immigrated from Rojava, especially from Afrîn canton, mainly for economic reasons. Owing to anti-Kurdish discrimination, they had clustered together in the northern neighborhoods of Aşrafiye and Şêx Maqsûd.

The leftist Kurdish freedom movement gained an especially firm foothold in the western cantons, with the 1979 arrival of the PKK in Syria and Syrian-occupied Lebanon. The PKK set out to win over the people in Kobanî, Afrîn, and Aleppo and gained early support in Aleppo. As a result of the PKK's strength there, in 2003 the PYD was founded in Aleppo. In March 2011, since many PYD activists were present in the city, the Kurdish movement accomplished a great deal.

The Armenian journalist Ewan Suveyda Mahmud lived in Aleppo for two years, starting in the summer of 2011, and is an important eyewitness to events there. When we sat down with her, we pressed her with questions, and here is what she told us.

Aleppo's Councils

The MGRK system in Aleppo existed in four neighborhoods: in Aşrafiye, in Şêx Maqsûd, which is much larger, and in an area that encompassed two neighborhoods, Hayderiye and Midan. While Aşrafiye and Şêx Maqsûd were home to working-class people, petit-bourgeois Hayderiye had many Arabs as well as Kurds, and in Midan, also better off, Kurds lived alongside Armenians. In the MGRK system, Aleppo had the same number of deputies as Kobanî and Afrîn.

Each of these four neighborhoods was made up of about thirty residential streets, each consisting of 100–500 households. They corresponded in size to the larger communes in Rojava, but here the residential street units were called councils. Day and night, hundreds of people worked to integrate all the streets into the new council system. Activists visited families in their homes until midnight, working five days a week, to win them over. No one was to be left out. In early 2012, the councils achieved regular, stable functioning, at which point youth commissions were set up in all four neighborhoods. Young people joined them in such numbers that subgroups had to be formed.

A little later, the women's councils were formed and became even more vibrant. Thousands of women participated regularly in women's council meetings and raised the gender question in the mixed councils and in society at large. Both the women's and the youth councils participated in the council system as commissions.

Upper-level councils were created at the neighborhood and cantonal levels and a few more at the residential street level. More commissions were founded as the need arose.

The commissions and councils in each neighborhood met in a people's house (*mala gel*), which would be open (and guarded) 24 hours a day, and any resident could come and raise issues with the councils. In 2012, the women's and youth councils built a center for the entire Aleppo region. A house for Kurdish-language instruction was built, which later, as the state was driven out, coordinated language instruction in the schools. A small but significant number of non-Kurds took part in the councils in Aşrafiye and Şêx Maqsûd, especially in the summer of 2012, Mahmud told us, "as the councils began working better and life was better organized. If not for the 2013 attacks, people would have accomplished much more, because in the councils they felt represented."

Aleppo's council system operated efficiently, Mahmud told us, since its areas of activity were well defined: "Compared with the council system in Cizîrê today, Aleppo's was very well structured and disciplined." One reason was surely the fervent political organizing, but another was perhaps the complicated political situation in Aleppo. As usual in the MGRK system, every council at every level had dual leaders, male and female, and together with the representatives of the existing commissions made up the coordinating board, which in turn represented the council at the higher levels.

A regular monthly calendar evolved. On the 20th of every month, the commissions at the lowest level (including the women's and youth councils) would meet. On the 21st of every month (or every two months, according to need and desire), the general assemblies of the communes would meet, for the whole population of a residential street. On the same day, the communes' coordinating boards would also meet (every month). Then on the 22nd, the neighborhood-level commissions (including women's and youth councils) would meet, and on the 23rd, the coordinating boards of the neighborhood councils. On the 24th and 25th, the neighborhood's people's council assembled, made up of the coordinating boards of the communes. On the 26th and 27th, the people's council of the Aleppo region met.

Clearly, much discussion had been necessary to set this intricate council system in motion, but Mahmud says it was "the only way they could develop effectiveness. It might seem that there were too many councils and commissions, but in an assembly democracy, that's necessary for decision-making and for bringing in the whole population. When thousands of people get involved politically, that's incredibly meaningful for the society and for political life."

Political discussion was intense in and around Aleppo, due to the advanced political organization and the interconnections among Kurds, non-Kurds and non-Muslims, and diverse political groups. In the residential streets and neighborhoods, weekly seminars and lectures were held, mostly practical in orientation but sometimes highly theoretical. Given the presence of a university in Aleppo, many students participated as well. The dynamism of the system between 2011 and 2013 can still be felt today, as Aleppo's MGRK system was the model for the structure in Rojava. And important activists in Afrîn canton's councils came from Aleppo, so Afrîn's system is running very well too.

The Defense of Aleppo Commune

Before the spring of 2012, the councils did not organize a strong system of defense because Aşrafiye and Şêx Maqsûd were not under attack. Mahmud told us, "The war was hardly felt in Aleppo, and the state remained present as always. The council system initiated some defense units, but they were secret. Their members were few, and they never appeared in public wearing military garb or carrying weapons. During the regular Friday pro-democracy demonstrations, for example, they stayed in the background, ready to protect the demonstrators against possible attacks."

But in the spring of 2012, fighters of the Ba'ath regime or the FSA took to shooting randomly, with no warning, into the Kurdish neighborhoods, injuring or killing people. The residents began to arm some of the youth through the council system, creating YPG units, but they weren't trained systematically or professionally and weren't able to cope with the attacks. Then suddenly as the war escalated, defense took priority over all other issues. The councils concluded an agreement with YPG commanders in Rojava: from that point, to serve in Aleppo's YPG, a person had to undergo basic military training in Rojava. Within a few weeks, experienced YPG fighters from the three cantons helped build strong forces in both major neighborhoods of Aleppo. According to Mahmud, "The purpose of defense was to protect the Kurdish neighborhoods against outside attacks."

The Aşrafiye and Şêx Maqsûd neighborhoods, she explained, "are located on an upland, and so they have strategic military importance ... That was additional security for the Kurds, useful for keeping them from being destroyed or expelled, or even worn down between the militarily far superior regime and the FSA."

But in July 2012, the situation changed almost overnight as the FSA and other armed opposition forces attacked Damascus and Aleppo simultaneously. Rebels from nearby rural areas invaded several neighborhoods, mainly Sunni Arab ones, and took control. In the next days and weeks, armed YPG set up roadblocks at all entry points into Aşrafiye, Şêx Maqsûd, Midan, and Hayderiye and posted guards. That put a stop to the FSA advance.

In a few weeks, the number of YPG units rose to four digits; they obtained weapons from the black markets and from Rojava. Then in the fall of 2012, the Asayîş [see 9.4] was formed, to handle internal security matters like criminality, violence against women, and extreme alcoholism. Their numbers were smaller, and they were chosen by the councils and held accountable to the Aleppo people's council. There was a clear separation between YPG and Asayîş. The YPG were not to move around in public unless it was necessary.

The war in Aleppo escalated in brutality and destruction—or rather, it did so outside Aşrafiye and Şêx Maqsûd, owing to the militant self-organization there. From the summer of 2012 to the spring of 2013, Kurds fled to the two neighborhoods for safety. "Even the city's elites sent their family members into the Kurdish neighborhoods," said Mahmud, "because they were the most secure. Mainly women and children came. The newcomers weren't armed and presented no danger, and the council system accepted them as long as that didn't change."

But the war couldn't leave the two neighborhoods in peace. They weren't in the center of Aleppo, but their strategic topographical position made them critical militarily. Both belligerents—the regime on one hand, and the FSA and other armed opposition groups on the other— pressured the YPG to take sides.

The FSA, flush with money from the Arab-Sunni Gulf States, began systematically buying up property in the Kurdish neighborhoods. FSA members purchased lodgings in the homes of Kurdish families— especially families that supported the center-right KDP-S and Azadî parties, and also families that were not political or not particularly integrated into the council system. FSA members took to carrying their weapons around outdoors—but the councils took notice and demanded that they cease doing so.

The councils also demanded that the FSA pull out of Şêx Maqsûd toward Aşrafiye. During Ramadan, on August 19, more than 3,000 people demonstrated in support of this demand. But the FSA didn't withdraw—instead, it fired at the residents from buildings. The YPG fought back, and in the hours-long battle, 13 civilians and several FSA fighters were killed. The day's fighting put the people on notice that they had to organize themselves better, both politically and militarily.

The hospital in northern Aleppo was closed, and most of the doctors had fled, so young people cared for the wounded—they had been instructed in basic wound care for a few months. But this and other battles drove the FSA out of Şêx Maqsûd and Aşrafiye. The controls at the entrances to the two neighborhoods were improved so that no one could just walk in. Over the next months, the FSA kept shooting into the two neighborhoods, but now from a distance.

Since the Kurds had not sided with the regime, the regime forces became increasingly brutal. The army intervened militarily, then began attacking targets with helicopters and planes, each time taking several lives. The YPG's defense actions caused many casualties among the attackers.

The hardships escalated rapidly, as Mahmud recalled. "The state shut down the electricity, and finding food and provisions became harder. There was a de facto food embargo. It became ever more dangerous to leave or try to come back. Sugar was five times more expensive than before. Sometimes due to the scarcity of diesel, there was no bread. Once there was no bread for five days. The winter of 2012–13 was very hard.

For heat, we burned everything, plastic and wood. Yet the people stayed in Aleppo—after all, many of them had lived there for sixty years."

The Kurds had often been accused of collaborating with the Ba'ath regime, but the regime refuted all those accusations through its behavior in Aleppo. In March 2012, the councils decided not to celebrate Newroz, the old Iranian new year and spring festival usually commemorated on March 20–21, because the state was bombarding all gatherings. But at Newroz 2013, the situation was excruciating. The Kurds controlled those two strategic upland neighborhoods, but the councils resisted being used by either one side or the other. The Kurds' neutrality angered both sides, the state and the FSA, which escalated their attacks. "Both the state and the FSA raised their pressure on the Kurds," Mahmud told us. "The embargo was tightened. Despite many promises to deliver food, sometimes nothing came. Once ten days passed with no bread. Rice was cooked for so long that we could feed it to the children as substitute milk."

The state targeted the FSA forces still in Aşrafiye and demanded that the FSA leave the neighborhood. Soon there were only a few FSA groups on the two neighborhoods' perimeter. The FSA insisted that regime forces were being allowed entry into the Kurdish-controlled neighborhoods and repeatedly fired on the houses. In 2013, the YPG was now a stronger force than it had been in 2012, but armed mainly with Kalashnikovs (AK-47s), it could hardly hope to equal either the state forces or the FSA in weapons.

Because of the embargo, the Kurds had little prospect of obtaining better defensive weapons. Almost nothing could arrive from Afrîn. Defending Aşrafiye and Şêx Maqsûd became all the harder because both neighborhoods were so densely inhabited. The YPG had to consider carefully its every action, due to its vulnerability.

In April 2013, the Aleppo people's council decided to evacuate most of the population to Afrîn and other parts of Rojava for safety, while it continued to try to hold on to northern Aleppo. The evacuation was poorly planned—people rushed out into the roadways. But some 400,000 were safely evacuated, some 75–80 percent of the population. Most of those remaining were young people.

In the summer and fall of 2013, the YPG defended Aleppo well, pushing back attacks by Islamic and other armed opposition groups, as well as parts of the FSA. But at the end of 2013, IS started to enter the city of Aleppo. In January 2014, armed opposition groups advanced against IS and drove it out of Aleppo and Azaz. In the spring of 2014, the YPG concluded a ceasefire with the FSA and other armed opposition groups. Al-Nusra, still present in the region, adhered to the ceasefire. As a result of the new circumstances, the areas that were not under regime control (Aleppo, Azaz, Idlib) could be supplied with food and other basic provisions over the border crossing at Azaz.

After the ceasefire, people moved back and forth between Aleppo and Afrîn, and hundreds, perhaps several thousand, Kurdish refugees returned to Aleppo. But most of them remained in Afrîn, because the city of Aleppo was by now a smoking ruin. The refugees settled in to their new locale and are integrated, politically and socially, into the council system. Since early 2015, the self-governed parts of Aleppo have repeatedly come under attack from jihadists. The new coalition Jaish Al-Fatah, led by Al-Nusra (Al-Qaeda) and heavily supported by Turkey, is continually trying to conquer the liberated parts of Aleppo, but the people of Şêx Maqsûd are maintaining their self-defense.

In Aleppo, Ewan Suveyda Mahmud told us, in summary, "we had a well-functioning system. Democratic Autonomy was speedily implemented, and the people became socially and politically active. The council system had a special dynamic in a city that was diverse not only ethnically and religiously but also politically and socially. It was much stronger here, at first, than in the three cantons of Rojava. Activists from Afrîn, Kobanî, and Cizîrê studied the system here and learned from it.

"Sadly, defense was the weak point, and also the fact that Aleppo is like a little island in northern Syria. Both the state and the FSA tried to sweep the Kurds into their murderous war, but the people took pride in not becoming a puppet for either side—even if it meant evacuating 400,000 people. The people of northern Aleppo wanted to remain neutral, not to kill or be killed.

"They tried so hard to keep their distance from the war and to endure the destruction … In January 2013, when Sakine Cansız, Fidan Doğan, and Leyla Şaylemez were murdered in Paris, they demonstrated in the tens of thousands, risking bombardment by the state to do so. They stand by what they have built. Wherever people from Aşrafiye, Şêx Maqsûd, Hayderiye, and Midan meet, they say proudly where they come from: that is, from the commune of Aleppo!"

6.5 The Supreme Kurdish Council (SKC)—Desteya Bilind a Kurd

Shortly before the liberation began, on July 11, 2012, the MGRK and the ENKS concluded the Hewlêr Agreement [see 4.4] and created the Supreme Kurdish Council (SKC), to ensure unity among Kurds. Eight days later the MGRK and YPG carried out the July 19 revolution, in which the ENKS played no role. A few days after Rojava's cities were liberated, the MGRK announced that the area affirmed the SKC as the highest political authority. Over the next weeks, the SKC convened many times to discuss the new administration in the liberated areas, even as the MGRK and its activists exercised the practical power in most of them.

In November 2012 the parties agreed on an addendum to Hewlêr, instituting a joint Kurdish military leadership. The ENKS demanded that in addition to the YPG, the self-government have a second military force, one set up by the ENKS. The MGRK and the YPG objected, saying that a second military force would lead to intra-Kurdish conflicts, as in South Kurdistan, where the two parties, the KDP and the PUK, had militias that actively warred against each other from 1994 to 1998. Instead of constituting a second force, the YPG suggested that the ENKS fighters, trained in South Kurdistan, should be integrated into the YPG.

But the ENKS rejected that idea. Further, it demanded more direct decision-making authority in the liberated areas, even though its parties had no notable institutions or grass-roots activists there. In fact, the ENKS demanded enough power for itself that it could overrule the council system and dominate it from the top down. To justify this demand, it invoked the Hewlêr Agreement.

The MGRK responded that the ENKS demands went beyond the Hewlêr Agreement. All SKC groups were free to collaborate with the district councils, but the MGRK council system must not be touched. The MGRK proposed that until the joint administration foreseen in the Hewlêr Agreement could be built, a transition period could be experienced.

Relations deteriorated after the summer of 2013, mainly because while IS, Al-Nusra, and parts of the FSA mounted massive attacks on Rojava's three cantons,[2] the ENKS and the Iraqi KDP remained uncannily silent and did not even permit aid to enter Rojava. The ENKS and the KDP seemed to expect that the MGRK would grow desperate and would have to turn to them for support and so would accept their demands.

As we think about the parties organized in the ENKS and their power politics, the following quote from Murray Bookchin may be appropriate to keep in mind: "Parties that do not intertwine with these grass-roots forms of popular organization are not political in the classical sense of the term. In fact, they are bureaucratic and antithetical to the development of a participatory politics and participating citizens. The authentic unit of political life, in effect, is the municipality, whether as a whole, if it is humanly scaled, or as its various subdivisions, notably the neighborhood."[3]

6.6   The Municipal Administrations

Close on the heels of the 2012 revolution, Rojava faced the pressing task of maintaining and improving public services. Before the liberation, municipal administrations (local authorities) had been relatively weak, installed and controlled as they were by the state in Damascus. When the state departed from Rojava, the council system did not dissolve the existing municipal administrations or dismiss their staffs. Instead, they retained the municipal officials so that services would continue without interruption. Trash removal, drinking water supply, sewage treatment, and traffic control had to function normally until they could be analyzed and improved.

Attack on the Qamişlo City Hall

The Qamişlo City Hall stands amid streets that are partly controlled by the regime and partly by the councils. When we arrived on May 10, we saw antitank barriers and guards outside. Security had been tightened as the result of an IS suicide attack two months earlier. In the entryway, we saw a photo of ten City Hall staff and visitors who had been murdered in the attack. The building had suffered massive damage, and some parts had collapsed. The two suicide attackers shot the guards at the entrance, then barged into the building and threw hand grenades into every room. The co-mayor Meaz Ebdulkerîm was wounded—when we met him, he was walking on crutches.

Rûken, the other co-mayor, had hidden in the bathroom during the attack, along with nine other women. One of the terrorists approached the bathroom door with a grenade, about to throw it in. A young man

---

who happened to be in the building—he worked for the municipal food distribution—spotted the attacker, threw himself onto him, and pinned him down until the grenade—which had already been activated—exploded. "He could have saved himself by jumping over the balcony," Rûken told us, "but when he realized that we women were in the bathroom, he saved our lives and sacrificed himself."

In addition to eight City Hall staff members, two civilians were murdered that day. One of them was Awaz, a young man who had come to register his marriage. One of Qamişlo's important women's activists, Helepçe Xêlil, was among those murdered. She was six months pregnant.

A few days earlier we had been in the Korniş neighborhood municipality hall. Hemrin Xelîl, one of the women in the neighborhood government—responsible for sanitation, water supply, bread, and electricity—said that Helepçe, who had worked there, "wanted to green the neighborhood, so children would have a place to play. We've opened a park near here, in her memory." She showed us the office of her murdered friend—her records and signature were everywhere, just as they had been "when I arrived here," said Xelîl. "Helepçe was educated in Amed [Diyarbakir] in North Kurdistan. She knew the ropes here better than anyone else—she understood what had to be done. We learned a lot from her."

Rûken shared her memories of the attack with us. "Blood was everywhere," she recalled, "body parts, cartridges. Hand grenades had been thrown into every room. Ten friends died—only those who were in the bathroom survived. It lasted thirteen minutes, but it felt like ten years.

"After three days, we came back and cleaned everything up. At first we almost jumped out of our skins whenever we even heard even a ballpoint pen drop. Once a light bulb exploded, and I almost lost my mind."

The martyrs:

Helepçe: co-mayor of Qamişlo (Rûken, has taken over her tasks)
Rewşen: ecology, gardens, and parks. Her goal was to green Qamişlo. The
   women in the city hall have taken over her work.
Emine: economics and finance
Fehed and Ali: foods inspection and distribution
Musa: city hall security
Ibrahim: price controls on food
Awaz and Ciwan: civilians. Awaz was at the City Hall to register for his
   wedding

Despite the terror from IS and others, the City Hall staff were not intimidated and those who survived returned as soon as possible to continue serving the people.

Figure 6.4　The martyrs of the Qamişlo city hall

Immediately, the councils placed the municipal administrations under the direct control of the district council's political commissions. From then on, all municipal administrations would be accountable to the district council. In the first months, the same personnel were replaced; those who had been very close to the regime, or who were repressive or nationalistic, were let go, as were most of the mayors. Dual leadership was introduced into the municipal administration, chosen by the councils of the neighborhoods or the city in plenary. All municipal staff were to meet regularly, to discuss agendas and hear the proposals of the people's councils. In this way, the municipal administrations were democratized relatively smoothly.

In the cities, the council system took over the existing buildings of the municipal administrations. In the countryside, where the Syrian state had run a municipal administration for every seven to ten villages, that infrastructure became part of the council system. In Qamişlo and Hesekê, however, the regime still controlled the city halls as well as equipment and much else. So in those two cities, the councils had to construct new buildings for the new municipal administration.

In the fall of 2012, in Qamişlo and Hesekê, trash removal became a problem. The sanitation trucks of the state-controlled municipal administration no longer collected garbage in the liberated areas, so within a few weeks mounds of trash were piling up in the streets. The situation was worsening by the day, so the Revolutionary Youth (Ciwanen Şoreşger) scrambled to put together a campaign, and with broad popular support, the accumulated garbage vanished from the streets in a matter of days. Fortunately, the dumpsites were in the liberated areas, but experienced personnel, trucks, and capacity were missing. It was an important moment, for the councils had to figure out carefully how to tackle the issue. But they rose to the challenge and soon organized both personnel and trucks on a permanent basis.

Scarcely was the garbage problem solved than the harsh winter of 2012–13 arrived, bringing dire heating problems. Rojava's heating system depends on oil, of which Cizîrê had plenty, but it had no petroleum refineries—for decades, more than half of Cizîrê's petroleum had been sent to the West Syrian city of Homs for refining. The new administration had hardly any diesel or heating oil in reserve, and the last of it was quickly used up. Only a little diesel smuggled from South Kurdistan was brought into Cizîrê, while inside Syria diesel was also smuggled, but the need far outstripped the supply and the price increased. Only the well-off could afford diesel for heating.

The rest of the population had to find other sources. First, unfortunately, they burned wood. They felled many trees, even in city parks and in villages. There was a systematic clearcut of trees in Cizîrê and Kobanî. In Afrîn, the tree cutting was less noticeable, because the area still has forests and many olive orchards.

By the summer of 2013, the councils finally succeeded in refining petroleum in greater quantities into diesel, thereby avoiding another total wipeout of trees the following winter. In fact, in 2014, some new city parks were laid out, and planted with trees. We visited a small park in the Qamişlo neighborhood of Korniş, which was opened as a memorial to Helepçe Xêlil, who had been murdered in a bomb attack on the Qamişlo City Hall in April 2014.

People's Municipalities

The municipal administrations are now known as "people's municipalities," and they have taken over basic services like trash removal, provision of drinking water, wastewater treatment, supervision and regulation of building construction, city planning, street organization, and traffic flow. They are now democratically controlled, directly accountable to the people's councils in the districts and also the neighborhoods and village communities, which approve all major decisions. They discuss issues and develop solutions, but they themselves have no political representation. They play no great role in the general political discussions, but just perform their strictly delineated tasks.

Qamişlo undertook a special restructuring of its municipality. In addition to establishing a metropolitan municipality for the whole district, it established municipalities for its six large neighborhoods, as is done in large cities in Europe. The staff for the metropolitan municipality was carried over from the previous municipal administration, but the municipalities' staffs have been put together anew, and their buildings were also newly built.

Due to financial shortfalls, the number of staff is limited, and only a few equipment purchases can be made. The embargo makes many things impossible. Remuneration for the staff is average for Syrian circumstances, and financing for the administrations comes mainly from the MGRK. Tax levies, once the main source of revenue, no longer exist. After the transitional phase of the revolution, a fee was imposed for construction approvals. Today, the most important revenue source is the fees levied for water, trash removal, and other municipal services. Charged to households, they amount to one or two dollars per month. The poorest families can be exempted, as decided by the municipality.

The people's municipalities are managing exceedingly well considering the circumstances. Just as before the revolution, they can repair damaged pipelines for drinking and waste water without great delays. In Dêrîk and Serêkaniyê, in the city centers, the streets are mostly quite clean, although sometimes a little trash is strewn about. In the outskirts, a lot of garbage sometimes piles up, but that's the case in many other Middle Eastern cities. Trash removal is still slow but is improving. In 2014, quite a few potholes in the city streets and on the main roads were filled in with asphalt. In 2015, many more roads in and around the cities of Cizîrê were blacktopped.

But the municipal administrations lack the financial and technical means to make greater investments in infrastructure. If the current political situation and the embargo continue for several more years, the situation could become critical. Long stretches of water pipe over long distances may have to be replaced, or the drinking water supply facility may have to be renovated, or high-value technical equipment and machines may have to be upgraded. Some things can be smuggled in from North or South Kurdistan, but not large machinery.

But the people's municipalities of Rojava differ from those in other countries in having the active support of the broad population, which can help overcome many challenges. On March 13, 2015, elections were carried out in Cizîre canton, in twelve districts (though in Til Temir this was impossible, due to IS). These elections were held for the "district municipal parliament." On October 11, 2015, in Afrîn canton, elections were held at the lower levels (not district level). Independent election commissions were created. Creating a list of voters was a challenge. The communes and neighborhood councils went to all the buildings and distributed election cards allowing a person to vote. Although not 100 percent of the population voted, the elections were a success considering that everything had to be set up anew. Never before had genuinely free elections been held in Rojava or Syria.

In the elections, candidates run as individuals, not as members of a political party. In the Cizîre canton, each district parliament consists of 15–31 persons. In Afrîn in total, 400 people were elected. The co-mayors are not elected directly but by these district or commune parliaments. (The exception is Qamişlo, which is divided in two districts. The district parliaments of West and East Qamişlo come together to elect their co-mayors.) The next elections will take place in 2017, that is, after two years.

The elected municipalities will hardly be transformed over time into structures like those in other countries. They still have unofficial responsibility to the people's councils. But they work together closely, as we can see almost one year after the elections. Often the activists on the municipalities' and the people's councils overlap, or the two structures want to work together as they understand themselves as part of a common broad political movement. This interaction will prevent the co-mayors from making unilateral decisions about the city. And as long as people join the MGRK structures, they will remain dominant in the society. The municipalities are open to further changes, depending on discussions among the people.

6.7   The Social Contract

In 2013, the MGRK council system was on a much firmer foundation than it had been the previous year. The democratic self-administration was taking concrete form and was meeting its various challenges. Popular acceptance had grown, even among those who didn't actually participate in council meetings. Everyone living in the three cantons who accepted the basic principles was free to participate in discussions in the council system.

Some political parties have kept their distance from the MGRK council system. Only a part of the weak left opposition—mainly the NCC—accepted it [see 6.2]. A significant minority of Rojava's residents still viewed the Ba'ath regime positively and considered participation in the MGRK to be an act hostile to the state. The Kurdish parties that were not part of the MGRK refused to join the council system, perhaps fearing they would disappear if they did.

Even more painfully, most non-Kurds remained aloof from the MGRK. To be sure, the Chaldean community in Dêrîk had decided to participate in the district council as part of TEV-DEM. As for the Syriacs, the Unity Party of Syriacs in Syria, by far the largest of the five Syriac parties, joined the council system, and through its active participation, some Syriacs began to have more positive attitudes toward the Kurds. During World War I, more than a few Kurds had participated in the genocide against the Armenians and Syriacs in Turkey [see 2.3], but the Kurdish freedom movement has regained the trust of many Syriacs, and through their participation in the MGRK, it is improving further. Still, many Syriacs remain aloof.

A number of Arabs joined as well, but taken together, all these groups represented no more than 20 percent of the non-Kurds. TEV-DEM felt that non-Kurds were joining too slowly. By now, it believed, the MGRK should have had the overwhelming majority of the population in Cizîrê behind it, as was the case in Afrîn and Kobanî.

One reason the non-Kurdish groups hesitated to join the council system was that they attributed little value to direct-democratic institutions and thought of politics in terms of parties (as most Kurds in Rojava had done up to 2011). And in Syria, parties and political organizations, almost without exception, are organized according to ethnic and religious identities. Since most people in Rojava are Kurds, these groups feared that participating in the council system would mean losing their identities.

At the same time, TEV-DEM wanted to gain more recognition for Rojava in Syria, the Middle East, and the world. But only Kurds in North and East Kurdistan, and some in South Kurdistan, were showing solidarity, along with a few leftist movements in other countries. Beyond that, Rojava received no regional and hardly any international support. On the contrary, Turkey, the South Kurdistan government, and the war parties in Syria had placed it under an economic embargo.

The MGRK realized that a direct democracy like Rojava's, with assembly elements, would scarcely be welcomed internationally: it was neither wanted nor understood, and confidence in such an experiment would be lacking. Unfortunately, internationally, a government with a traditional parliament, made up of conventional parties, would be more likely to be perceived as more effective. People within Syria who were not ready to accept the council system might accept a parliament with elected representatives and conventional parties. And people internationally who did not accept direct-democratic structures were more likely to accept a more traditional system as well.

The MGRK proposed a "transitional administration" with a "common/representative parliament." All of Rojava's people, without exception, regardless of ethnicity or religion, would have a place—it would include as many groups and people as possible. The MGRK would appeal to all political parties (as long as they were not religious fundamentalist or fascist), including the ENKS, as well as other organizations, and groups to join.

The first round of discussions addressed the principles for the new joint comprehensive administration. A social contract was sketched out, which in October 2013 was presented to the public for comment. A dynamic unfolded such as the region had never before seen. The discussions went on for three months, and suggestions were collected. TEV-DEM held dozens of conversations with groups outside the MGRK, and in the end, more than fifty organizations of Kurds, Arabs, Syriacs, and others came together.

But the ENKS refused to participate, stubbornly holding to the view that the MGRK represented only a small part of the population, that it had had no right to legislate, and that it could work only through the SKC. (But even a strong SKC would have lacked legitimacy, as under its auspices non-Kurdish people would not have been represented.) The ENKS's refusal to participate was, at least in part, the result of pressure from the KDP government.[4]

Three parties in the ENKS coalition thought this objection went too far. They had concluded that the new transitional administration was the best option for serving the interests of all the peoples in Rojava. In late 2013 and early 2014, three leftist parties—the Democratic Leftist Party of Kurds in Syria (Partiya Çepa Kurdî li Surîyê, PÇKS), the Kurdish Leftist Party, and the Democratic Kurdish Party of Syria (PDK-S)—decided to leave the ENKS and announced that they would join the transitional administration. However, before the three parties could leave, the ENKS excluded them. Thereafter, more small Kurdish parties joined the transitional administration, parties that belonged neither to the MGRK or to the ENKS—including the Communist Party of Kurdistan and the Green Party of Kurdistan.

Guaranteeing Human Rights

In January 2014, a commission considered all the hitherto submitted proposals for a social contract and compiled a draft. In its very first sentence, it affirms the system's emancipatory and gender-equal character: "We, the people of the Democratic Autonomous Regions of Afrin, Jazira and Kobane, a confederation of Kurds, Arabs, Assyrians, Chaldeans, Aramaeans, Turkmens, Armenians and Chechens, freely and solemnly declare and establish this Charter, which has been drafted according to the principles of Democratic Autonomy."[5]

The Social Contract, we must point out, does not reflect the MGRK council democracy that has been in place since 2011. It does not mention the MGRK by name. It is not very revolutionary or libertarian. But it is the product of fifty parties and organizations, brought together from a state just emerging from dictatorship. It was formulated in such a way that all those participating could agree. It represents a compromise, but one that is relatively positive. All fifty groups, for example, agreed to reject the nation-state and the centralized regime, and all fifty agreed to gender equality, democracy, environmental, youth, and social rights. Perhaps one or another aspect is missing, and some things still appear a little vague, but in comparison to European constitutions, the Social Contract is not only progressive but one of the most advanced in the world.

The Social Contract assigns no particular leadership to the Kurds but instead emphasizes the society's multicultural (ethnic as well as religious) character. It establishes Kurdish, Arabic, and Aramaic as the three official languages in Cizîrê. In Kobanî and Afrîn, the official languages are Arabic and Kurdish; if needed, others can be adopted, either locally or across the canton. The contract expressly protects the rights of smaller ethnic and religious groups. It recognizes Ezidism as an equal religion and sets firm minimum quotas for the representation of Syriacs and youth.

Interestingly, the Social Contract does not officially refer to the self-governing region as "Rojava." Rather, it speaks of the three cantons, or autonomous regions. The first articles states: "The Charter of the Autonomous Regions of Afrin, Jazirah, and Kobane is a renewed social contract between the peoples of the Autonomous Regions … The Autonomous Regions are composed of the three cantons of Afrin, Jazirah and Kobane, forming an integral part of the Syrian territory … The Canton of Jazirah is ethnically and religiously diverse, with Kurdish, Arab, Syriac, Chechen, Armenian, Muslim, Christian and Yazidi communities peacefully co-existing in brotherhood."[6]

The Social Contract states that the three cantons are to be governed on the basis of Democratic Autonomy and are to become part of a democratic Syria. They are to serve as models for all of Syria. The contract invites the rest of Syria to participate: "All cities, towns and villages in Syria which accede to this Charter may form Cantons falling within Autonomous Regions" (Article 7). Neighboring cities and districts may either join the existing three cantons or establish their own autonomous administrations.

In terms of human rights, the Social Contract goes further than comparable documents when it states that it "holds as inviolable the fundamental rights and freedoms set out in international human rights treaties, conventions and declarations" (Article 20). We know of no state or region that in its constitution makes a blanket recognition of all international human rights agreements. The Social Contract guarantees the right to "free and compulsory primary and secondary education" (Article 30), as well as the rights to "work, social security, health, adequate housing" (also Article 30), and to strike (Article 34).

Article 37 is perhaps unique in the world: "Everyone has the right to seek political asylum. Persons may only be deported following a decision of a competent, impartial and properly constituted judicial body, where all due process rights have been afforded." As for the economy, it is "directed at providing general welfare [and] at guaranteeing the daily needs of people and to ensure a dignified life. Monopoly is prohibited by law. Labor rights and sustainable development are guaranteed" (Article 42).

6.8 The Democratic-Autonomous Administrations (DAAs)

In the beginning of 2014, the United Nations, the United States, and Russia were organizing an international conference, known as "Geneva II," to be held at the end of January. For months, the MGRK had sought to ensure that the Kurds would be able to participate, but none of the powers were interested. Even after months of diplomatic efforts, the door remained closed.

Several days before the Geneva II conference was to begin, the three cantons declared Democratic Autonomy as a way of sending a signal to the participants. They accepted the Social Contract. On three separate days, they issued their own declarations of Democratic Autonomy: on January 21 in Cizîrê, on January 27 in Kobanî, and on January 29 in Afrîn. Hundreds of thousands of people celebrated in the streets of Rojava's cities.

Simultaneously with the declarations of Democratic Autonomy, each canton formed a transitional administration, also known as a democratic-autonomous administration (DAA). Each DAA has a legislative council (*meclîsa zagonsaz*, a local/regional parliament), to be elected for four-year terms. The legislative council elects an executive council (a regional authority) with two co-chairs. These organs, together with the supreme constitutional court, constitute the administration of a canton.

Within the DAAs, the executive councils have allocated "ministries" (in Kurdish, *vezalet*) politically, to the parties, so that most parties received at least one ministry, to ensure the active participation of all. As a result of negotiations, many new ministries were created, to widen party participation. Cizîrê's DAA, for example, has 22 ministries, as many as Kobanî and Afrîn combined. The MGRK parties, although they are by far the most decisive in the cantons, have fewer than half the ministries in Cizîrê. And the PYD holds a minority of ministries in the three cantons.

Initially the principle of dual leadership was not applied to the ministries, because the non-MGRK parties and organizations had few women as active members, and they objected to a "division" of power. As a result, almost every minister has two deputies, at least one of whom must be a woman. That was obligatory if the minister was a man, and unfortunately most were.

Our visit in May 2014 took place five months after the declarations of Democratic Autonomy. In Amûdê, we met with the Cizîrê co-president Ekram Hesso and several ministers. The setting was informal, and we were able to pose challenging questions, even to the two Syriac and Arab deputies. We asked the ministers how many staff each ministry had. Less than ten, we were told.

What had they accomplished so far? we asked. Several of the ministers who were from non-MGRK parties—those for environment and tourism, for social affairs, and for municipal administrations—emphasized that the difficult conditions of embargo and war limited their means and possibilities, so they relied on the strong MGRK system and indeed preferred to develop joint projects with it. After all, before the establishment of the transitional administrations, the MGRK had organized most of the area's issues.

Regrettably, the ENKS continues to operate politically against the Rojava self-government regime, lobbying against it and against the PYD, and alleging connections with the Syrian regime.[7] According to a document published by WikiLeaks, the ENKS leader Abdulhakim Bashar passed on information to the CIA and the Syrian intelligence service at least for the year 2009.[8] And finally, the ENKS's parties openly support the embargo against Rojava. As Mohamed Ismael, an El Partî leader, told us, "We can't allow any aid to enter Rojava, because the PYD brings all the goods under its control and then distributes them to buy approval from the people." The ENKS's logic is simple: anyone who joins the council system must belong to the PYD.[9] Following this logic, the councils' efforts to coordinate aid and distribute it to the neediest is actually the PYD confiscating it for its own political interests.[10] This is a deliberate distortion.

During our visit, the first camp for refugees from other parts of Syria was established, in Cizîre, near Dêrîk. The living conditions there were arduous. While Dijwar Ehmed Axa (of the Kurdistan Communist Party) appeared everywhere in the Kurdish media, it was the MGRK council system's commissions which were doing most of the work concerning the refugee camp. Both sides regarded the collaboration as positive.

In the summer of 2015, Cizîre and Afrîn decided that from that point onward their cantonal governments must have a woman and a man as co-heads. In Cizîre, these were the Arab man Sheikh Hamedi Daham and the Kurdish woman Hediye Yusîv. In Afrîn, Osman Sheikh joined Hevî Mustafa as co-chairs of the executive council. In Kobanî, still extremely affected by the war, this change not has yet taken place, as Enver Muslîm is still the sole head of the executive council.

At the time of writing, some two-and-a-half years have passed since the establishment of the DAAs. No elections for them have yet been held, due to the war. But the 2015 municipal elections held in Cizîre and Afrîn [see 6.5] were an important experience that paved the way for future DAA elections.

Meanwhile, as many other parts of Syria have descended into hell, the three cantons have seen mainly positive developments. The people have established common administrations on their own initiative and have taken crucial steps to overcome ethnic and religious prejudices. Considerable trust has developed among Kurds, Christians, and Sunni Arabs. This point is very important, as in the Middle East and surrounding regions, governing powers usually instrumentalize religions and ethnicities to stir up conflicts. The very fact that diverse groups came together voluntarily and share democratic self-administration is unusual for the region.

The three cantons are now in the process of establishing relations with groups outside the original three cantons. In October 2015, military successes in Cizîre and Kobanî cantons led to the establishment of the Syrian Democratic Forces (SDF). In December 2015, the next relevant step was the foundation of the Syrian Democratic Council (Meclîsa Demokratîka Suriya, MDS) in Dêrîk city, as its political wing, to work for Democratic Autonomy in the liberated areas and the implementation of a federal system.[11] This step gave the three DAAs and Syria's democratic-left forces a strong new voice. As of mid-2016, most international and regional reactionary powers at least mention the existence of a third force apart from the Islamist-nationalist opposition and the chauvinist-dictatorial Ba'ath regime. Most important of all, a growing part of the population of Syria is taking notice of the MDS, even if the majority do not yet support it.

6.9   The Federal System of Rojava/Northern Syria (FRNS)

In early 2016, with military successes of the SDF, the liberated territories outside the three cantons were quickly expanding, and better coordination was needed. The three cantons, in turn, needed a stronger common association at the Syrian, regional, and international levels. So the cantonal DAAs, the MDS, and recently liberated communities discussed how to better develop a more coherent system for everyone within the enlarged territory.

As a result, on March 17, 2016, 31 political parties and 200 delegates met for two days in Rimelan. They represented the DAAs, recently liberated areas outside the cantons, and not-yet-liberated areas (like the Shehba region between Kobanî and Afrîn), supported by the MDS. The meeting issued a declaration for a Federal System in Rojava/Northern Syria (FRNS), written in Arabic.[12]

The declaration creates the new federation and emphasizes that it considers itself part of Syria, and that its formation is not a step toward separation. The three cantons will continue to exist as part of the federation, and communities from recently liberated areas may choose to join, or they may choose to become part of a growing democratic Syria without joining the federation. Although the three cantons will coordinate with the rest of the federation, the federation will be the official body. A new Social Contract is in preparation. Women's freedom is the essence of the new system. Ethnic and religious diversity is, as always, crucial. Social classes, indeed workers, are mentioned as important. The founding meeting elected a coordinating body of 31 people and 2 co-chairs.

The Assad government, the Syrian National Coalition, and Turkey immediately condemned the declaration. So did the United States, although less vociferously, saying it would require Syrian-wide acceptance. Interestingly, given its closeness to the Ba'ath regime, Russia welcomed the declaration. Their varying reactions may indicate a growing rift in the approaches to Rojava among these allies; since March 2016, news reports have highlighted differences between Russia and the Assad regime on several issues.

Issuing the declaration gave new expression to how the Rojava Revolution will move forward. It proposed a political solution for resolving the Syrian war and by its very existence, has forced others to present their own ideas. Federation, broadly defined, makes sense as a proposal for decentralization and democratization. It may also eventually reduce the political and military conflicts around Rojava, in the rest of Syria, and in Iraq and North Kurdistan.

6.10 The MGRK and the DAAs

The three cantons owe their existence to the MGRK, as do the three DAAs. Today, approximately two-thirds of the people of Cizîre and more than 90 percent of the people of Afrîn participate in institutions that the MGRK founded since 2011, meeting in groups on a regular basis and making decisions affecting their lives. In Rojava, everyone benefits from this system, even if they choose not to participate directly. Diverse non-MGRK sectors of the society, which are all welcome to participate, have acknowledged the critical role that the MGRK has played. By mobilizing thousands of people around its political ideology, and showing that prejudices can be overcome as people work together, it has gained enormous prestige.

After the Social Contract was approved in January 2014, the relationship between the MGRK and the new DAAs was much discussed. How could these two be brought together? What would be the role of the council system and its commissions in relation to the DAAs' legislative councils, executive councils, and ministries? Would it not have been possible in 2013 to insist on only the MGRK system, and not create the DAAs, and to enlarge its social base over time? Would the council system be put on the back burner for short-term political gain? Was it simply a

Figure 6.5 A TEV-DEM meeting in Kobanî in 2015

transitional system? What will be its role in the FRNS? What attempts are being made to strengthen the MGRK's council system?

These questions are particularly important for the supporters of direct, grass-roots, radical democracy. In practice, the relationship between the MGRK and the DAAs has been positive, but there is currently no satisfactory answer to questions about the long-term role of the council system.

The first thing to note is that when the MGRK called for a common autonomous administration for all of Rojava in September 2013, it had not exhausted the discussions about its own problems and contradictions. The fact that a higher body of government was founded regardless carries the problems and contradictions over to a new level, and they have become more and more apparent as time has gone by.

Recall that the MGRK initiated the process of founding the DAAs because of the issue of legitimacy: the need to bring into the political structure the widest range of people as possible. A sizeable portion of the people (up to 45 percent in Cizîre canton) refrained from participating in the council system due to their prejudices and because they could not make sense of its processes.

But now people are getting acquainted with the DAAs, with the MGRK councils and communes, and with the Kurdish freedom movement itself, both in its active practice and in the principles it advocates. Our impression from the interviews we conducted is that all who have been actively involved in a council or commune feel energized by their participation. After the DAAs were founded in January 2014, the MGRK continued to function regardless of the existence and functioning of the ministries. It acted as a part of the transitional administrations and supported them in every possible way. But when the ministries developed projects, it was mainly MGRK activists who ran them. There was no other way because up until then the council system had been in control at the cantonal level. After the DAAs were founded, with their legislative councils, the MGRK system became less active in order to avoid a dual decision-making structure. The DAAs now make decisions at the cantonal level. The MGRK councils coordinate with the DAAs there by means of the commissions and also TEV-DEM. The main agenda at these meetings focuses on the activities of lower-level commissions, where the MGRK councils are still involved.

Before the DAAs were established, the commissions attached to the council system had all developed structures in their eight areas, including large-scale public companies. They have continued working in the eight areas in line with the DAAs. But over time the public companies have been officially handed over to the DAAs' ministries. The Asayîş, the YPJ, and the YPG, once part of the council system, are now also components of the DAAs.

But we should not think of the council system as separate from the DAAs or from the new FRNS. The ministries and the commissions cooperate with one another. For example, in practice the functions of the public companies are still carried out more or less by activists of the MGRK. How these public companies will be run over the long term is under discussion. One option is to give them an official role; another is to transform them into cooperatives with a public mandate.

The founding of new communes has not been neglected. The organization of communes in Afrîn canton was completed in summer 2015, while in Kobanî it restarted after the defeat of IS. The number of communes in Cizîre canton is increasing rapidly, but there is still a long way to go. In the regions newly freed by the Syrian Democratic Forces, where the majority of the people are not Kurdish, the offer to establish Democratic Autonomy and thus communes is brought to the people step by step. Insisting on communes is insisting on radical grass-roots democracy. The proliferation of communes in Rojava in 2015, as well as the development of a communal economy, are the expressions of an alternative to capitalist modernity, developed slowly but steadily. The growth of communes helps to alleviate concerns about the erosion of the MGRK council system. The DAAs have issued laws that support the communes and cooperatives, another instance of cooperation.

Our second visit to Rojava in early 2016 revealed that the people organized around the MGRK still have their revolutionary fervor. But we believe the relationship between the MGRK and the DAAs (and now the FRNS) should be formalized and its processes detailed. Although today the system seems to be running smoothly, a formal written framework supported by the public would be useful in case of conflicts or unexpected problems.

In this regard, in the summer of 2015, a process discussion was held, looking for a common solution. The formula discussed in early 2016 was that the councils represented at the level of the cantons (as TEV-DEM) should participate in the legislative council with a 40 percent quota. Whether this formula will pass and how it will be implemented remains to be seen.

Notes

1. Cizîrê canton districts include Dêrîk, Til Koçer, Çil Axa, Girke Lege, Tirbespî, Qamişlo Rojhilat, Qamişlo Rojava, Amudê, Dirbesiye, Serêkaniye, Til Temir, Hesekê and Til Hemîs. Afrîn canton's districts include Afrîn, Cindirês, Reco, Bilbilê, Şêrawa, Mabeta, Şêra and Şiyê. As Kobanî is being restructured, it is still too early to name its districts.
2. GuneyYildiz, "Kurdish-Jihadists Clashes Fracture Syria Opposition," *BBC*, August 18, 2013, http://bbc.in/28Rc2FJ.
3. Murray Bookchin, *The Rise of Urbanization and the Decline of Citizenship* (San Francisco, CA, 1987), p. 245.
4. Aldar Xelil, "Xelil: Rojava bütün ezilenler icin örnek bir devrimdir," *ANF News*, November 16, 2013, http://bit.ly/1DAlsCU.
5. Charter of the Social Contract, January 29, 2014, http://bit.ly/28PfEc2. A more accurate translation of "Autonomous Regions" is "Democratic-Autonomous Administrations."
6. Ibid.
7. Nilüfer Koç, "Die Rückkehr des hegemonialen Krieges in Kurdistan," *Kurdistan Report*, no. 175 (September–October 2014), http://bit.ly/1 MFMmcs.
8. US embassy in Damascus to Secretary of State, "No Dividend on SARG-Kurdish Backchannel Talks," *WikiLeaks*, November 25, 2009, http://bit.ly/1IHhEBg. SARG refers to "Syrian Arab Republic Government."
9. This assertion is questionable. In May 2014, the PYD in Rojava had, by its own account, about a thousand members. Its aim is not to increase that number but to advance the democratic process in Rojava. More than 15 parties are represented in the transitional government.
10. Nick Brauns, "Embargo gegen die Revolution," *Kurdistan Report*, no. 171 (January–February 2014), http://bit.ly/1cJL6rE.
11. Many members of the MDS were previously engaged in the National Coordination Body for a Democratic Change, which was initiated in 2011 but remained ineffective within Syria. Fewer MDS members were involved in the Syrian National Coalition.
12. "Final Declaration of the Rojava Northern Syria Democratic Federal System Constituent Assembly," *Kurdish Question*, March 17, 2016, http://bit.ly/28YG8Ko.

7

Civil Society Associations

Many people have difficulty distinguishing conceptually between a society and a state. Antonio Gramsci once defined "civil society" as the basis of the bourgeois state,[1] as an embattled ground. Gramsci assumed that civil society was an instrument of the ruling class, used for producing hegemony and thereby consent, which has to be conquered by the revolutionaries in the war of position. Today, civil society organizing by labor unions and associations is said to manufacture consent for the hegemony of Capitalist Modernity in a limited way, which neutralizes it as a means of political participation. Ever since Francis Fukuyama predicted "the end of history," neoliberal capitalism has ensured its own hegemony by ruling out possible alternatives.

Today in capitalist countries, civil society has the role of limiting the opposition produced by capitalist modernity—so that the state in Europe rejects the most humane treatment for refugees and settles instead for cost-free "civil society" engagement. Representative systems like parliamentary ones weaken active participation of people in the political process and bring forth a mass of people passively governed. The current representative systems, especially in Europe and the United States, reflect a systematic de-politicization of civil society; political self-expression has largely been reduced to quadrennial elections and people to objects of governance.[2] De-politicization is part of a strategy of ensuring political hegemony by instilling resignation and political apathy in the population and thereby averting disruptive social conflicts.

The Kurdish freedom movement, by contrast, sees the state as a means of extracting profits for the benefit of certain social groups or classes; it seeks to isolate people and inculcate a fixation on authority.[3] For the movement, the challenge to the state potentially comes from society, which for thousands of years the state has colonized and subordinated in its own interests.[4] The Kurdish movement, in its anti-statism, thus draws on Gramsci's concept of civil society in proposing to strengthen civil society for the purpose of overthrowing the state. In contrast to the abortive Bolshevist strategy of seizing state power, Öcalan posits, like Gramsci on the ideological, political struggle for civil society, a "war of position" beyond military confrontation.[5] Through empowerment, civil society tries to free itself from the hands of the state and its religious, economic, and administrative structures and so to build a counter-hegemony and to activate individual parts of the society to represent civil society in councils and communes.

For decades, the Ba'ath dictatorship politically excluded civil society, but today a politicized civil society, through Democratic Autonomy, is nurtured precisely to keep statism at a minimum and even avoid it altogether.[6] Such a process does not develop on its own; rather, a large network of civil society associations is working out solutions to social problems in all realms of Democratic Autonomy. Civil society associations actively perform educational work as well as organize society. All these associations have their own charters and have the right to organize within the population and to send voting delegates to the boards of TEV-DEM.

Fedakar Hesen, of Rojava's Union of Civil Society Associations, defines the role of civil society in Democratic Autonomy: "Rojava and especially Cizîrê possess great wealth, both above the ground and below it. Under the state system, all this wealth belonged to the state, and nothing belonged to the society. The state had no use for the society. Consider the case of oil: it was drilled and pumped here but taken elsewhere to be refined. None of the profits went to the people. Oil, having been sucked from the people's ground, was then sold back to the people at a high price.

"Anyone who wanted to build a house had to get approval of the Ba'ath regime, and that was usually not forthcoming anytime soon. You couldn't even lay out a garden without state approval. You couldn't plant a tree. Obviously our present autonomous system also requires certain arrangements, but in contrast to the state, here the goal is to establish an ecological society. The state did nothing to benefit the society, but the system of autonomy does.

"Today in Rojava, civil society is sharply distinguished from the former state system. It puts the will of the people front and center, where the regime did not. Moreover, officeholders in all the institutions of civil society are subject to imperative mandate. Under the Ba'ath regime," says

Hesen, "the state wanted any decision made at the top to be implemented below, even at the level of households. Even if a decision made no sense for a given household, it had to be implemented. The state wanted a society of slaves, dispossessed from their culture. Democratic Autonomy, however, respects the views of society and seeks to create social self-governance. This is the goal of civil society organizing as well."

So when we speak of Rojava, we must broaden the classical notion of civil society associations. Our delegation noticed how much we had been committed to this old notion when we visited the Union of Civil Society Associations. We had expected an association of human rights and humanitarian aid organizations, but instead we found an organization made up mainly of occupational groups. In representative and bourgeois-parliamentary systems, labor unions and other associations press for improved working conditions as a question of power, but in Democratic Autonomy, these institutions have representation at the different council levels. As far as we could determine, the tasks of civil society organizing in Rojava are more broadly defined. Civil society associations have representation on the councils, even to the point of dedicated quotas.

7.1 Union of Civil Society Associations—Saziyen Cîvaka Sîvîl (SCS)

Civil society associations work in all areas but especially in the economy. "Here in the city," according to one report, "every family operates a workshop or a shop or is in some way involved in trade. The civil society association ensures the unity of the people and prevents violations or infringements of the law." Democratic Confederalism's critique of the state and its support for a communal economy is one of the key principles of the Union of Civil Society Associations (SCS): "The state system exploited the society's labor power and trampled the rights of workers. Under Democratic Autonomy, civil society associations solve problems according to principles of moral politics and an ecological society. The unity of society is the foundation. These associations hold society together. They ensure the unity that is needed to satisfy everyday social needs. Of course, they do this as part of democratic, communal life. They are how society organizes itself."[7]

In the economic association, shops, companies, cooperatives, and workshops combine to negotiate working conditions and to ensure social responsibility. Social responsibility involves, among other things, controlling food and fuel prices, so that everyone, including refugees, is adequately nourished. For example, the association set the price of heating oil at a 5-lira difference in Dirbesiyê (in Arabic, Al-Darbasiyah), and Tirbespî. In the communalized economy, economic self-organization helps prevent the pursuit of profit maximization, which in the capitalist economy is so destructive, and it defends the rights of workers.

"Under the Ba'ath regime," said Hesen, who is also co-chair of the Hesekê district council, "it was impossible to demand workers' rights. You couldn't open your mouth about low wages, rights violations, anything like that. If you did, you were prosecuted. Those who demanded their rights were thrown in prison, charged with 'seeking to divide the state.' But Democratic Autonomy considers violations of workers' rights to be criminal offenses. Here everyone has the right to a life in an ecological and democratic society."

One social problem that the SCS solved was a conflict between taxi drivers and minibus drivers. Minibuses regularly drive outside the city, but they were bringing their passengers directly to their front doors, which meant the taxis lost a lot of income. So the SCS decided to establish a central bus station in each city center, which the minibuses could easily access.

Democratic Autonomy proposes that all professional groups join such civil society associations, where they can jointly solve problems and hold members accountable. Remziye Mihemed of the Qamişlo People's Council told us that membership dues are 100 lira per month (about 40 US cents), which is spent on essentials; participation is voluntary. Teachers' commissions will tackle, say, the problem of teacher-inflicted violence and hold teachers accountable. Traders' commissions protect businesses and ensure that the prices of basic foodstuffs are not driven up. Local services commissions, which are connected to the council system, are responsible for the supply of water and electricity. A variety of commissions are closely linked to the council system, Mihemed told us.

Here once again we see the difficulty of defining "civil society association" in a society that aspires to be completely civil. The councils and the civil society associations not only manage the vicissitudes of the war but offer concrete ideas about new forms of economy and society [see Chapter 12]. While visiting the SCS in May 2014, we learned that some

32 civil society associations in Qamişlo had recently consolidated—associations of taxi drivers, merchants, workers, and others.

7.2 Culture and Art—Çand û Hûner

As we have seen, representing and advancing Rojava's different cultures is a principle of Democratic Confederalism.[8] Culture and Art is a civil society association dedicated to advancing culture. Founded in 1988—long before the revolution—it was initially organized illegally. Today it aspires to establish cultural academies in every city of Rojava, networking the cultural institutions of the diverse ethnic and religious groups confederally.

Culture and Art strives not only to preserve and maintain traditional cultures but also to create a new emancipatory culture based on the new political and social situation. It addresses social issues, even presenting them in theatrical productions. As of October 2013, for example, Amûdê's Culture and Art Academy had some one hundred active members who gave lessons and worked on dramatic productions. We watched a play, performed by Amûdê's Culture and Art youth group, that dealt with the problem of flight from Rojava to South Kurdistan's camps, Turkey, or Europe: its message was to encourage people to stay in Rojava rather than leave. Most of the plays performed by Culture and Art are original.

The Culture and Art academy in Serêkaniyê was founded in early 2014 and had 170 members as of May, including numerous Arabs and Chechens. The academy has facilities for theater, media, and literature; it has a children's area as well and is home to the musical group Koma Şehîd Yekdar, named after a martyr who fell in Aleppo.

Culture and Art is organized on the principle of mutual learning and teaching, and every learner is encouraged to become a teacher. People of all ages participate. It runs its own libraries, in close cooperation with its academies. It has transformed former regime buildings into cultural centers, and major state facilities are now open to the people for cultural and theatrical performances. Part of the work is the foundation of a new film commune.

7.3 Revolutionary Youth Movement—Tevgera Cîwanên Şoreşger

The Revolutionary Youth Movement is a direct descendant of the Youth Commission of Syria, which opposed the Ba'ath regime, and its members are now making significant contributions to the development of Rojava's self-government. During the revolution, according to Harun Bozan, a member of the board, "we … held demonstrations in every district, every village, and every city and played an active role in the uprising. But establishing the communes and councils was very important. We weakened the state system with our actions, even as we built the new institutions." The Revolutionary Youth "differed from the other youth movements in that we offered an alternative to Assad. The others said only, 'Assad should go away,' but they didn't know what should happen after he went away." Ideologically, they "mobilized around the philosophy of Chairman Apo. As Apo-istic youth, we knew exactly how to use our energy, our activism, and our youthful spirit in the service of the revolution."[9]

The Revolutionary Youth built meeting halls in towns and villages. In the "City of Youth," they reclaimed premises from the Ba'ath regime and put them to use for social self-organization. Youth theater groups perform in venues that only recently were the inaccessible offices of the regime.

Today the Revolutionary Youth still organize protests—for example, against the KRG's embargo. They publish at least one newspaper in every city and conduct seminars in the communes. But as a young person in Dêrîk explained to us, "Our work is different from that of the commune in general. The commune is there to solve problems of water and electricity supply as well as family problems. But we organize youth for the revolution. Many young people have little information about the revolution and its goals."

They see their main task, we were told, as advancing not only their own education but that of society in general, especially political education, history, democratic values, and women's liberation. Teens from different backgrounds come together and learn from one another. The courses are self-organized and aim to turn the students into teachers. Fridays are dedicated to political education; other nights are for movies, remedial courses, and sporting events.

In Kurdistan, the term "youth" is rather broad and may include people from 12 to 27. Those aged 18 and older play another important role: defending their communes and neighborhoods against the attacks of IS and other terrorist groups. "We organized our self-defense units street by street," Harun Bozan told us. "We trained these groups. They functioned as guards and carried out protective measures. If the people were under attack, we saw to their safety."

Representative systems typically see young people as needing to be administered to, but in Democratic Autonomy teens play a central role in the self-government and are a key transformational part of society. Following the model of Democratic Autonomy, the Revolutionary Youth consists of a mixed-gender organization—Kurdish Students of Syria (Xwendekarên Kurd li Suriye)—and an autonomous organization of women and girls, the Revolutionary Women (Jinen Şoreşger).[10] The struggle of youth is directed toward a social revolution and against the oppression of youth by the elderly, that is, the gerontocracy: "The gerontocratic system equates age with experience and concludes that older people have more experience and therefore should have more right to participate in decisions and decision-making processes. Gerontocracy finds expression in institutions, in the manner in which society is managed and by whom. It is also reflected in the society's internal perspective on young people. We present ourselves as young people against this system. Experiences are not only associated with age, because ways of life, ideology, and the implementation of ideology in life are important. It depends on conviction and will. We take our stand against this gerontocratic system in our independent and autonomous organization. Education is also a very important part of our defense, so as to raise awareness among the youth, so that they are capable of participation in the construction of their system with their own identity. We also have our own academies organized by youth that serve for our self-education."[11]

The organization governs itself by the council principle, but it is also an integral part of the council system at all levels, sending delegates who participate in deliberations and decision making. Finally, it is also a parallel autonomous communal organization that reaches to the trans-regional level.

7.4 Association of Families of Martyrs—Saziya Malbatan Şehîdan (SMS)

Vital to any society at war is an institution that cares for the families of those killed in action. In Rojava, the Association of the Families of Martyrs (SMS) offers psychological support for families, keeps them

Figure 7.1   Memorial day for martyrs

socially active, and shares in their mourning. It offers funeral services and gravesite tending; it also provides material support, even food for widowers, widows, and orphans. SMS also organizes support for families of murdered civilians.

In May 2014, in Qamişlo alone, there were 400 families of martyred YPG/YPJ fighters. In addition, we were told, the struggle of the Kurdish guerrilla forces HPG and ARGK, in the North Kurdistan mountains, left 250 martyrs. The SMS makes no distinction between those killed in action in the HPG/ARGK or in the YPG/YPJ, and it cares for their families no matter where they have fallen.

We observed SMS staff visiting families not only to express sympathy but also to determine their needs and involve them in social activities. The SMS are politically active and participate in protests against the embargo.

7.5   Human Rights Commission—Komela Mafên Mirovan (KMM)

Human rights activists in Rojava face a major challenge: they must document and investigate massacres committed by groups that are fighting Rojava, and they must subject Rojava's security forces to the same scrutiny. Rojava's forces, the Asayîş and Sutoro, are made up of volunteers, and due to the war, much of their training takes place while their service is ongoing. But in every society, the monitoring of security forces is key to the protection of human dignity.

The Human Rights Commission (KMM) was founded to perform that monitoring. It educates the security forces through weekly awareness trainings on human rights; it carries out extensive inspections. As the KMM's Axîn Amed explained to us, "To prepare our reports, we visit prisons of the Asayîş, always unannounced. We have found no cases of torture. We spontaneously visited the Asayîş headquarters in Qamişlo. We will investigate any allegation of torture." In our observation, allegations of torture are systematically investigated and any abuses are not concealed but rather penalized.

With regard to detention and custody, we observed a surprising openness in the security forces. Without any prior permission, we had access to all kind of Asayîş stations and detention and custody locations when we requested it. Even Human Rights Watch confirms its free access to prisons and institutions in its report on Rojava.[12] But due to the uniqueness of Rojava's situation—that is, the revolution and the war— another problem arises. While the security forces are more than willing to allow inspections, local human rights commissions lack staff and support to conduct them, as so many resources have to be concentrated on the war.

7.6 Civil Society Organizing

Rojava is creating a new form of society without a state. This chapter has sketched only a few selected civil society associations; we could have highlighted many more. But certain principles are common to all. The people organize in communes; they form commissions; and they work with democratically legitimate organizations such as Heyva Sor for health care, Kongreya Star for women, and many others. As we have seen, Rojava is not a statist society but rather a civilian—that is, of the *civitas*—citizen-designed society.

So the classical nongovernmental organization (NGO) does not apply to Rojava, precisely because everything is civil, from the communes to the civil society associations, which are interconnected with the council system. The associations contribute their knowledge to the institutions of self-government and highlight any errors and shortcomings, thereby promoting social development and complementing the democratic self-administration. They are independent of it, yet their voting representatives contribute to it at all levels.

A few NGOs do exist that have nothing to do with either the state or the self-administration. They are generally critical of the self-administration, presumably because they are tied to the right-wing ENKS party bloc. Hence their influence on society is much more limited than that of the associations listed above. We did not visit them, so we cannot say anything about them, but Fedakar Hesen of the SCS observes: "We have only recently begun to construct the system of Democratic Autonomy. The system of civil society associations also exists. During the creation of the system, some errors and problems may well occur ... But the work is gratifying, so even though this system is new, people are willing to work for it on a voluntary basis.

"Under the Ba'ath regime," he continues, "no one was able to speak up for their rights. But today when the workers raise an issue, they notice that their right to do so is protected, so they begin to participate more energetically." Today, the challenges to civil society organizing lie in the transition from a population patronized by the regime to a people who are engaged and socially and politically involved at all levels. Another is the lack of expertise in urban planning and energy, especially since many trained personnel have left the region. But our delegation witnessed a great enthusiasm for the establishment of this new system and a willingness to face all challenges, using the principles of criticism and self-criticism and imperative mandate.

Notes

1. Antonio Gramsci, *Gefängnishefte* (Hamburg, 1991–99), vol. 4.
2. Antonio Negri and Michael Hardt, *Declaration*, http://bit.ly/1Ny3yjT.
3. Abdullah Öcalan, *Jenseits von Staat, Macht und Gewalt* (Neuss, 2010), p. 263.
4. Abdullah Öcalan, *Democratic Confederalism*, pp. 12–13, http://bit.ly/1AUntIO.
5. See Tanil Bar-on, "From Marxism and Nationalism to Radical Democracy: Abdullah Öcalan's Synthesis for the 21. Century," *Kurdish Issue*, April 25, 2015, http://wp.me/p4jvjX-d8.

6. Öcalan, *Jenseits von Staat, Macht und Gewalt*, p. 263.
7. Nergiz Botan, "Rojava Devriminde sivil toplum nasıl çalışıyor?," *ANF*, August 21, 2014.
8. "Doğrudan demokrasiyle toplum irade ve güç olur," *Yeni Özgür Politika*, December 23, 2010, http://bit.ly/29yXYU5.
9. Harun Bozan, a member of the Revolutionary Youth board, interview, "Rojava'da devrimin öncüsü ve savunucusu gençler," *Yeni Özgür Politika*, May 21, 2014.
10. Ercan Ayboğa, in *Yeni Özgür Politika*, June 28, 2014.
11. Hanna Kohlmann and Michael Knapp, "Wir haben jung begonnen und jung werden wir siegen," *Kurdistan Report*, no. 183 (January–February 2016), http://bit.ly/28R4SFX.
12. "Syria: Abuses in Kurdish-Run Enclaves," *Human Rights Watch*, June 19, 2014, http://bit.ly/28R8s2N.

8

Defense: The Theory of the Rose

"The terrorist militia IS has exposed the worthlessness of the military superiority of states as well as the emptiness of their values ... For with their unprecedented fighting spirit, they have demonstrated their moral superiority for the whole world, and they have tested the credibility of the global community. The Kurds may lose a city, but the global community has already lost all its values."[1]

Precisely because Rojava strives to be a radical democracy and rejects the profit-oriented capitalist economy, and precisely because the many women in the ranks of the defense forces contradict patriarchal claims to rule, Rojava came under attack by ISIS and its allies. Starting with the defense of Kobanî in September 2014, the women fighters became a symbol, demonstrating a new role for women in the Middle East, achieving victory over "evil,"[2] and exposing the militaristic, patriarchal violence and the lies of both the NATO states and their Islamist partners. International enthusiasm for the YPG/YPJ has been enormous. The American YPG volunteer Jordan Matson posted on his Facebook page that he'd received thousands of questions from around the world asking how to join the YPG.

But by September 2014, the YPG and YPJ had already been waging an armed resistance against radical Islamic militias, Jabhat Al-Nusra and ISIS, for two years. Some 600 fighters had been killed, to no reaction from the world public.

8.1 People's Protection Units (YPG)—Yekîneyên Parastina Gel

In 2004, after the Qamişlo uprising was brutally crushed [see 4.1], the severe repression convinced many Syrian Kurds that they needed a self-defense force. So they began to create units, illegally, so that the next time the Assad regime attacked, they would be ready to mount reprisals.

Figure 8.1 A YPJ and YPG muster

The first units of the YXG [*see* 3.3] were "an unofficial force consisting of small groups of young people," as Şîlan Karaçox, a commander in Cizîrê canton, recalled: "Sometimes they carried out actions when the regime attacked the Kurds, such as when someone was arrested."[3]

In July 2012, according to Sîpan Hemo, another commander, the self-defense force "played its role in the liberation of the Kurdish cantons." In Dêrik, the YXG clashed with regime forces [*see* 4.6], but in the end the regime withdrew, and "the revolution of July 19 was proclaimed."[4]

Neither the Turkish state nor KRG president Massoud Barzanî could prevent PKK activists from traveling to Rojava to join the YXG and help build it up. One of them was Xebat Dêrik, a former PKK commander, who realized that with the fighters now numbering in the thousands, a new organization was necessary. It was at his initiative that the YXG was restructured into the YPG in the summer of 2012. At its founding conference on New Year 2013, the YPG declared that it was not associated with any party but was solely under the Supreme Kurdish Council (SKC), representing all the people of Rojava. "We began to separate the political and military forces from each other," Dêrik recalled.[5]

The first camps and a training academy were set up. Among the ranks of the YPG would soon be not only the Kurds but Syriacs, Arabs,

Turkmens, Chechens, and other social groups, as well as people of different belief systems and political tendencies.

The expanded defense force turned out to be absolutely necessary. In the summer of 2013, the first anniversary of the revolution, the war began: Jabhat Al-Nusra, IS, and parts of the FSA were all involved in attacks on Serêkaniyê [see 8.4], soon to be followed by attacks on places in Afrîn, Kobanî, and Hesekê.[6]

Figure 8.2 YPG and YPJ fighters at Serêkaniyê

8.2   Women's Protection Units (YPJ)—Yekîneyên Parastina Jin

"It feels as if we've been released from prison."

When the YXG was founded in 2011, it was a mixed-gender force—two out of three members of the general command were women. Şîlan Karaçox, a cantonal commander, told us it took a long time for society to accept the participation of women in the defense forces: "By 2011 there were still only a few women. Much trust was needed for the families to let their daughters join. Sometimes they demanded that their daughters stay with a certain female commander. That was a very long discussion, but finally it was understood that a liberation of the society could be achieved only through the liberation of women."

Women who fought in the PKK women's army, the YJA Star, began returning to Rojava, where their decades of military experience was needed, initially for training.[7] "At first a few of us lived together in a house," Karaçox recalled, "and we had to teach the young people how to handle a weapon. Men took to the weapons quickly, but for women it was harder and more alien, so we placed special emphasis on it. Then came theoretical discussions about what defense is, and how people can protect themselves. This process gave the families trust, and so more women came to us."

With the July 2012 revolution and the transformation of the YXG into the YPG, thousands more women streamed in. Since women fighters were considered essential both to the defense of Rojava and to the struggle for women's liberation, autonomous women's units were created in early 2013. The YPJ was founded on April 4, 2013, in parallel to the YPG. All women who were previously in the YPG's mixed units automatically became members. Şîlan Karaçox told us that "initially there was one women's battalion per canton; then each neighborhood got one." Soon every district had a YPJ center, and several women's defense academies were built.[8] New women's units were created almost daily.[9]

The YPJ fights on the same level as the YPG. In May, the first YPJ fighter fell in the defense of Afrîn city: Meryem Mihemed (Şehîd Şîlan),

Figure 8.3   A Syriac YPJ fighter at Serêkaniyê

who had been born there in 1991. The current situation demands that all of Rojava's people be ready to defend themselves and the accomplishments of their new society, if necessary by arms. The journalist Berfîn Hezîl reported in a radio interview in October 2014 that some 50 percent of all women of every age in Rojava had received weapons training.[10]

A Revolutionary Transformation

Fighter Mizgîn Mahmoud told an interviewer, "As a young Kurdish woman, I am ready to accept my responsibility in the Kurdish revolution So I had no fear of signing up with the YPJ to help make the people more secure. I worked both at the control points and in the city. I'll tell my children about it one day. We're building this country for our children, so they can govern themselves, defend themselves, and be educated in their own tongue in their own schools."[11]

In October 2014, Destan, a YPJ fighter at Kobanî, told the ANF journalist Sedat Sur, "I had never thought that a woman could be coequal with a man. In our family, men were always dominant, and I considered it entirely normal and accepted it as legitimate ... Only in the YPJ did I come to understand that male dominance is not a normal part of life but on the contrary, that it goes against the natural order. This realization awakened an enormous feeling of freedom within me ... The greatest use of this conflict, in my eyes, is the break with the feudal values in Kobanî." Ronahî, a young YPJ militant, has said that people gradually got used to seeing armed women in the streets, and now the image of woman has changed vastly: "I can hardly believe this is happening. It feels as if we've been released from prison."

In some areas, the participation of women no longer warrants even a discussion. "We have our own system," Şîlan told us. "In Afrîn, Hesekê, and Serêkaniyê we performed our own independent missions. Our system is self-sufficient.[12]

"In wartime, we work with the YPG. In any decision, at least 30 or 35 percent of women have to participate. In Kobanî, there were just as many women fighters as men, but in Afrîn it's 35 to 40 percent women. Kobanî is very feudal, so at first it was difficult, but then the dam burst and women's enlistments exploded. In Qamişlo too, every neighborhood— there are six all together—has at least one women's unit, and most have a battalion."

At Kobanî, said Destan, "Women fought at the front. One can say that they have implemented the strongest blows against the ISIS gangs. Many women died in heroic resistance." For example, in early October 2014, as the situation in Kobanî became grim owing to the lack of anti-tank weapons, the YPJ fighter Arîn Mirkan stopped a tank by throwing herself into the air and detonating herself with hand grenades. She has become a symbol of the resistance. "It's now our job to continue their battle and that of all those who have been killed in action, especially the women," said Destan.

With the battle for Kobanî, Rojava's female fighters attracted attention from the international public, who reacted with astonishment. Sensational Western media reported that a woman, Meysa Abdo, co-commanded the front at Kobanî. One reason is surely that armed women fighters break a taboo, since weapons are the symbol of male domination. They also signal a transcendence of gender differences, and insofar as they are perceived as a threat to men, they endanger male privilege.

How do men in the YPG react to it? We asked one female fighter. "They have to accept it," she told us. "That's the philosophy of our movement. Men have been running things for five thousand years."

Non-Kurdish women have joined the YPJ as well, said Bengîn Melsa, a commander at Serêkaniyê. "Most come because they want to defend the cantons. Once they've been in for a while, they understand the goals of the fighters better, they get to know us better, and they gain awareness. We have only a few Arab and Syriac women in our ranks. The Arabs have many problems with the language, and they're often very withdrawn, much more so than the Kurdish women. They're more strongly influenced by patriarchal institutions. It takes a long time for them to open up."

Nonetheless, the feudal concept of marriage still dominates the thinking of many families in Kurdistan. They find it possible to support the decision of their daughters to join the movement only because they know and trust that the cadres don't get involved in romantic relationships. The Kurdish movement has discussed the subject extensively, over decades. One reason cadres are barred from romantic relationships is the commitment to equality among comrades. In romantic relationships, one inadvertently privileges one's partner, contradicting this concept.[13] Zaher Baher, of the Haringey Solidarity Group in London, who visited Rojava in 2014, notes that "the women and men we spoke to believed that [love, sex, relationships] are not appropriate at this stage as they are involved in revolution and have to give everything to the revolution in order to succeed."[14] In the 2014 Australian film *The Female State*, Cûdî Osse says that the fighters do not love weapons, death, and war, and would be glad to love, but now they must give top priority to the defense of their country. In this respect, YPG/YPJ cadres must be distinguished from Asayîş, who are sometimes married and go home to their families.

8.3   Legitimate Self-defense

The YPG and YPJ adhere is the principle of legitimate self-defense (as does the HPG guerrilla army in North Kurdistan), according to which all military activity is of a reactive nature. When the forces are attacked, they retaliate but they also leave open the possibility of political engagement.

"Our theory is the theory of the rose, a flower that defends itself," said Çinar Sali of TEV-DEM. "Every being has to create methods of self-defense according to its own way of living, growing, and connecting with others. The aim is not to destroy an enemy but to force it to give up its intention to attack. Guerrilla fighters discuss this as a defensive strategy in a military sense, but it works in other areas as well. It's a method of self-empowerment. The YPG and YPJ attribute great meaning to defense. National armies serve the state, but they leave the people without defense."

The principal task of defense is to protect the achievements of Democratic Autonomy, but it bears an ideological and political charge as well: to educate people in the ideas of Democratic Autonomy and disseminate the ideas further.

Normally, the YPG/YPJ do not fight on the offensive. In Qamişlo, for example, the airport is still controlled by the Assad regime. The forces could certainly drive it out, we were told, but that could escalate the conflict and might lead to a bombardment of the city. On the other hand, when the regime attacked YPG checkpoints near Hesekê, the YPG retaliated. Recently the thinking has evolved: if the majority of the population (Kurdish or not) of a region that is under IS or Al-Nusra control supports liberation, then the YPG/YPJ, or more recently the Syrian Democratic Forces [*see* 8.10], as happened in Til Abyad and Shaddadi—will do so.

Self-defense became critical after the liberation of 2012, when, as YPG spokesman Redur Xelîl recalled, Rojava came under acute threat from several sides: "As long as the regime and other armed groups didn't attack us, we didn't attack anyone. But since July 16, 2013, we have been attacked by Al-Nusra and ISIS and other Islamist groups, from Dêrîk to Afrîn. And the Turkish army attacked us. Turkish sharpshooters killed two of our friends. They openly supported the Islamists and attacked us directly."[15]

On July 7, 2014, due to the ominous situation in Cizîrê, the legislative council introduced conscription: all men (initially) between the ages of 18 and 30 now have to complete six months of basic military service. For women participation is voluntary, since drafting women is not yet socially accepted. The aim is that in the case of an emergency, everyone will be ready to defend their village or district. After the decision was announced, thousands of young people registered with the YPG/YPJ. By November 2015 in Cizîrê canton, Kurdish, Arab, and Syriac youth had cleared seven areas.[16]

In Afrîn canton, conscription was instituted in early 2015 with the first 200 youths over age 18. These self-defense units (*erka xweparastinê*) are not components of the YPG/YPJ, but can join at any time. Usually, *erka xweparastin* enter a newly liberated area after the YPG/YPJ and handle logistics. They are the only units that wear bulletproof vests and helmets.

Also in early 2015, the defense commissions [*see* 6.3] systematically established self-defense units (*hêzen parastina cewherî*) in the village and neighborhood communes, comprising civilians of every age. All members of Qamişlo's defense commissions, for example, came together, chose their leadership, and organized military training. The task of the *hêzen parastina cewherî* is to monitor streets and neighborhoods and support the Asayîş. In battles, they handle the rearguard tasks. The YPG/YPJ, the Asayîş, the *erka xweparastinê*, and the *hêzen parastina cewherî* together constitute a coherent defense network.

8.4   The Liberation of Serêkaniyê

On May 11–13, 2014, we visited Serêkaniyê, a predominantly Kurdish city on the western edge of Cizîrê canton, home to Kurds, Arabs, Syriacs, Armenians, and Chechens. The city uniquely expresses the sorrow and oppression of the Kurdish people, as before Kobanî it was known as the "fortress of resistance."

The city was cut in two in the 1920s, when the colonial powers drew the Syrian-Turkish border through it [see 1.2]. The Syrian-occupied southern portion was renamed Ras Al-Ayn and the Turkish northern part was called Ceylanpınar. Surrounding the city are Arab villages, built during the Arab Belt resettlement program of the 1960s.

In November 2012, up to 3,000 heavily armed Al-Nusra and Ghuraba al-Sham units crossed the Turkish border and entered Serêkaniyê.[17] Hardly any YPG units were in the city, only 39 YPG fighters, and they were cut off from supplies. The regime had withdrawn its forces. The YPG decided to exercise restraint, since it didn't want to be seen as fighting on the side of the regime against the FSA. After four days of fighting, Al-Nusra and FSA units occupied Serêkaniyê. Large portions of the population fled.

But then the Islamists began to destroy the homes of Syriacs and Armenians—and even to oppress the Arab population. They instituted a reign of terror, publicly executing both supposed and real adherents of the regime, bullying and mistreating the residents. Only the eastern quarter of Serêkaniyê, Sinah, continued to resist.

A few days after the invasion, on November 18, Al-Nusra attacked a YPG control point, and some of its supporters burned a flag of the Supreme Kurdish Council. Talks were to be held, but when Abid Xelîl, the co-chair of the people's council, showed up for the meeting, the jihadists murdered him.

So the YPG troops declared war on IS and Al-Nusra, although at the time no one believed they could prevail. Over the next months, intense clashes followed, alternating with ceasefires. Thirty-five YPG fighters died.

About five kilometers outside Serêkaniyê lies the town of Til Xelef (in Arabic, Tell Halaf), which has a largely Arab population. On the edge of the town stands a hill, also known as Til Xelef; it is an internationally famous archaeological site from the late Neolithic. An entire epoch—the Halaf period, from the sixth millennium BCE—is named after it for the pottery found there. In antiquity, the Aramaic palace of Kapara stood at Til Xelef. Al-Nusra and IS occupied the hill and used it as an artillery emplacement from which to bombard the village.

Meanwhile, a battle for position was taking place between the YPG and units of Al-Nusra. Sometimes only fifty meters lay between the lines. Heavy weapons were used. The village suffered heavy damage, as the people and the YPG defended it. When the jihadists realized they could not prevail militarily, we were told, they resorted to a strategy of terror. They mounted suicide attacks, in the village and in front of the City Hall in Serêkaniyê. Eleven people died, six of them civilians. The suicide bombers came from Algeria.

After five cycles of ceasefire and open warfare, the YPG finally became strong enough that in June 2013 it mounted an offensive. "With the fight for Serêkaniyê," said Sîpan Hemo, the YPG's local supreme commander, "we showed Rojava that we were able to protect the people. Crucially, we liberated the holy places of all denominations and saw it as our task to guarantee the safety of people of all ethnicities and religions. Then Syriacs began to join the defense units. Thousands volunteered, sometimes armed only with sticks and stones."[18]

The YPG offensive drove Al-Nusra from the city, along with the war profiteers who had joined the jihadists in hopes of booty. The jihadists seem to have sold off many cultural goods from Til Xelef—Asayîş determined that two truckloads of archaeological findings had been removed. The people of Serêkaniyê, who had suffered greatly under Islamists' brutality, welcomed the YPG victory enthusiastically.

Daily Life of the YPJ at Serêkaniyê

We were fortunate to be able to spend two days in a mobile women's unit on the front at Serêkaniyê. We shared their daily life: standing watch, playing sports, eating together, rotating troops at the front, making contact with people.

The independent YPG units started out as 15–20 cadres fighting in mixed units, but once the YPJ was formed, the women's units fought independently. The YPJ units consisted of about thirty women and were stationed near contested areas in Cizîrê as needed. "Most of the women could never have imagined that they would be fighters one day," Dîlan told us. Eighteen-year-old Sakine Cansız told us that right after her training, she fought at Til Hemîs and was wounded—she showed us the bullet wound in her leg. When we asked whether it was normal to go directly from training to the front, she said, "I wanted to, because there were so few there, and we were many young people."

The women are well trained and politically educated—the training lasts six months. Every woman in the battalion could be a commander at the front, explained 23-year-old Melsa, who had been wounded twice. Commanders were not elected but are chosen by the leadership.

Figure 8.4   Hevala Melsa, of the YPJ, at Serêkaniyê

Jihadists believe that if they are killed, they go directly to Paradise. "Each of them," YPJ commander Rûken Jîrik told us, "wears a key to paradise around his neck, and a spoon on his belt in order to eat with Muhammad. When they go into battle, they're pumped full of amphetamines, and the crazy ones behind them drive them forward." Willing to commit suicide, "they have no fear of death, as they think they are going to Paradise." But "if they're killed by a woman, they think they won't go to Paradise," Melsa told us. "They're afraid of women," said another fighter. "When we fight, we trill loudly, so they'll be sure to hear our voices."

Around Til Xelef, Melsa told us, there were supporters of Islamists among the Arab population: "A week ago we carried out an operation around Til Xelef with two hundred YPG/YPJ fighters, going to every individual house, to search for weapons and hidden fighters. Some of the Arabs support IS. The problem is that the Arabs have no unified, shared position."

The commander of the battalion, Avesta, showed us the positions at Til Xelef where her unit had fought the IS gangs. "We were hunched here for twenty-four hours, it was July and very hot. The drinking water came to us hot enough to cook with. The friends brought water, bread, and food at night in cars. Many died along the way or were wounded." The border crossing at Ceylanpınar was only one hundred meters away.

Figure 8.5   The ruined village of Keşte, near Til Xelef, May 2014. The inhabitants are returning only twenty days after the YPG/YPJ liberated the village

Çiçek says the battle over Serêkaniyê "was a war of position. Between us and the enemy there lay at most fifty meters. Day and night we stood across from each other. Sometimes they attacked, sometimes we did … Everyone wanted to be up front, to protect the others. The surrounding area is very level, and we didn't know how we were going to defend ourselves. Until we figured it out, there were many casualties.

"Whenever someone was killed, we took their weapon. When there was no fighting, we sang. Between skirmishes we did training, we read and discussed the roles women play in this war. To show the enemy our resolve, we called out to them, and they got afraid. Our morale was very high. The units at the front rotate frequently so they won't be tired. We were very disciplined, to avoid needless casualties. Whenever anyone fell, we immediately talked about it, and about why they fought, so that morale wouldn't waver. We helped the new ones."

Til Xelef was liberated in November 2013. "When the gangs were here," we were told, "they tortured and mistreated the people. But now that the YPG is here, the residents said, they can sleep well."

"Orhan is in Paradise"

Traveling west from Serêkaniyê, our delegation wound through cornfields and villages until we reached Til Xenzir (Tall Khinzir), a fortified hill that the YPG and YPJ had recaptured from the jihadists a month earlier. It was the farthest west we could go; some 60 miles (96 kilometers) farther, beyond the sparsely populated Arab-settled strip, lay Kobanî. We climbed the hill, and from the top we could make out the jihadists' positions in the suburbs of the small city of Mabruka and hear the sounds of mortar shells.

Little more than a stone's throw away, to the north, lay the Turkish border. Now that Til Xenzir is no longer under the control of the jihadists, tanks have been brought up to the Turkish border. At night, the hill is floodlit from Turkey, making it easier for the gangs to observe the movements of the YPG there. There is sporadic fighting.

The commander at Til Xenzir pointed out a village, across the Turkish border, where the gangs' black market takes place. There, under the eyes of the Turkish Army and the Turkish state, the jihadists openly sell the booty they have plundered from the villages of Rojava, everything from faucets to house doors. Whenever they occupy a village, they grab everything portable—even fuses, and cables ripped from the walls—and destroy the rest.

They can cross the border into Turkey whenever they feel the need. Dozens of witnesses in the YPG and YPJ have seen it happen—just a few days before we were there, 22 trucks crossed over. Witnesses in North Kurdistan also report seeing wounded jihadists in the Turkish hospitals. Meanwhile Turkey has sent more than a thousand trucks into Syria, delivering weapons directly into the hands of IS and Al-Nusra.[19]

We repeatedly saw jihadist units in vehicles meet each other at the Turkish border and exchange things. On January 22, several Al-Nusra vehicles crossed the border into Rojava and killed two YPG fighters. The country they were crossing from, it should be pointed out, is a NATO state, some 30 miles (48 kilometers) distant from where German soldiers were stationed.

Some fighters from the local YPJ battalions showed us knives that the jihadists had left behind. "They used them to slit the throats of dead YPG fighters," Avesta, a YPJ commander, told us. "Among the dead were some Turks, and one had a cell phone. We picked it up and called his home, and a Turkish voice answered, 'Is this Orhan?' We said, 'Orhan is now in Paradise.'"

8.5   The Liberation of Til Koçer

At the other end of Cizîrê canton, in March 2013, Islamists of Jabhat Al-Nusra overran Til Koçer (in Arabic, Al Yarubiya) and the surrounding villages. They occupied the town, with its border crossing, and drove out the local population, which was predominantly Arab. They cruelly slaughtered those who refused to leave their homes and uploaded videos showing decapitated corpses onto the Internet. Those who fled went to Dêrîk, Qamişlo, and Rimelan, where the residents accommodated them with shelter in schools, mosques, churches, and the people's houses (*mala gel*). Everyone pitched in for them, collecting blankets, groceries, baby food, and medicines. Meanwhile, the Islamists made Til Koçer and the surrounding villages into a base.

When a delegation of ninety tribal leaders asked the YPG to drive out the occupiers, its request did not fall on deaf ears. Local people guided the YPG forces approaching the area. The Islamists had mined the entrances to the city, but advancing in the darkness, the units deactivated the mines. House by house, they moved into the city center. "We had to proceed very carefully," explained Silvan Afrîn, a YPJ commander. "The town's population is mostly Arab. If a child were to die as a result of something we did, it could turn the whole tribe against us." When they finally met up with the Islamists, the battles were fierce, lasting three or four hours. Arabs fought alongside the YPG/YPJ, against the jihadists. During the fighting, five or six YPG/YPJ fighters fell, compared to dozens of Islamists.

The liberation took ten days, but in late October 2013, Til Koçer came under YPG/YPJ control.[20] The terrorists fled, abandoning tanks, cars, heavy artillery, and other war materiel. By liberating Til Koçer, the YPG/YPJ won the hearts of the residents, many of whom then enlisted.

Again and again, people told us that Al-Nusra and IS gangs defiled the very name of Islam. They had no real project for this region—they came only to plunder and murder. Everyone—Kurds, Arabs, Syriacs, or Ezidis—was ready to defend the country. In many places, civilians, young and old, took up arms to help beat back the Islamist gangs.

Melsa, age 23, took part in the liberations of Serêkaniyê and Til Koçer and several other actions. In her most recent injury (she has been wounded several times), a slug passed through the left side of her waist. "That happened a month ago in Serêkaniyê," she said, as she showed it to us. "It doesn't matter anymore. We've been wounded so often, it's as if we're running through water but we don't get wet. We free an area, then go someplace else."

"After we freed Til Koçer," Melsa said, "we found the city to be incredibly filthy. The Islamists hadn't built anything, only plundered and robbed and ruined. Everywhere we came across their drugs and their trash. That's why the local people call them çete, 'gangs.' When the townspeople came back, they welcomed us, embraced us, kissed us. Some gave us gifts, a pitcher of yogurt or some cheese they'd made."

Figure 8.6   A mobile YPJ unit at Til Koçer

After the liberation, some Arab women even wanted to fight. "The women here are confined to their houses—it was initially very hard to make contact with them," explains Rûken Afrîn, from Yekîtiya Star [*see* 5.3]. "But after the liberation of Til Koçer, a dam broke, and a few women joined the YPJ."

Several Arab battalions of YPG and YPJ were created in Til Koçer. "Everything for us has turned around 180 degrees," said one of the new fighters. "It's so much better than it was under the Assad regime. That's what all the Arabs here think." Rûken Jîrik, a YPJ commander, explained to us that she is a descendant of *abid* (Arabic for "slaves") who served the Arabs in this region. The slave system hasn't been entirely abolished here, so the rescue by the YPG/YPJ was a double liberation. "Now we can't even accept everyone who wants to join," added Rûken. "There are so many, we can only proceed step by step."

We had a chance to get to know some of the new Arab women fighters—they had just completed their basic political and military training but hadn't yet been deployed. They wore headscarves with their military uniforms, which looked rather strange at first. Bêrîvan (a Kurdish *nom de guerre*) told us that after Til Koçer was liberated, her father brought her to the YPJ himself—he wanted her to have a strong position in society the way the Kurdish women did.

None of these women had any fear of war. "Our women are normally at home 24 hours," Bêrîvan told us. "At first we were afraid to pick up a weapon with our hands. But we like the friendship, the interactions. We hope the project of Democratic Autonomy will have an effect throughout Syria."

8.6 Training and Induction

Şehîd Şîlan Women's Military Academy

Each of the three cantons has a women's military academy, named after Şehîd Şîlan Kobanî (also known as Meysa Bakî), a PYD leader who was killed in an attack on Mosul on November 29, 2004. All the trainees are cadres. They receive a comprehensive education in history, politics, nature, society, weaponry, and more.

One morning, one of the authors visited the Şehîd Şîlan academy in Cizîrê, out in the countryside. It was the first women's military academy in Rojava, founded just after the YPJ conference. It's very important for women to have their own armed force, trainees explained, and to be able defend themselves.

Tolhildan, age 20, had enlisted in the YPG in 2011, even before she was old enough to fight. She has six siblings—one sister is in the YPJ and a brother is in the YPG. Her father is a PYD member. She fought at Serêkaniyê and Til Koçer. Ararat, age 20, with nine siblings, had also joined the YPG in 2011. Her goal is to defend the country and its women. Her mother is in Yekîtiya Star, and she has a brother in the YPG. She fought at Til Hemîs, Serêkaniyê, and Hesekê. She sees no difference anymore between men and women in the armed forces. Now in the YPJ, she is a press spokesperson, and she has training in video and photography. But all knowledge is to be collectivized, she emphasizes, and fighters will teach one another.

Serhildan, age 21, another member since 2011, has six siblings. Her father does communal work; her mother and a sister are in Yekîtiya Star, and a brother is in the YPG. She says she was naïve when she joined— the political education was difficult for her. She didn't understand much, even though she had finished twelfth grade. After eight months of education and training, she saw combat at Hesekê and Til Hemîs. She doesn't think much of the IS fighters: "They can't fight. They don't resist. They run away."

Figure 8.7   A student at the Şehîd Şîlan Women's Military Academy

Jîn, also 21, also joined in 2011, in Til Temir. "The gangs attacked our village in October 2011," she says. "A relative of mine was killed. I wanted to study, but when the revolution began, I wanted to join. My mother was afraid for me, and both my parents said, 'You can't do that,' but we argued all night, and I joined anyway. Physically I had no problems, I'd already done heavy work in the village. At Til Temir, the attackers arrived in cars. We were only a few people, but when we fought back, they ran away and left the cars behind. They had heavy weapons, but they didn't know how to use them properly. Sometimes Arab villages support the gangs.

"I became a team commander, and now I'm a *taxim* [platoon] commander. In a battle, the commander goes up front. The farther up front you are, the harder you have to fight. The difference between women and men is that the men go up front immediately. But women consider a tactic carefully so we never run away. Feelings of comradely love run very high in battle. There is a lot of mutual aid and support. A friend once threw himself into the line of fire to rescue me."

Şehîd Jînda Defense Academy

"Defense is the most important thing."

When we visited the Şehîd Jînda Defense Academy, a class was in session with 25 fighters, 12 of them women. The teachers, mainly female, had fought in the north with YJA Star. Most of the instruction that day was political. Every morning, the students rose at 5 o'clock, did sports, and then the classes began at 7.

No matter what topic we brought up, everyone said that the defense of Rojava is the most important thing now. But once a place is liberated, it can't be protected with a standing armed force, they said, since troops are needed everywhere. When IS attacks, everyone has to grab their weapons, not only the YPG but also the Asayîş and even civilians, the experienced fighters told us. They participate resolutely, they said, as long as cadres are there to provide leadership.

In the kitchen, we found two men cooking and cleaning. "It's normal for us," said one of them. "I do it at home too. I'm married and have two children." Nineteen-year-old Cila from Hesekê chimes in that some of the men couldn't cook at first, but they taught each other. Relations between the female and male *hevals* is relaxed and comradely. Almost all the fighters have numerous siblings and cousins in the movement or in the YPG or YPJ; most of their families have martyrs already. The Arab commander Şirîn tells us that after a cousin of hers was killed, opinion in the village shifted toward support for the YPG.

Figure 8.8   An Arab YPJ fighter undergoing officer training at the Sehîd Jînda Academy

YPG/YPJ Centers

In all the larger cities, the YPG and YPJ have a center (in Kurdish, *navend*) where people can enlist. The *navend* also represents the military forces externally, and they act as interlocutors between families and their children in the YPG/YPJ. After completing a basic military education, the fighters are assigned to handle security in the access roads; Islamist suicide bombers have been known to enter the Kurdish areas in vehicles.[21]

At the YPJ *navend* in Serêkaniyê, we asked Bengîn Melsa, a commander, who could join. "If someone is too young or an only child, we don't accept them," she said, "or if many of their family members have been martyred. A health issue could also be a ground for rejection. And we generally don't accept mothers. Only a few women have left their husbands and children to fight with us. In very rare exceptional cases, we accept a 14- or 15-year-old who is threatened with a forced marriage, or who faces family violence, and who has fled to the YPJ. But a girl that young can't be deployed to fight till she's 18." Girls under 18 participate in daily YPJ life and get to know the movement, its principles and ideology, but they don't participate in military actions.

In June 2014, the YPG and YPJ signed an international convention banning the acceptance of people under 18 into their ranks (and others banning anti-personnel mines and sexual violence).[22] A delegation of the Geneva Call led by Pascal Bongard visited Rojava and found that enforcing the law pertaining to the participation of under-18-year-olds still had difficulties, because in isolated cases, under certain circumstances, the YPG accepts them.

8.7 Equipment, Units, and Tactics

Those who join YPG/YPJ militias to defend their home cities receive a monthly stipend of about $150, if they have family; those who join as cadres, or movement militants, don't earn anything. All fight mainly with light weapons, that is, Kalashnikovs, RPG handheld anti-tank grenade launchers, BKS machine guns, and Russian-made Dragunov sniper rifles. Dushkas, or heavy machine guns, mounted on pick-ups are also used. And the fighters have a few tanks seized from the Islamist gangs or left behind by the Syrian Army.

The three cantons have a defense board president. The forces' organizational structure is borrowed from the PKK guerrilla army. A platoon (*taxim*) consists of eight or nine people; two platoons form a unit (*bölük*), and two units form a battalion (*tabur*).

The YPG and YPJ are a typical guerrilla army: they attack quickly, then withdraw quickly. They concentrate their forces, then disperse to lay ambushes. But this tactic isn't always useful on Rojava's flat terrain. To protect villages and cities, they dig ditches with bulldozers, so they can shield themselves from mortar attacks and other heavy weapons. They install armor on buildings and farm machinery for use as military equipment. In urban warfare, they smash through interior walls in order to move through buildings safely. In Kobanî, the IS gangs had the advantage of being better equipped, while the defense forces had the advantage of local knowledge.

But the YPG/YPJ's decisive advantage is that they are defending their country and their families and share a common vision. The other side has some staunch fighters as well, but many are mercenaries, and most have little connection to the region or its inhabitants. When we attended a funeral for martyrs in Dêrîk, we met a fighter from Germany who had been trained as a sharpshooter. She told us the IS fighters are poorly trained and mostly inept. "They come to die," she said. "They're drugged with stimulants. In Cezaa, two hundred of us faced six hundred of them, but we beat them."

8.8   Serêkaniyê Today

By the time we visited Serêkaniyê in May 2014, the war-scarred city was being rebuilt. About 80 percent of the population had returned and were trying to build a new life despite the terrible lack of supplies. Its financial situation was grim, since trade was still cut off by the embargo.

Two weeks before we arrived, the City Hall had been damaged by a bomb attack. Everyone was still talking about it—the horror, the injuries. The staff showed us videos, taken afterward. We could see body parts strewn amid the destruction.

While the walls and windows were being repaired, the municipal administration was housed in temporary quarters. Meanwhile, the staff struggled to meet the people's most pressing needs. A staffer from the finance division, about 20 years old, explained to us, "We work for no pay. Our city was destroyed, and we want to help. Some people donated furniture for the municipal administration, so now we have a chair, a table, and a desk. At first we didn't know what we were doing, but we're learning." The council system was up and running, and there were councils in every village community, connected to the district council. Kurds and Arabs were rebuilding the city together, step by step. The system of communes and dual leadership was introduced in Serêkanîye as in other places, so the city now had one Kurdish male mayor and one Arab female mayor.

One important task for the municipal administration was to distribute lands formerly owned by the regime. The councils allocated them first to Kurds who had no land or property as a result of the Arab Belt policy. Often the families of martyred fighters were given land, too, depending on family size. In the Serêkaniyê district, about 10,000 *dunams* of land have been distributed so far (a *dunam* is 1,000 square meters), with prioritizing for agricultural cooperatives.

Wheat and cotton are Serêkaniyê's main crops. Water for irrigation must be pumped from 200–500 meters below the surface, and the pumps need to be powered by electricity, which had been cut off. Currently, they use diesel generators, the diesel refined from the oil pumped in near Rimelan. The larger generators keep noise and environmental damage to a minimum and ensure a continuous power supply, but there aren't enough of them. Still, the fields are very productive. Thirty percent of the income from the farmland goes to the councils, while 70 percent stays with the agricultural workers.

Only a few new economic projects had been realized by the time of our visit, among them a women's bakery. Suleyman Pote, an economics spokesperson, described the plans for the district's economy. A market is being organized for cooperatives; prices are to be 15 percent below normal. Because of the embargo, machines for processing cotton aren't available, but a cooperative textile factory is to be constructed, so that the cotton can be processed and clothing produced locally.

8.9 The Liberation of Girê Spî

In 2012, IS jihadists occupied Girê Spî (Til Abyad), a city of 15,000 amid 500 villages and the towns of Suluk and Ain Issa. The city lies in the gap between Kobanî and Cizîrê cantons, 100 kilometers west of Serêkaniyê and 60 kilometers east of Kobanî. The Turkish-Syrian border divides the city, with the northern part, occupied by Turkey, now called Akçakale. Because of Girê Spî's important strategic location, the southern, Syrian-occupied part was Arabized as early as the 1960s, and a large portion of the local Kurdish population was expelled.[23]

Girê Spî was crucial for the jihadists to hold because the direct supply link from Turkey to Raqqa, IS's Syrian capital, ran through the city. On June 15, 2015, the YPG and YPJ, in a joint operation with Burkan Al-Firat and some fractions of the FSA were able to liberate the city and its surroundings.[24] That victory was significant, because it meant that Kobanî and Cizîrê could now be geographically connected and that Cizîrê could provide Kobanî with support.[25] And the victory deprived IS of that direct link to Turkey.[26]

In October 2015, Girê Spî declared Democratic Autonomy and officially became part of the democratic-autonomous administration of Kobanî canton. The Kurdish woman Leyla Mustafa and the Arab man Mansur Salum were elected co-chairs of its executive council, and commissions were chosen. All ethnicities in Girê Spî—Kurds, Arabs, Turkmens, and Armenians—are represented in these working groups.

The Liberation of Şengal

In the summer of 2014, IS terrorist militias were approaching the city of Şengal, in northern Iraq, preparing to attack the 350,000 Ezidis who lived there [see 2.1]. Serbest Babirî, the head of the seventeenth section of the ruling KDP in Iraqi Kurdistan, declared, "The Peshmerga will defend the people of Şengal to the last drop of blood." But the Peshmerga withdrew without warning. Some 11,000 Peshmerga and their 200 commanders not only proved unavailable to defend the Ezidis, they proceeded to disarm them. As for the KDP, it failed to evacuate the Ezidis, leaving them to their fate at the hands of IS. "How often in history have the Ezidis been sold and betrayed," a Ezidi sociologist said to us.[27]

On August 3, 2014, IS attacked Şengal city and occupied it. It murdered or enslaved thousands of Ezidis and captured and enslaved thousands of women and girls. (After Şengal's liberation, numerous mass graves would be discovered.)[28] Tens of thousands of Ezidis fled to nearby Mount Şengal.[29] But there they were trapped, without food or supplies. As horror mounted, the YPG, the YPJ, and the PKK opened a protective corridor for the trapped Ezidis and rescued 200,000 of them, bringing them to Cizîrê. Every automobile in the canton, private or otherwise, was driven to the border to transport the refugees to safety. Many Ezidis fled, but some 6,000 remained at the Newroz refugee camp, near Derîk.

On the morning of November 12, 2015, a major military operation to liberate Şengal began. Participants included the resistance units of Şengal, the Yekîneyên Berxwedana Şengalê (YBŞ) and the Yekîneyên Jinên Êzîdxan (YJÊ), the Ezidi women's unit; the HPG and YJA Star (PKK forces); the YPG and YPJ from Rojava; and Peshmerga units. Seventy-five hundred fighters took part in the liberation, which succeeded in routing IS.

A total of 170 PKK and YPG fighters were killed while liberating Şengal, yet in the days after the liberation, the Peshmerga claimed the victory was theirs and denied that PKK forces had even participated.[30]

For IS, the loss of Şengal, like that of Girê Spî, was a strategic defeat. Then when the YPG/YPJ cleared Hesekê of jihadists in the summer of

2015, it lost direct control over the route between Mosul and Raqqa. Still, the Ezidis remain insecure: on November 25, 2015, terror militias of Jabhat Al-Nusra and the allegedly "moderate" Ahrar Al-Sham attacked the Ezidi village of Basufan in Afrîn canton with heavy weapons.[31]

8.10   The Syrian Democratic Forces (SDF)

On October 10, 2015, the formation of the Syrian Democratic Forces (SDF; in Arabic, Qūwāt Sūriyā ad-dīmuqrāṭīya; in Kurdish, Hêzên Sûriya Demokratîk) was announced. The thirty forces participating in this umbrella military alliance include the YPG/YPJ, the Al-Sanadid Forces,[32] Syriac Military Council, the Burkan Al-Firat Operations Center, Suwar al-Raqqa, Shams al-Shamal, Lîwa Al-Selcuki, Brigade Groups of Al-Jazira, Jabhat Al-Akrad, Jaysh Al-Thuwar,[33] Lîwai Al-Tehrîr, and Lîwai 99 Muşat.[34] The foundation of the SDF was Burkan Al-Firat. Complementary to the SDF, the political alliance Democratic Council of Syria was established on December 10, 2015.

The SDF is a unified fighting force, comprising Kurds, Arabs, Syriacs, and all other Syrian ethnicities. Its declared goals are the liberation of Syria from IS and the establishment of a self-governing democratic Syria. The SDF comprises all the self-defense forces of Cizîrê canton and as well as about five thousand Arab fighters in the Syrian Arab Coalition.

Within only a few days in mid-November, the alliance was able to liberate an area of 1,362 square kilometers in southern Hesekê, which included the cities of Xatuniye (in Arabic, Al-Khatuniyah) and Hol (in Arabic, Al-Hawl), as well as 196 villages.[35] The Arab populations welcomed their liberators jubilantly.[36] On February 19, 2016, the SDF freed Al-Shaddadi, the last major city under the control of IS in Hesekê province.

In May 2016, the SDF began an operation to liberate Raqqa. The leading commander, Rojda Felat, explained that this operation's goal is to free much of the area north of Raqqa and take control of the roads connecting IS with other areas it occupies. The local people, mostly Arabs, have implored the SDF to free them from the yoke of IS. By conducting this operation, the SDF is responding to this demand of the people.[37]

For the Federal System of Rojava/Northern Syria [see 6.9], the priority must now be to liberate the 98-kilometer stretch of land that stretches along the Turkish border between the cantons of Afrîn and Kobanî/ Cizîrê. The area, also known as Manbij, had been in the hands of IS since January 2014. In July 2015, Turkey stipulated that the Euphrates River was a "red line" across which the YPG/YPJ could not advance into Manbij. Should the Syrian Kurds dare to cross the river, they would be attacked by the Turkish military. So in late October 2015, when YPG fighters showed signs of crossing the Euphrates in boats, the Turkish Army attacked several times.

At the beginning of June 2016, the SDF began a comprehensive operation to liberate Manbij. The operation was named "Abu Leyla" in memory of a beloved commander from an Arab tribe who was killed by IS at the beginning of the operation; he had played an important role in the liberation of Kobanî. Within a few days, the operation had brought under its control the route connecting Jarabulus and Raqqa as well as more than a hundred villages.[38] It liberated Manbij on August 12, 2016.

The SDF and US Special Forces

In early October 2015, the United States officially gave up on its ambition to train "moderate rebels" to fight IS and Assad.[39] A few days later, the US Army apparently supplied the SDF with weapons and ammunition.[40] It went on to station 50 special forces in Rojava, and for the liberation of Raqqa and Manbij, it added 250 more. But a few hundred ground forces cannot fight a war. The brunt of the fighting lies with the SDF.

As of June 2016, Turkey was preventing the United States and the SDF from carrying out a joint operation to take Raqqa. It had offered to mount such an operation itself, but it did not happen. Turkey's aim was to create a counter-weight to the SDF in northern Aleppo and Manbij under the maxim "All brigades that aren't on the list of terrorist organizations should unite under the name Northern Army (Jaysh as Simal)." To groups dependent on Turkey that "don't join this structure," Turkey threatened to "withdraw its support and put them on the terrorism list."[41]

Turkey had long used its İncirlik airbase as leverage on the United States, permitting its use only on its own terms. But the United States made itself independent of this pressure by building up an airbase in Rimelan. It is obvious that the United States supports the SDF operation only for its own propaganda purposes, because it wants a military victory in Syria against IS, and because of the US elections in November 2016.

At the end of May, US fighters wearing insignia of the YPG and YPJ were seen in Raqqa, according to a US Army spokesman. They were not authorized to do so, and they were ordered to remove them immediately. Perhaps some uninformed soldiers believed they were fighting on the side of "the good," but this is not the case. The United States continues to stand by its NATO partner Turkey. One has only to look at how the United States averts its eyes from the war crimes of the Turkish government in North Kurdistan, even as the Turkish Army repeatedly shelled Rojava. The US participation with the SDF allows IS and Assad to portray the SDF as a puppet of US imperialism, possibly to the detriment of the SDF.

The United States does not support the Rojava project politically, even though it is a federal state itself. It did not recognize the declaration of the Federal System of Rojava/Northern Syria on March 17, 2016, although Russia did. Many observers feared that the United States would force Rojava to make compromises in its radical democratic project. Still, as of June 2016, Rojava was benefiting from US air support, no matter what American intentions may be. The risk that Rojava cannot endure alone, without the support of the US Army, in total isolation, is of course great, although Russia has offered to help.[42]

8.11   The Significance of the YPG and YPJ

Clearly Rojava would not exist without its self-defense forces. Had they not been created, the Kurds and their allies would long ago have been driven out. All the groups threatened by IS recognize this fact; hence nearly all the Arab tribes, loath to submit to IS dictatorship, are increasingly coming around to support the self-defense forces.

The international media regularly underplay the accomplishments and sacrifices of the YPG and YPJ. They even tend to label all Kurdish fighters as Peshmerga. But the YPG/YPJ's military achievements—especially their determined defense of Kobanî against IS—have also won them, as well as the PKK, international recognition as a significant force in the Middle East. The participation of women in the armed struggle is strategic (and contrasts with the Peshmergas' combat exclusion of women).[43] Gender equality in other parts of society in Rojava would be unattainable without it. The women's struggle for a radical transformation of gender roles is taking place in the heart of a revolutionary

Middle Eastern culture. The existence of the women's forces highlights, in the eyes of the global public, the progressive character of Democratic Autonomy, and it has broadened international solidarity with Kobanî.

The YPG and YPJ fight with far greater motivation than do the mercenaries of IS and Al-Nusra, who are mostly unwilling recruits pumped up on drugs. Much suffering could have been avoided if comparable self-defense units had been established everywhere in Syria, not just in the Kurdish areas. Hanife Hisên explained to our delegation in May 2014 that PKK leader Öcalan had been critical on this point: "Why have you only organized in the Kurdish areas?" This requirement has been answered now with the founding of the SDF, the Democratic Council of Syria.

Still, areas liberated by the YPG/YPJ often find themselves between a hammer and an anvil. Thousands of miles of border must be defended, and the embargo is forcing people to emigrate. And while the jihadists fight with modern materiel and weapons, mostly seized from US-equipped groups, the weapons used by Rojava's defense forces are ancient. The fighters have neither helmets nor bulletproof vests. "Give us, at long last, more weapons!" implored a YPG commander at Hol. "We are fighting with Kalashnikovs and machine guns against IS, with its heavy weapons and tanks."[44]

As a result of this imbalance, Rojava's casualties have been too high. As of the summer of 2016, an estimated 4,000 fighters have been killed. These deaths would not have occurred had the Western states, the Gulf monarchies, and Turkey not initially armed the most radical forces of the Syrian opposition, including the group now known as IS. Even today, in view of the attacks in Paris and Brussels and beyond, the United States and Europe continue indirectly, via their NATO partner Turkey, to support Islamist groups like Ahrar Al-Sham, which continually attacks Afrîn canton, and Jabhat Al-Nusra—forces that are ideologically and organizationally indistinguishable from IS.[45]

Even with ancient weapons, the YPG and YPJ continue to fight undaunted. They are defending not only their homes but their long-held dream of Democratic Autonomy. As the commander at Hol said, "We're fighting for all of you!"[46] The world, including the United States and Europe, must recognize that in the Middle East there is simply no alternative to democratic self-government.

Notes

1. Aras Masif, "Kobanê und die Heuchelei des Westens," *Kurdische Nachrichten*, October 8, 2014, http://bit.ly/1Spt6D8.
2. Andrea Seibel, "Der kurdische Widerstand verkörpert das Gute," *Die Welt*, October 18, 2014, http://bit.ly/1QEU64b.
3. Fabio Bucciarelli and Eduardo Matas, *Rojava: A Newborn Country*, 2014, vimeo.com/79114978.
4. Michael Knapp, "Die Verteidigungskräfte von Rojava—YPG/YPJ," *Kurdistan Report*, no. 172 (March–April 2014), http://bit.ly/1duOmrM.
5. "YPG: Kürdistan devrimi ve demokratik Suriye için savaşıyoruz," *Yeni Özgür Politika*, January 20, 2014, http://bit.ly/1NjIdef.
6. "Jihadists Expelled from Flashpoint Kurdish Syrian Town, NGO Says," *Now*, July 18, 2013, http://bit.ly/28YKvE3; Violations Documentation Center in Syria, "Under a Scorching Sun," August 2015, http://bit.ly/28QY7Dr; "Angriffe Al Qaida naher Gruppen auf kurdische Selbstverwaltung," *Civaka Azad*, n.d., http://bit.ly/28OxlLO.
7. Given women's longstanding participation in YJA Star, the young author Dilar Dirik writes that for her generation, armed female Kurdish fighters are not unusual: Dilar Dirik, "Western Fascination with 'Badass' Kurdish Women," *Jin, Jiyan, Azadi* (blog), February 17, 2015, http://bit.ly/1IvKPVd.
8. CENÎ Informationsdossier zu Rojava, November 13, 2013.
9. *ANF*, March 9, 2013; *ANHA*, August 30, 2013; *Kurdpress*, October 4, 2013.
10. "Frauen kämpfen um's Überleben und gegen religiösen Faschismus," *Global Dialoge—Women on Air*, radio broadcast, October 14, 2014, http://bit.ly/1QEVNi1.
11. "Die Revolution in Westkurdistan—Teil 8," *Civaka Azad*, n.d., http://bit.ly/1PpKLr3.
12. Balint Szlanko, *Among the Kurds of Syria*, film for Hungarian television, October 2, 2013, http://bit.ly/1G5010S.
13. Anja Flach, *Frauen in der kurdischen Guerilla: Motivation, Identität und Geschlechterverhältnis* (Cologne, 2007), pp. 113 ff.
14. Zaher Baher, "The Experiment of West Kurdistan (Syrian Kurdistan) Has Proved that People Can Make Changes," *Libcom.org*, August 26, 2014, http://bit.ly/18rMBsZ.
15. Bucciarelli and Matas, *Rojava: Newborn Country*. On Turkish incursions, see "YPG: Turkish Army Attacks Rojava Territory and Kills a Citizen," *ANHA*, November 17, 2015, http://bit.ly/28TQZBL; "Turkish Army Continues Attacks on Rojava, Leaving Two Children Killed," *ANHA*, February 16, 2016, http://bit.ly/1TKAtaW; "Turkish Army Attacks Qamislo with Mortars," *ANHA*, April 5, 2016, http://bit.ly/22bxVD9, and many others.
16. "Sê sal ji Şoreşa 19'ê Tîrmehê," *ANHA*, July 13, 2015, http://bit.ly/1NVKtGQ.
17. "In Syria, Clashes Between Arab Rebels, Kurds," *Washington Post*, November 28, 2012, http://wapo.st/28UkMwB.

18. Jonathon Burch, "Kurds Seize Town on Syria-Turkey Border, Ankara Concerned," *Reuters*, July 18, 2013, http://reut.rs/1KFgXFK; Knapp, "Verteidigungskräfte von Rojava", and David Wagner and Giorgio Cafiero, "In Kurdish Syria, a Different War," *Foreign Policy in Focus*, September 5, 2013, http://bit.ly/28OEmYG.

19. For a comprehensive review of Turkey's links to ISIS, see David L. Phillips, "Research Paper: ISIS-Turkey Links," *Huffington Post*, March 7, 2016, http://huff.to/1Iaatvo, which contains many links. For other coverage of Turkish links to other groups as well as ISIS, see Allen McDuffee, "Activists: ISIS Is Now Launching Attacks from Inside Turkey," *Atlantic*, November 29, 2014, http://theatln.tc/1FIBSUA; Bassem Mroue, "Islamic State Group Attacks Kobani from Turkey," *Associated Press*, November 29, 2014, http://apne.ws/11DS506; Barney Guiton, "'ISIS See Turkey as Its Ally': Former Islamic State Member Reveals Turkish Army Cooperation," *Newsweek*, July 11, 2014, http://bit.ly/28X1kR1; Natasha Berland, "Senior Western Official: Links Between Turkey and IS Are Now 'Undeniable,'" *UK Business Insider*, July 28, 2015, http://huff.to/1Iaatvo; Humeyra Pamuk and Nick Tattersall, "Exclusive: Turkish Intelligence Helped Shop Arms to Syrian Islamist Rebel Areas," *Reuters*, May 21, 2015, http://reut.rs/1mt9pzG, among many other examples.

20. Carl Drott, "Arab Tribes Split Between Kurds and Jihadists," Carnegie Endowment for International Peace, May 15, 2014, http://ceip.org/1DWrs3a.

21. Szlanko, *Among the Kurds of Syria*.

22. "Syrian Kurdish Armed Non-state Actor Commits to Ban Anti-Personnel Mines, Sexual Violence, and Child Recruitment," *Geneva Call*, June 16, 2014, http://bit.ly/1S49Xon.

23. Elke Dangeleit and Michael Knapp, "Tall Abyad/Girê Spî: Angelpunkt im Kampf gegen den IS," *Telepolis*, July 2, 2015, http://bit.ly/1QDkadR.

24. Burkan Al-Firat (Euphrates Volcano) is a coalition of diverse resistance groups under the command of the YPG/YPJ for the purpose of liberating the Euphrates region. Its formation was proclaimed on September 10, 2014, five days before IS attacked Kobanî. Members include, among others: the YPG/YPJ, the Al-Tawhîd Brigade, Liwa Thuwar ar-Raqqa, Shams Al-Shamal Brigade, Seraya Jarabulus, Jabhat Al-Akrad, Siwar Umunaa El-Reqa, El-Qesas Brigade, und Lîwa al-Jihad Fî-Sebîlillah: "YPG und FSA gründen gemeinsames Angriffzentrum," *Kurdische Nachrichten*, September 10, 2014, http://bit.ly/1SUiagz.

25. Dangeleit and Knapp, "Tall Abyad/Girê Spî."

26. In late May 2015, the Turkish newspaper *Cumhuriyet* had made available pictures and films that prove that the Turkish intelligence service MİT had delivered weapons to IS. President Erdoğan then denounced the editor-in-chief, Can Dündar, and at the end of November 2015, Dündar was arrested. In May 2016, he was sentenced to five years and ten months' imprisonment for "leaking secret information of the state": "Devlet işi yapıyorduk," *Cumhuriyet*,

June 11, 2015, http://bit.ly/1O24Ok9; "Amnesty International Calls on Turkey to Release *Cumhuriyet* Journalists," *Today's Zaman*, December 18, 2015, http://bit.ly/1TWcJxQ.

27. Hakim Fehmi Ibrahim, Ezidi sociologist in Bielefeld, personal conversation, December 2015.

28. "Weiteres Massengrab nahe Sindschar entdeckt," *Tagesschau.de*, November 28, 2015, http://bit.ly/1lEhW2x.

29. Föderation der Ezidischen Vereine e.v., "Sengal ist befreit—die Befreiungsaktion Sengals ist ein wichtiger Schritt für die Menschlichkeit," *Civaka Azad*, November 13, 2015, http://bit.ly/1IoE4hJ.

30. "Barzanî: 'Nur die Peshmerga haben Shingal befreit, keine andere Einheit war beteiligt,'" Êzîdî Press, November 13, 2015, http://bit.ly/1TIjNhi.

31. "Syrien: Terroristen attackieren êzîdîsches Dorf Basufan," ÊzîdîPress, November 25, 2015, http://bit.ly/1NNoAuS. See also "Al-Qaeda Militants Bomb Kurdish Villages near Aleppo," *ARA News* November 14, 2015, http://bit.ly/1J2Zt4G.

32. The Al-Sanadid Forces are a militia of the Şammar tribe (the largest Arab tribe in the region, with about 1 million members on both sides of the border). Al-Sanadid was founded in early 2015 by the tribal leader Sheikh Hamidi Daham, to support the YPG/YPJ in the struggle against IS. It is led by Hamidi al Hadi's son, Bandar al Humaydi: "Al Sanadid Forces: 'We Go Wherever the YPG Goes,'" *ANHA*, July 15, 2015, http://bit.ly/1QloVtR.

33. Revolutionaries' Army, involving Jabhat Al-Akrad, Lîwai 99, Special Operations Center 455, Lîwa Al-Selcuki, Ahrar Al-Zawiya, Lîwa Sultan Selîm, Lîwa Şuheda Al-Atarib.

34. "Declaration of Establishment by Democratic Syria Forces," *Kurdish Question*, October 15, 2015, http://bit.ly/1J3aVxj.

35. "HSD veröffentliche eine Bilanz über die Operation im südlichen Hesekê," *ANF*, November 16, 2015, via ISKU, http://bit.ly/1IoFmJC.

36. "Heseke QSD Koyluler Karsilama 1," *ANF*, November 27, 2015, via YouTube, http://bit.ly/1RKHoiS.

37. "Kurdish-led SDF Launches Offensive on Syria's Raqqa," *Al Jazeera*, May 25, 2016, http://bit.ly/1TKAtaW.

38. "Arab-Kurdish Coalition Captures More than 105 Villages and Farms from ISIS as part of Manbij Operation," *ARA News*, June 15, 2016, http://bit.ly/28VVOQt.

39. "Lavrov: Little Doubt US Arms Delivered to Syrian Opposition to Fall into Terrorists' Hands," *RT*, October13, 2015, http://bit.ly/1lWItYr.

40. Roy Gutman, "Syrian Arab Militias Dispute They Received U.S. Airdrop of Ammunition," *McClatchy DC*, October 20, 2015, http://bit.ly/1RKH6Jo; "Declaration of Establishment by Democratic Syria Forces," *Kurdish Question*, October 15, 2015, http://bit.ly/1J3aVxj.

41. *ANHA*, May 16, 2016.

42. "Operation in Rakka—neue strategische Phase," *ISKU*, May 25, 2016, http://bit.ly/28V41Po.

43. In Iraq, in the uprisings against the Ba'ath regime before 1991, a few women fought in the ranks of the Peshmerga; see Peruin, interview by Oliver Piecha, "Ich war dort die einzige Frau," *WADI*, late autumn 1993, http://bit.ly/1LgcqNx. The best-known female fighter was Leyla Qasim, who was executed in Baghdad in 1974; her portrait hangs in many YPJ institutions today. But currently the Peshmerga excludes women from combat: Judith Neurink, "No Frontline Deployment for Female Kurdish Troops," *Rudaw*, September 28, 2014, http://bit.ly/1dLbZw8.

44. "Kurdische Terroristenjäger: Diese Kämpfer treiben den IS vor sich her," *T-Online*, December 2, 2015, http://bit.ly/1NN9OHt.

45. Thomas Pany, "Syrien: 'Neue Möglichkeiten' der USA Ahrar al-Sham?" *Telepolis*, September 22, 2015, http://bit.ly/28VYYnt.

46. "Kurdische Terroristenjäger: Diese Kämpfer treiben den IS vor sich her," *T-Online*, December 2, 2015, http://bit.ly/1NN9OHt.

9

The New Justice System
Consensus Is Key

The revolution in July 2012 rendered the Syrian justice system obsolete. The people, and the political movement behind them, clearly rejected not only the Ba'ath regime, with its state security apparatus, officialdom, and intelligence agencies, but also, and less visibly, the judicial system and its personnel.

But as important as removing the old system was determining what the new one would look like. In any society that is not free of domination, that is not yet fully emancipated socially or in gender terms, so-called "crimes" are committed, even at the most basic level, especially against the background of war—conflicts, violence, theft, and robbery—which a society must address.

A striking feature of Rojava's system is the existence of the peace committees (in Kurdish, *komîteya aşîtî*), sometimes referred to as peace and consensus committees, at the two basic levels of the MGRK council system. They ensure social peace in the residential streets and the neighborhoods, and resolve cases of criminality and social injustice. In the 1990s, under the Ba'ath regime, activists in Syrian cities with Kurdish majorities formed the first peace committees. The state considered them a threat to its monopolistic justice system, so they ran clandestinely, parallel to the existing system. Even with the increased repression after 2000 and especially after 2004, however, they continued to operate, albeit in smaller numbers and limited areas.

It was because of the long experience of these peace committees that, after the Syrian uprising began in March 2011, Kurdish activists were able to establish them in great numbers at the neighborhood and village community levels. And after July 2012, they were set up at the residential street level as well. Those cities and villages that had had experience with peace committees experienced no chaos or confusion in delivering justice and became the go-to places for settling civil and criminal cases. In the localities where they had not previously been created, usually they were set up quickly.

Figure 9.1   Guards at a courthouse in Dêrîk

9.1   Structure

After the liberation that began on July 19, 2012, justice commissions (in Kurdish, *dîwana adalet*) were established for each district at the instigation of the TEV-DEM. In the first few weeks, the justice commissions consisted of groups of lawyers and opinion leaders in the communities who took charge of the liberated courts and prisons. One of their first steps was to free political prisoners. Next, they took up the cases of prisoners who had been convicted on nonpolitical charges (except for murder), such as theft. They sought a consensus between the parties, and when it was achieved, the prisoners were released. The prisons were soon emptied. Meanwhile, the justice commissions recruited judges, lawyers, prosecutors, jurists, and others who had broken with the regime to serve on the peace committees, and the people's councils elected or appointed others.

The justice commissions were crucial for the establishment of the new system. The justice commission of Cizîrê, the largest canton, has eleven members, while the ones in Afrîn and Kobanî have seven each. They carried out wide-ranging discussions with the people's councils about the new justice system; they coordinate with the MGRK council system and are accountable to it.

The peace committees, created at the commune and neighborhood/village community levels, constitute the basis of the new justice system. The aim of the peace committees is not to condemn one or both sides in a proceeding but to achieve consensus between the conflicting parties. Only in very few cases at the neighborhood level, after long discussions, have decisions been made by majority, but they are exceptions. If possible, the accused is not ostracized through punishment or incarceration, but rather is made to understand that his or her behavior has led to injustice, damage, and injury. The matter is discussed among the parties at length, house visits may be made, and witnesses brought in, in the belief that achieving consensus and rapprochement will lead to a more lasting peace.

If a peace committee at the commune level is unable to achieve consensus, the case may be taken up to the peace committee at the neighborhood level, where consensus is again sought. The peace committees do not handle murder cases—those go directly to higher-level bodies.

At the level of the commune and neighborhood, the peace committees have a dual structure. Mixed committees are responsible for resolving conflicts and handling crimes, while women's peace committees handle cases of patriarchal violence, forced marriage, plural marriage, and so on; they are directly linked to Kongreya Star [see 5.3].

At the next level up, the district, are the people's courts (*dadgeha gel*); they too were brought into existence by the justice commissions. The judges (*dadger*) who sit on them may be nominated by a justice commission or by anyone in the jurisdiction. The district-level people's councils advise on nominations; seven people are elected for each people's court. Nominees need not have a juridical background, and usually several of those chosen do not. Unlike other societies, Rojava considers it far more important for judges to be individuals who can represent the people's interests.

The upper levels of Rojava's justice system may resemble those in other states, but the base is much more democratic. At the close of a case in the people's court, one of the parties may bring the case to an appeals court (*dadgeha istinaf*). Rojava has only four appeals courts, two in Cizîrê and one each in Kobanî and Afrîn. At this level, the judges must be jurists; they are chosen by the people's court at the canton level. There is only one cantonal court (*dadgeha neqit*) to cover all three cantons.

Finally, there is a constitutional court (*dadgeha hevpeyman*), whose seven justices ensure that the MGRK council system and the people's courts and the DAAs observe the Social Contract and the laws. In each canton, people's court attorneys (*dozgeri*) as well as other prosecutors work on behalf of the public interest.

Also at the summit of the judicial system is the justice parliament (*meclîsa adalet*). Each of the three cantons has one, and they consist of 23 people: three representatives from the justice ministries, founded in January 2014; eleven from the justice commissions, seven from the constitutional court, and two from the bar association. One member of the justice parliament speaks publicly. The fact that the transitional administrations have only three representatives, and thus little legal influence, is an important contrast to conventional justice systems.

The justice parliaments have the responsibility of ensuring that the judicial system meets the needs of this fast-changing and democratizing society. Their top priority is the further elaboration of the judicial system. Its structure remains only skeletal, and many details and practices have yet to be decided upon. They face the huge challenge of instituting new legal foundations based on the Social Contract. At the same time, they scrutinize existing Syrian laws, regulations, and guidelines. If a law is found to discriminate or exclude, or if it contradicts the Social Contract, it is rewritten to correct these problems and make it democratic. If such a revision is not possible, it is deleted and replaced with a new law. The reason for starting with Syrian law is that three cantons consider themselves part of Syria.

The justice parliaments also advise on pending technical and administrative questions. Lawyers' concerns are discussed there, and solutions developed. The proceedings in the justice parliaments are carried out through discussions, and while there is sometimes controversy, their members have not disagreed completely. They have had to work quickly to build a functioning justice system. The necessary discussions will continue in the coming years, when peaceful times will hopefully prevail.

The law academy in Qamişlo follows the discussions from a neutral distance. Established in 2013, the academy's first objective is to train people for the justice system. It too scrutinizes existing Syrian laws, regulations, and guidelines, and supports the justice parliaments' work in this field. It critically analyzes the justice system and proposes changes.

9.2 Peace Committees

The communes, at the level of the residential street, elect members of the peace committees [see 6.3]. At the level of the neighborhood or village community, the people's council (comprising the communes' delegates) chooses the peace committees. The upper levels in the council system have no peace committees.

A peace committee consists of five to nine people, with a gender quota of 40 percent. Most members are not traditional magistrates, since they are elected democratically and with gender parity. But they usually have experience in mediating disputes. Most are over forty years old. Their procedures are not spelled out in detail. Rules and principles have developed in practice over the years and to some extent are transmitted verbally.

Parallel women's peace committees exist to guarantee that in cases of patriarchal violence, decisions are made free from patriarchal influence. Women were the driving force in creating these structures. A man who commits patriarchal violence against a woman can be sentenced to between six months and three years in prison or community service. Even if the woman retracts her complaint, the convicted person has to serve at least six months in prison.

Other sanctions against those convicted of crimes may include a period of education, lasting until the trainers are convinced that the person has changed; work in a cooperative or public service; exclusion from the commune; social isolation—for some people the hardest of all; boycott, if the convicted person has a shop; temporary relocation to another neighborhood; and exclusion from some public rights.

9.3 Procedures

In the new justice system, an arrested person is viewed not as a criminal to be convicted but as someone to be rehabilitated. The objective is not only to determine whether the person has committed the crime but to understand the reason behind it. Numerous people are involved in the discussion, not just a small, elite group. The approach is unlike anything in either capitalist and parliamentary systems or in Real Socialist states. Only small radical democratic movements and communities like those of the Zapatistas in Chiapas offer a similar alternative.

In the new justice system, a small but important change is in the arrangement of the courtroom. Everyone in the room sits at the same level, and the categorical division of lawyers, defendants, and visitors is rejected as it is a reflection of hierarchical thinking.

In terms of sentencing, the death penalty has been abolished, it goes without saying. A penalty of life imprisonment (the maximum term has been temporarily set at twenty years) can be imposed only in cases of murder, torture, or terror. As of May 2014, this penalty had been handed out only twice in Cizîrê: once for a man who murdered a woman in a barbaric way, and once for a man who tortured and murdered a member of the Asayîş.

Prisons have been reconceived as educational institutions, and once the means are available, they are to be transformed into rehabilitation centers. The justice commissions are especially concerned with prison conditions: as one member explained to us, "We've already deprived the prisoners of their freedom; we don't want to punish them further with onerous prison conditions."

The peace committees are becoming more accepted by the wider society, as non-Kurdish people increasingly turn to them for conflict resolution. Their effect has been positive, since quarrels and dissension are declining, and crime, especially theft, is on the wane. As of early 2016, the number of cases handled by the peace committees and people's courts has declined; reliable figures are hard to come by, but every interview partner in Rojava emphasized such a decline. Such crime as exists is concentrated at the urban peripheries, where the organizational level of MGRK system is relatively weak. Because of the work of the women's movement, "honor" killings have noticeably abated.

In such soil, social solidarity and cohesion can grow, as has been the experience of several years of revolution in Rojava. Today, if the majority of the people are acting in solidarity, founding cooperatives, and making decisions together, it is partly because the work of the peace committees has been successful.

9.4 Justice Platforms

Starting in the fall of 2014, the people's courts came under intensive criticism. According to the critics, they were beginning to resemble the courts in existing hierarchical justice systems. Instead of a broad social participation, a small group of people were making decisions about the people on trial, as if they had some special power. This practice, it was pointed out, could result in the general population feeling alienated from the people's courts, even though the people's court judges are elected and even though they act with the best intentions.

By comparison the peace committees, composed of volunteers, solved problems much more satisfactorily and resulted in longer-lasting outcomes. The reason for this was that the peace committees met the parties and witnesses several times in different locations, even in their homes—that is, in non-official places. Their processes were and are much more immediate than those of the people's courts.

A long discussion in summer 2015 came to the conclusion that greater public participation was needed for resolving conflicts at the community level. To this end, the decision was made to establish "justice platforms." Now, if a peace committee at the commune or neighborhood level cannot solve a case, it can apply to the justice commission to convene a justice platform. For a justice platform, up to 300 people, from related communes and councils, civil society organizations, social movements, are assembled to hear the presentation of a case and discuss its resolution. If one evening is not enough, the people will meet together again, even repeatedly. The community discusses the causes of the "crime" comprehensively. They decide on a solution, if possible by consensus, but if that is not possible, they vote. Justice platforms take recourse to voting more often than peace committees do, owing to the large number of participants in the justice platforms. This is reasonable, since achieving consensus is much more difficult when there are many participants, and since the justice platforms are more open to objections by individuals or small groups.

At a justice platform, certain things are understood. Very personal matters are not discussed. Cases are not to be used for propaganda. No one is considered guilty until a decision is made. Transparency is important, and attempts are made to limit emotionality.

The justice platforms cannot eliminate the need for people's courts altogether; the people's courts will not be abandoned. Rather, the justice platforms are a kind of experiment in the democratization of the justice system. Later in 2016, the justice platforms will be assessed, and the people will be able to decide whether and how to proceed with them. We consider the justice platforms a challenging but interesting tool to overcome tendencies of alienation and bureaucracy, and to develop participation for justice systems all over the world. To be sure, they require a great deal of energy on the part of people. But they could become one of the many aspects of the Rojava Revolution that libertarian, left, and democratic movements and peoples of the world consider for themselves.

9.5 Asayîş

As the revolution in Rojava unfolded, one of the tasks of the new council democracy was to establish a force that would fit the people's aspirations and avoid the kind of party militias that plague South Kurdistan. The result was the Asayîş, whose name translates as "security forces." Security forces defend society and as such are to be distinguished from police, which defend the state. As one instructor from the Asayîş academy in Rimelan emphasized, "We see ourselves as the security forces for the defense of the society, not of the state." The role of the Asayîş is to make possible the free and self-determining activity of everyone within a diverse society.

Physical safety is essential for a free and self-determining life. So in Rojava, if a city is attacked either by IS or by Al-Nusra, the Asayîş will defend it alongside the YPG and YPJ. They counter spies from the Assad regime, from Turkey, and from the KPD. Many people told us, "Without the Asayîş, none of us could live here."

As soon as we arrived in Heseke district in May 2014, we saw what they meant. Regime troops were trying to advance toward the self-governed zone, but the Asayîş were resisting them. Two Asayîş, among others, were killed while defending Heseke's Kurdish neighborhood.

Accompanied by a young comrade, we climbed onto a roof and got a good view of this large city of 500,000. At that time, about 35 percent were under self-government. (Heseke has since been almost entirely liberated.) Some 2 kilometers from where we were standing lay the part of Heseke controlled by jihadist gangs. Much of its population had fled from the terrorist regime, among them Berfîn, a young woman from the divided city. She explained to us that she could not walk around over there in a T-shirt, because the jihadists had imposed an exceptionally rigorous yet arbitrary form of Sharia, enforced by violence, including dismemberment. Many times in Hesekê, as in Serêkaniyê, we saw people smoking who had had fingers cut off. The relative peace and social freedom in the cantons protected by Asayîş have a special meaning, for in spite of the war, Rojava, thanks to the Asayîş, is one of the safest places in Syria.

Internal Security

To handle "internal security," the Asayîş intervenes in conflicts that the peace committees can't resolve, often involving assaults and violence but also drug dealing. Connected and accountable to the people's councils, Asayîş cannot detain a suspect longer than 24 hours without a court order. Rojava's justice system, as we have seen, is oriented not toward punishment but toward re-socialization and education. In Amûdê, we met an Asayîş member who had previously been imprisoned: while there, he had become so enamored of Asayîş principles that he joined the force. His story is not unique.

To ensure that an arrest does not in itself constitute punishment, the Asayîş strive to maintain the best possible prison conditions. We observed this ourselves when we visited the alleged terrorist Bashar Abdulmecid Mussa while he was in prison in Tirbespî. We asked him about the conditions of his arrest and detention. He told us the Asayîş were treating him very well. He allowed us to inspect his body, so we could see that he had not been harmed physically. He was in contact with his family. His relatively relaxed demeanor excluded, for us, the possibility of force or mistreatment.

In order to guarantee that the rights of prisoners are respected, the Asayîş allow visiting human rights organizations unlimited access to prisons, as is testified in a Human Rights Watch report of March 2014. When an Asayîş member oversteps or violates protocol, the consequences are immediate, ranging from suspension to a judicial proceeding and imprisonment.

We could not find any evidence that Rojava had political prisoners. We asked about their existence whenever we spoke to Asayîş, courts, and councils, and also asked dozens of activists and other people we met in Rojava. This was partly motivated by the fact that the Human Rights Watch report of March 2014 stated that, when people belonging to oppositional parties of the ENKS had been arrested for committing crimes, their parties often made the allegation that these detentions were political.[1] Based on our investigation, however, we find it credible that there are no political prisoners, and that the Asayîş would benefit from more public outreach to counteract such reports.

For the Asayîş, education is of highest importance. Even after members finish training in the academy, they return every 15 days for continuing education in human rights. The Human Rights Commission [see 7.5] educates and oversees the Asayîş.[2]

Structure and Organization

As of May 2014, Rojava had 110 Asayîş stations and approximately a hundred roadside control points (probably more today), from which vehicles could be searched, say, for explosives and weapons. Asayîş members more or less live in the stations where they work and go home only rarely. They wear no insignia of rank, and collegial relations are considered important. Their work is mostly unpaid—they receive their clothing, their food, and a small expense allowance of about $125 per month. They usually hold down a second job. They lead a collective life in service to the people and the system of Democratic Autonomy, having joined out of a desire to protect society.

The head of the Asayîş in Qamişlo, Heval Ahmed, described himself to us as a Communist, explaining that the force's command structure is democratic, which means that each level chooses its commanders. Once a month, there is a big meeting where new commanders can be nominated and elected. Each unit consists of 30–45 people and is subdivided into smaller units, which elect their leaders as well.

To address problems of aggressive behavior, the Asayîş have structures for systematic criticism and self-criticism. To prevent the emergence of hierarchy, the commanders regularly stand before their units and not only self-criticize but receive criticism from members.

The Asayîş are a mixed-gender institution—as of May 2014, women made up about 30 percent of the force. But there are also separate women's units, Asayîşa Jin, that intervene especially in cases of patriarchal violence and domestic abuse. The principle is that women

Figure 9.2   Asayîşa Jin, women's security force, at a checkpoint in Tirbespî

can talk to other women more easily and openly. Some women would feel very inhibited, for example, about reporting a rape, or an episode of domestic violence, to mixed or all-male Asayîş members. They have far fewer inhibitions about talking to young women. Asayîşa Jin units are closely tied to the women's councils.

Notes

1. Human Rights Watch, *Under Kurdish Rule: Abuses in PYD-run Enclaves of Syria*, June 19, 2014, http://bit.ly/1Fo93Da. See also "PYD Responds to Human Rights Watch Report," *Peace in Kurdistan*, July 2014, http://bit.ly/1edIeVm.
2. "Asayîş birimlerine 2 bin insan hakları broşürü," *ANHA*, December 3, 2015.

10

The Democratization of Education

Soon after the revolution, Rojava's educational system became more diverse, open, democratic, and participatory for students and teachers alike. The primary step was the blossoming of Kurdish-language instruction, first in community spaces and then in schools organized by the Kurdish Language Institute (Saziya Zimanê Kurdî). In May 2014, we visited the Celadet Bedirxan Academy for Kurdish Language, History, and Literature (AZDW, Akademiya Ziman, Dîrok û Wejeya Kurdî ya Celadet Bedirxan) in Qamişlo, where we had an extended talk with Berîvan and Dildar, two longtime activists.

The academy stands on a hill in the outskirts of Qamişlo, on a spot formerly occupied by the Institute for Agrarian Economy; the building is ringed by great expanses of land, still available to staff and students for farming. The location, Berîvan explains, "creates an environment somewhat isolated from the city, suitable for study." The academy coordinates the whole education system of Cizîrê canton, provides materials for instruction, and trains teachers.

Figure 10.1   Kurdish-language instruction in Serêkaniyê

10.1 Before and After the Revolution

Rojava's Kurdish education movement originated, Berîvan explains, in 1993, when Abdullah Öcalan, then living in Syria, proposed that the Kurdish language be taught in private homes. In many places in Rojava, the proposal was taken up. The Syrian state's intensified repression after 1999 disrupted Kurdish-language instruction, but it continued surreptitiously—ten or fifteen teachers and students would meet, each time in a different home to avoid detection.

Meanwhile, in the late 1990s, in the refugee camp in Maxmur (Makhmur) in South Kurdistan, a specific school system was established beyond the reach of the KDP and PUK. Maxmur, home to around 12,000 North Kurdish refugees, became a place where Kurmancî—the dialect spoken in Rojava—was taught. Here, the Kurdish freedom movement had an opportunity to take steps toward establishing an emancipatory education system. After March 2011, it became possible to teach Kurdish openly in Rojava, and eleven teachers from the Maxmur camp spent a year doing so.

With the founding of the MGRK [see 6.2], Kurdish-language instruction spread to more places, now coordinated by an education policy. Volunteers taught in many villages, and private instruction became more common in urban apartments. The teachers were those who had had studied Kurdish before 2011—that is, who had been able and willing to risk it. In early 2012, the MGRK assigned language schools to specific buildings: "We even transformed stables into schools, if we had no other options."[1] Not only children and teenagers, but people of all ages attended classes. Where the demand was great, groups were divided by age.

The existing teachers taught as many classes as they could, but in 2011 only a few dozen people were really equipped to teach the language well, Dildar and Berîvan explained to us. That wasn't enough for 3 million people—they could reach maybe a few thousand at most. Something had to be done, and fast. So, as soon as students learned how to read and write Kurdish and became familiar with the grammar, they began to teach it themselves. Kurdish-language classes self-propagated.

The July 2012 liberation, explained Berîvan, "provided us with a new situation, with previously unimaginable possibilities." That summer, to meet the growing demand for teachers, "the MGRK's bodies decided that many hundreds of teachers would be trained." In September 2012, Kurdish-language instruction did indeed begin in most schools, especially in Afrîn and Kobanî, and in the Kurdish neighborhoods of Aleppo. By comparison, Cizîrê was much weaker because the MGRK's organizational level was less developed there, and thus fewer Kurdish teachers existed. In addition, many areas of Cizîrê were not liberated until the fall of 2012. But a year later, the situation changed in Cizîrê, and in almost all schools with a Kurdish population, Kurdish-language instruction was offered.

In 2012 and 2013, when Kurdish-language instruction was introduced, it was an elective subject. The education movement thought it important that Kurdish students enroll on their own initiative, Dildar and Berîvan told us. But reality surpassed expectations: almost all the Kurdish students signed up. The very fact of learning Kurdish was exhilarating to them, resulting in good progress. But a few Kurdish students didn't enroll, Dildar notes. Parents who support the ENKS forbade their children to study Kurdish for ideological reasons. Nevertheless, a considerable number of these children defied their parents and enrolled in Kurdish-language instruction.

In the fall of 2013, the AZDW was founded in Qamişlo to systematically train teachers and develop the intended new education system. Similar academies were created in the other two cantons: the Viyan Academy for Kurdish Language and Education in Afrîn, and the Ferzad Kemanger Academy for Kurdish Language and Education in Kobanî. Language instruction still had many weaknesses in 2014, but soon after our visit to the AZDW, on May 26, the second session of teacher training was completed. Since then, many sessions have been conducted.

As of May 2014, Cizîrê had some 1,300 Kurdish teachers, and Afrîn and Kobanî another 900 each, totaling 3,100. Women make up 80–90 percent of the teachers, most of whom had never taught before. Since teaching is now their main occupation, they receive an honorarium from the MGRK—around $100 per month, which is worth a great deal in Rojava. Teachers in Cizîrê who were employed before the revolution still draw wages from the Syrian state— in Kobanî and Afrîn, no teachers are paid by the state anymore.

The academies and the education movement generally would like not only to see Kurdish-language courses taught in schools but to see all subjects be taught in good-quality Kurdish and to prepare all students for a life of working toward a democratic, ecological, and gender-equal society.

10.2 Reconstruction and Pedagogy

After the liberation, Rojava's schools continued to use Arabic as the general language of instruction. But they dropped the course from the curriculum that taught about the Ba'ath ideology and Syria's ruling political system. Previously, students had had to participate in "patriotic" marches, singing together in support of Assad—that too was eliminated. "It was toxic for the students, absolutely unacceptable," Dildar says. Statues of Assad Junior and Senior were removed, as were all Ba'ath flags and images. The school administrators objected, but the state wasn't in charge anymore, so they couldn't call for help. Gritting their teeth, they resigned themselves to the changes. "A few administrators wouldn't give up the fight," Dildar told us, "so the MGRK gave them compulsory leave." If they change their views, they can return to service.

As of our May 2014 visit, the MGRK and the education movement had not entirely replaced the former school leadership, or transformed the system. By early 2016, the transformation was much farther along, moving slowly but surely based on widespread discussions in Rojava, so as to be well-grounded and long-lasting. Probably too, the education movement didn't yet have the capacity to change everything without sowing confusion.

Schools that have few or no Kurdish students initially didn't offer Kurdish-language instruction, except on request. But after the winter of 2013–14, several schools with mainly Arab students asked for it. When the new school year started in September 2014, it was offered in these schools. Dildar was gratified, for it showed that Democratic Autonomy was gaining ground among non-Kurdish population groups. She was right; the request from non-Kurdish communities continued for the following two education years.

A further important development has been the introduction of Aramaic-language instruction in schools with many Syriac students. This started in September 2013, in the Dêrîk district, where the local Syriacs established a language and education institute and private schools giving instruction in their native tongue. This was actually less challenging than the Kurdish-language situation because, under the Ba'ath regime, the

Syriacs were permitted to have private language courses. But Dildar and Berîvan welcome the prospect that Rojava's many other ethnic groups— Armenians, Turkmens, and Chechens—will soon go a similar route. Meanwhile during the 2015 school term, the majority of Syriac children in Rojava were taught in their native tongue.

The education movement worked hard to persuade the school administrators to accredit Kurdish-language instruction as fulfilling degree requirements. At first they balked: the Syrian interior ministry sent letters warning them not to do it—Dildar and Berîvan have seen such letters. But finally in the summer of 2013, in the liberated regions, Kurdish was listed as a course on many students' certificates. That moment was historic, because it forced the Syrian state to accept Kurdish-language instruction. Its meaning should not be underestimated, says Dildar. Eventually the education sector in the rest of Syria will also have to officially recognize instruction in Kurdish and other languages.

10.3 The Academy for Kurdish Language, History, and Literature (AZDW)

At the Academy for Kurdish Language, History, and Literature, we watched as forty young teachers were being trained. Fortunately they were enthusiastic, because had they not been, they surely would not have been able to endure studying for eleven hours every day for more than three months. Since our visit, more than seven sessions have been completed, which has resulted in many educators with improved approaches.

In the schools, the language is usually taught for four to ten hours each week, in two stages. First, students learn grammar and spelling; then they learn about the history of the language. They learn better that way, says Berîvan. If there aren't enough teachers, two classes may be merged.

The teachers-to-be also study Kurdish history and literature, the history of assimilation, pedagogy, Democratic Nation ideology, and women's science (*jineolojî*). They initiate study groups, some of which continue beyond the term, like one that focuses on regional history and archaeology and organizes visits to archaeological sites.

We asked Dildar and Berîvan how the students, and the people generally, accept the Roman alphabet, which is used in Kurdish-language instruction. Both answered that it's absolutely no problem and is not challenged. In fact, many are happy about it as it has the added value of providing an early introduction to the Latin alphabet.

One group of teachers has begun to develop a Kurdish dictionary, taking on the laborious task of compiling a comprehensive collection of Kurdish words. General students and families are getting involved, as well as a group of elders between ages 50 and 70, who learned the language as children and retained it despite the Ba'ath regime's assimilationism. The group are determined that the shortcomings of existing Kurdish dictionaries used in other parts of Kurdistan will not be repeated here. For some concepts, Kurdish terms exist, but they don't have much currency and the Arabic equivalents are used instead; the group's goal is to revive the Kurdish terms for general use. Teachers and students also establish groups on other subjects on their own initiative, for the long term, and for objectives not easily achieved.

Apart from Kurdish-language instruction, the AZDW has the goal that all primary school classes will be taught in Kurdish as soon as possible and secondary school classes in the near future. In the fall of 2013, some schools in Afrîn were selected as a pilot project. Two years later, most primary schools in Afrîn decided to teach mostly in Kurdish. (In Kobanî, preparations had begun, but the IS attack in September 2014 jettisoned all such plans.) In Afrîn, mathematics, sports, handicrafts, and history-social studies have been taught in Kurdish for more than two years. The experience has revealed two difficulties. The first is that the proper translation of Arabic terms used for all these lessons requires patience, persistence, and time. The second, more challenging, is that statist, hierarchical, patriarchal-sexist, and racist content and thinking are hidden in the curriculum taught to children for many decades. Eliminating expressions of that content is possible only with an alternative language. Rojava aims to do this in steps, starting with the fall 2015 term.

The AZDW's third main working field is to prepare three crucial lessons for the secondary and higher educational level in the Kurdish language: "Democratic Nation," a summary of the Rojava revolution for children; "Geography and History," challenging in a new language, and "Culture and Ethics," equally so. Activists at the Mesopotamian Social Sciences Academy in Qamişlo have participated in a workshop to help prepare these materials.

At the AZDW, teacher-student relationships are unconventional, and sharing and collective behavior are valued. The so-called "staff" do not consider themselves teachers—instead, they regard themselves and their students as equals. Everyone lives, cooks, plays sports, and cleans up together during the sessions, which last several weeks. The land surrounding the academy buildings is used for agriculture so that the community doesn't lose contact with the earth. Several fields (about five acres) have been planted with fruit trees and vegetables, and a clever irrigation system has been devised.

Problems and challenges remain, as Dildar and Berîvan were quick to tell us. The schools have nowhere near enough books, notebooks, and other materials. The few available books and study materials are used and reused. The embargo imposed by Turkey, the KRG, and the Islamists prevents much of anything from entering Rojava. It was only at the end of 2015 that the first book was published in Rojava, a harbinger of a full independent education policy [see 10.3].

10.4 Academies

The education system under the Ba'ath regime created a mentality that is a handicap to the revolution today. The curriculum was dictated by the central state, allowing no leeway for local initiatives or self-rule. Directors and teachers at state schools instilled fear of authority in the students, and breaking this mentality and replacing it with the new paradigm will take a long time.

The academies, by contrast, are centers of "people's education" that have played a crucial role in setting up the new society. They can be established whenever activists and social movements feel necessary, they are oriented to meeting the basic needs of the broad population, and they are open to everyone, educating activists and all interested people. They work from the principle that knowledge arises in relationship and in production processes and must be given back to society, for which the academies are a tool. Doing so requires changing educational methods, the use of buildings and tools, and even the daily life at academies, based on sharing and companionship.

In Rojava, as of this writing, academies have been founded in the following subjects: Self-defense, Women, Youth, Ecology, Asayîş, Economy, Free Ideas and Thinking, Urbanization, Law and Justice, Sociology, History/Language/Literature, Policy and Diplomacy.[2] The ideology commissions of the MGRK system are in regular contact with the academies.

Nurî Dersîmî Academies

Every large city of Rojava has a Nurî Dersîmî Academy, named after an important Kurdish intellectual. Nurî Dersîmî (1893–1973) fought for the Kurdish people's rights to their culture and language and never bent under the Ba'ath regime persecution and repression. Dilgesh, a young man who teaches at the Nurî Dersîmî Academy in Rimelan, explained to us that the academies are intended to transmit liberatory values to the people. They teach everything from the local languages to philosophy, history, and science. Even European philosophy—Descartes, Plato, Nietzsche, and Marx—is on the curriculum.

The academy in Rimelan is housed in a fashionable building that was formerly home to the directorate of the state oil company. It's a clear manifestation of the revolution that venues of the former power elite have been converted into cultural centers, people's houses, and educational institutions.

Dilgesh told us that the writings of Öcalan, with his ecological, democratic, gender-liberated paradigms, have a central place in the academy's curriculum. The lessons make repeated reference to Rojava's new social and political system, to its democratic ethics and councils, and to women's history.

Dilgesh thinks the revolution will place society on a new moral and political basis. "We want to think freely now, without boundaries, and question everything," he says. "Our goal is to broaden [heretofore] limited school learning and to enable people to perceive themselves as conscious subjects." The academy offers no technical education but rather a kind of holistic education in which natural science plays an important role.

Classes consist of 15–20 participants, who come from all parts of society, for sessions of 10–25 days; payment is by donation. The participants usually room at the academy itself, which is surrounded by a tree-lined garden. Their cultural and even political heterogeneity is highly significant, for basic values are being transmitted here. Not only individuals but whole communities attend, then pass on what they have learned to others.

The academy's leadership consists of six people. Like the teaching staff, half of the leaders are women. Dialogue is central to the pedagogy, and the teachers think of themselves as students as well. Lessons take place almost every weekday. Every two days, the teachers evaluate the work, addressing the problems of the school and the teachers and balancing critique with self-critique. This process ensures that the faculty keep developing.

The Nurî Dersîmî Academies are associated with the people's councils and therefore with TEV-DEM, and so they are part of the system of Democratic Autonomy and the institutions of democratic self-government. Their main problem is that due to the war, people are struggling to survive, and most regard education as having only secondary importance. But the teachers say they are committed "to organizing and politicizing the people in spite of everything."

10.5 Outlook

Several months after our first visit, IS attacked Kobanî, whereupon all the educational institutions in Kobanî were destroyed. The school buildings were gutted, and the education system so painstakingly created is in a shambles. During the occupation, many refugees from Kobanî continued their lessons in the Suruç (Pîrsus) camps of North Kurdistan.

But as of the fall of 2015, almost all the students are back in Kobanî, and they are getting their education in rehabilitated school buildings, a priority for reconstruction. Out of 900 teachers before the IS occupation, the majority (750) have returned; out of 300 schools before the occupation, 257 have reopened.[3] The Kobanî self-administration had done everything possible to limit the loss of education to one year.

Several academies were also re-established in 2015, like the Women's Education and Science Academy, important for activist women. These commitments to reestablish the education system underlines the strength of the political structures in Kobanî that were developed before 2014 and continued during the IS occupation.

Afrîn and Cizîrê have been less affected by destruction and have progressed. As of 2015, in places where Kurdish children are in a considerable majority, 306 schools have been organized for teaching all classes (except Arabic-language instruction) in Kurdish from the first to the third grade. The Afrîn pilot project (mentioned above), in which several schools are teaching all classes in Kurdish up to the eighth grade, is under way.

But in Cizîrê, establishing Kurdish as the main language in primary schools has run up against challenges. Many Arabs, Syriacs, and other groups accepted it, but in the city of Dêrîk, where the ENKS has many supporters, parents protested. Having mainly Kurdish as the teaching language, they argued, would make it difficult for their children to find jobs in the future. ENKS members demonstrated, shouting slogans against the MGRK and the PYD.[4] In our view, the ENKS wanted a reason to protest Cizîrê's democratic-autonomous administration. But after a few days, the situation calmed, and the announced change was implemented.

In Kobanî, the people continue to rebuild the schools despite the closed borders that prevent the import of essential construction and education materials. On February 1, 2016, the community opened the first school for disabled and special needs students, to great enthusiasm. With 15 students enrolled, the school will teach Kurdish and computer skills among other subjects. The school is led by the teacher Suleyman Mahmoud, who is himself blind and a specialist in teaching blind and otherwise disabled students. The opening of this school speaks volumes about the people of Kobanî's wish to support the most vulnerable in the community. Despite immense difficulties, their community is providing their disabled and disadvantaged members with opportunities, to ensure that they are not only included as members but are visible and celebrated as contributors. Kobanî re-pooled its limited resources so that this much-needed school could be built. Its very existence is a strong political and ideological statement to the world.[5]

This small step alone suggests the broad dimensions of the transformation in Rojava's education system since the revolution. It is just one important contribution to the long-term aim of devolving education to the society itself.

Notes

1. Dilbilimci Dêriki, "Rojava'da dil devrimi silahlı mücadele ile başladı," DIHA—Dicle Haber Ajansi, April 13, 2014.
2. "Dorşin Akif ile Söyleşi," Zan Enstititü, http://bit.ly/1V4WdKO.
3. "Kobani Ready for New School Year," ANHA, September 29, 2015, http://bit.ly/1UhoF25.
4. "Rojava Revolution Has Created the Ground for Kurdish Education," ANHA, October 29, 2015, http://bit.ly/28UK1Rl.
5. Hawzhin Azeez Facebook Page, February 2, 2016, http://bit.ly/28UCm2C.

11

Health Care

Developing a sustainable, free health care system constitutes an expression of Democratic Autonomy. Rojava's Social Contract affirms the right to health care for all in Article 30. But the international embargo on Rojava [see 12.3] has had a disastrous effect on medical care, far more onerous than on other sectors. Hundreds of thousands of people are gravely affected, as Dr. Agirî in Qamişlo, who has helped coordinate health policies in Rojava since the revolution, explained to us. One doctor in Amûdê asked, "What help is it to a baby whose mother has no milk, that Barzanî has a problem with Rojava's self-government? We don't receive any infant formula!"

11.1 Before and After the Liberation

Before the liberation, Syria's health care system was under government control. Care was free of charge, but service was poor in some rural areas.[1] State hospitals had been declining in quality since the 1990s, and neoliberal reforms in the health sector allowed the wealthy to find treatment at private clinics with private doctors.

Then came the 2011 uprising, and in early 2012, Rojava established new health committees at the district level to discuss how, if the state should somehow collapse, health care could continue and be rebuilt on a social basis. These committees networked and came up with practical ideas. Once the liberation began, they proved highly valuable and their creation was a wise strategic move.

Although the 2012 revolution terminated state authority in Rojava, the hospitals and other public health facilities remained open, and doctors did not emigrate (although over the next two years, many would). While the MGRK system assumed control over other state and public institutions and services, it did not take over health care facilities. Rather, the health committees coordinated health policy, in consultation with the MGRK and TEV-DEM.

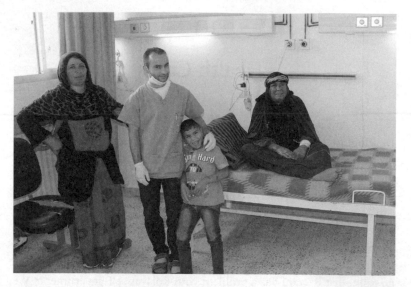

Figure 11.1   Inside a hospital in Dêrîk

11.2   Health Assemblies

In each district, the health committees established a health assembly (in Kurdish, *meclîsa tendurustî*). The health assemblies coordinate health policy in most districts in the three cantons. In the recently liberated areas, preparations are currently under way for assemblies there as well. Two health assemblies may exist in one district, depending on the organizational strength, as in Dirbesiyê.[2] All meetings are open to the public and are recorded in writing and even on video. All members, in accordance with the 40 percent gender quota and the co-chair system, elect the health assemblies' coordinating bodies.

The health assemblies are the most important bodies when it comes to Rojava's health policy. Participants in them include doctors (both from the public hospitals and from the private clinics and practices), pharmacists, laboratory technicians, and hospital staff, as well as medical-sector and humanitarian aid organizations such as Kurdish Red Crescent (HSK). Importantly, numerous Arabic and Syriac doctors participate in the health assemblies. The women's councils ensure that women are not disadvantaged vis-à-vis the men in the health sector and have the same rights, working conditions, and opportunities.

The health assemblies have set as a goal that each big city in the three cantons will have a fully equipped hospital. Hospitals currently exist in Afrîn, Dêrîk, Kobanî, Qamişlo, Hesekê, Girê Spî, Serêkaniyê, and Hesekê. Six are under the supervision of the health assemblies and continue to function despite the growing shortage of doctors.

In Kobanî, the 2014 IS attack and occupation destroyed the facility there, which was almost finished, but now a new hospital is under construction. With international support, a blood bank has been established. The hospital in Dêrîk was undamaged and is in use. The hospital in Serêkaniyê was looted when Al-Nusra occupied the city, but its re-equipment was organized in 2015. The hospital in Hesekê provides poor service and is used only reluctantly by the people.

In 2013, hospitals and clinics proved unable to adequately care for all the war wounded, so small hospitals were established for this purpose. The Qamişlo military hospital, established in 2014, treats up to 26 patients. Similar hospitals were constructed in Afrîn and Kobanî in 2014–15.

In small towns, community health centers rather than hospitals make basic health care widely available. The health assemblies aspire to open at least one in every district. They are supported by the MGRK system. The centers can do almost everything except perform major surgeries. (The private clinics dating from before the revolution are not of good quality and concentrate on surgery, according to Dr. Agirî. That they are expensive goes without saying.) The doctors work voluntarily for about two to four hours a day, after their other jobs. "For those patients who can afford it, we charge an average of 200 Syrian pounds [just over one US dollar] per treatment," we were told. (No one is denied care for lack of money.) "Half of that goes to the doctors, and the other half to the health center. Private doctors charge 700 Syrian pounds [$3.70], which is unaffordable for many people." In the community health center in Amûdê, all the commission doctors work one day for free.

Health centers are often set up in traditional buildings, which means they are chilly in the winter and relatively warm in the summer. Non-medical considerations and economics, Dr. Agirî stressed, are being taken into account in all planning.

The health assemblies offer regular seminars and workshops on health and medical issues, for popular education. They are conducted in the people's houses (*mala gel*), women's houses (*mala jinan*), and youth centers. Thousands of young people have completed a comprehensive first aid course, so they will know what to do in case of emergency.

Since 2014, health seminars have been introduced into the schools as well. Seminars for women have been implemented in cooperation with the Free Women Foundation of Rojava [*see* 5.6] in Qamişlo. Since the fall of 2014, international volunteers have been supporting regular educational seminars in Rojava.

Kurdish Red Crescent (Heyva Sor a Kurdistanê, HSK), with 180 employees in Cizîrê canton (as of May 2014), helps the health assemblies organize medical and other humanitarian aid. In the larger towns, HSK offices accept donations of clothing and other necessities, which it then distributes under the supervision of the health assemblies.

Figure 11.2 A team from Heyva Sor (Kurdish Red Crescent) coping with shortages

11.3 Challenges

But Heyva Sor is hardly in any financial condition to meet the needs of Rojava's society, especially when it comes to the refugees from other parts of Syria. The need for medical supplies is urgent, Dr. Agirî emphasized to us, yet the embargo blocks shipments across the Turkish-Syrian border. Hospitals and health centers are so lacking in technical equipment that some surgeries can't be performed because the operating rooms are unusable.

Medications too are scarce, particularly for patients with diabetes, hypertension, and liver ailments. Quite a few surgical operations are performed with little or no anesthesia. In Qamişlo, a pharmacy that sells prescription drugs at wholesale prices is probably the most affordable in all of Syria, but many items arrive late or not at all. Medications sold on the black market are prohibitively expensive. Although the councils have set price controls, this doesn't affect the price of black-market medications.

In 2013, people in Nisêbîn and Mêrdîn, in North Kurdistan, took to the streets and demanded that the Turkish government permit medications and supplies to be transported across the border into Rojava. They ultimately forced the government to concede, as Ayşe Gökkan, the former mayor of Nisêbîn, told us. Starting that spring, supplies and medications could legally be imported. They have to pass through controls by the Turkish Red Crescent, after which local authorities in North Kurdistan transport them across the border, where health assembly staff receive them. The aid is then distributed to hospitals, health clinics, and pharmacies, with an effort to supply all facilities equally.

A third problem, as Dr. Agirî mentioned, is the insufficiency of doctors. Those who practice in Rojava are good overall, but there are not enough of them. Under difficult wartime conditions, many doctors have fled, knowing that they would easily find work in other countries. The region needs specialists in breast cancer, as well as neurosurgeons and vascular surgeons.

The war is felt everywhere in Rojava, but the wounded at the fronts suffer most from the insufficient care. Injured YPG or YPJ fighters sometimes die because they receive no treatment. After being wounded, they are immediately taken to the nearest clinic or hospital, but the health care workers are overburdened, and equipment and medications are insufficient. Again, an influx of experienced medics from around the world could contribute a great deal.

11.4   Health Assemblies and the DAAs

In each canton, the health assemblies established a high-level administrative body, the health council, that coordinates the health services and activities on a broad scale. Although not subordinate to the MGRK, the health councils work closely with TEV-DEM, with the neighborhood people's councils, and with the communes.

In 2014, the DAAs created health ministries. The health assemblies and councils became part of them. They retain an autonomous structure and are self-determining, and their statutes and programs attach great importance to democratic and participatory processes as basic to success. Yet their connections to the health ministries are a much-debated issue. Health assemblies make decisions in consultation with TEV-DEM and the MGRK system, and they implement them. Although they are officially sub-organizations of the health ministries, the health care professionals in the health assemblies discuss, decide, and act. The health ministries provide opportunities, based on decisions from the health assemblies. The relationship is defined in accordance with the revolution's principles of radical-base democracy.

Well-attended health congresses have been held in the level of districts and cantons. On March 2, 2014, a Medical Congress in Qamişlo discussed herbal healing methods, affirming the need to retain the memory and legacy of traditional medicine. It also emphasized bottom-up organization.

In mid-September 2015, the Cizîrê Health Congress, held in Dirbesiyê, decided to open a health academy and to establish educational committees in each health sector, thus improving the quality of health education. In early 2016, the first health academy opened in Kobanî.

On December 25, 2015, the First Kobanî Health Congress issued a document summarizing Rojava's health policy. It highlighted that health care is essential "for the construction of ... an ecological society"; that women are "the avant-garde of health care"; that "a natural health perspective" is essential; that health care as "commodified by capitalist modernity" has manufactured demand for dubious services and made people dependent on them. Democratic Modernity, it continues, "based on the socialization of health and health care in the community," is not only self-sufficient but also necessary to building Democratic Autonomy.[3]

The Health Congress discussed and made decisions about strengthening women's health care, by expanding the activities of women's committees in the health assemblies; establishing of diplomatic committees to increase support from abroad; establishing student health committees—that is, providing opportunities for students to gain better access to current information and follow developments internationally; establishing more community health centers in small settlements (below the district level); and developing alternative, herbal medicine and healing as a critical connection to past experiences.[4]

After talking with activists, we can state that in the field of health care the Rojava Revolution is following its original core values. Despite war and embargo, the health system has been improved due to its participatory approach. By improving the health sector in connection with a successful defense of society, the Rojava Revolution may create a health care model of similar importance to that of Cuba.

Notes

1. Anand Grover, "Substantial Progress on Health in Syria, But More Needs to Be Done, Says UN Expert, 2010," UN Human Rights Council, http://bit.ly/29c3gT3.
2. "Zerg Health Assembly Was Established," ANHA, December 31, 205, http://bit.ly/1tvkJP7.
3. "Kobanî Health Congress Announced Final Declaration," ANHA, December 27, 2015, http://bit.ly/1OvQmln.
4. "Health Congress Resulted in Signfiicant ... ," ANHA, November 18, 2015, http://bit.ly/23i85zB.

12

The Social Economy

12.1 Under Ba'ath Colonization

Under the Ba'ath regime, Rojava was one of Syria's poorest regions, exploited quasi-colonially.[1] Yet the three cantons are wealthy in natural resources, fertile soils, and minerals, including petroleum. Agricultural production here accounts for about a third of Syria's economic strength.[2] Dr. Ahmad Yousef of the Afrîn DAA says Rojava could feed two or even three times its current population, yet still 60 percent of Syrians living below the poverty threshold are Kurds from Rojava.[3]

The regime forced each canton to produce its leading agricultural commodity and little else. Thus Cizîrê was forced into a monocultural cultivation of wheat (and to a lesser extent cotton), such that it provided up to 50 percent of all Syrian wheat, making it the country's breadbasket. But Cizîrê was barred from vegetable production and fruit cultivation. Any tree planting had to be approved by three ministries, which made it all but impossible. (This policy was instituted for "security reasons" in the context of the Arab Belt program.) The overall appearance of Cizîrê's landscape reflects this policy: it looks like a single huge wheatfield.

As for Kobanî and Afrîn, they were and are mostly given over to fruit and olives. Afrîn supplied 25 percent of Syria's olives.[4] About a third of the arable land in Kobanî had been used to cultivate wheat.

Cizîrê also has oil wealth, constituting 50–60 percent of Syrian oil production. Drilling began in the 1960s, extracting petroleum of a heavy grade. By 1995, Syrian production reached its peak. Since then, its reserves have shrunk, and oil production has slowly but surely decreased. If the current war had not broken out and domestic demand continued to rise, Syria would not have been able to export any more oil by 2020. Cizîrê's petroleum fields also have significant amounts of natural gas.

In pre-war Syria, all goods produced in Rojava were shipped outside the region for processing. The petroleum and gas pumped here were piped

Figure 12.1 Oil, wheat, and animal husbandry in Cizîrê

to big state refineries in Homs. Despite its wheat production, Rojava had no large flour mills—the wheat was transported to other parts of Syria. Cotton picked in Rojava was shipped south for textile processing. Then the milled flour, processed fruit and vegetables, textiles, refined oil, and other goods were brought back into Rojava for consumption.

This arrangement reflected the colonizing nature of the Syrian state. The regime systematically neglected the region and deliberately kept it poor, as Dozdar Hemo, Cizîrê's economic development adviser, told us in May 2014. Neither the state nor the private sector invested in the economy. "It would have been impossible to assemble three sewing machines for a textile workshop," explained Remziye Mihemed, the canton's finance minister, "because a day or two later, regime functionaries would storm in and shut it down. And the regime routinely prevented people from working in groups, to perpetuate their dependence on itself."[5]

Syriac, Armenian, and some Arab men could find employment relatively easily. Syriacs and Armenians were mostly handicraft workers, skilled laborers, or shopkeepers and were less oppressed by the regime. As for the Arabs, resettled here under the Arab Belt program, the state gave them preferential treatment in the allocation of land and work. The salaries the regime paid to its bureaucrats and security forces constituted a significant stream of cash in Rojava.

But many Kurds had no choice but to leave Rojava altogether. Hundreds of thousands emigrated to the large Syrian cities to earn a living so they could provide for their families back home. The largest émigré community was concentrated in Aleppo, more than half a million in all.

12.2 Effects of the Liberation

After the liberation of July 2012, the councils had the task of ensuring that the economy didn't collapse and that basic provisions remained available. The fact that councils had already been in place for at least a year turned out to be a great advantage. And the MGRK's economics commissions at the district level also proved a boon. The system's first post-revolutionary task was to maintain basic supplies, via the municipal administrations. It succeeded by gradually incorporating existing institutions into the council system.

The councils also imposed price controls. On the second day of the revolution, the economics commissions set price caps on the markets and on businesses, to prevent speculators from hoarding food and medications in order to profit when prices later rose. The price controls guaranteed that everyone would pay the same for food and diesel. In Afrîn, the price of flour soared during one winter, rising from 3,000 to 6,000 Syrian pounds per bag. Subsequently the cantonal administration set the maximum price at 4,100 pounds. Flour sold for anything higher was confiscated. In 2014, the wheat harvest was greater than expected, and two flour mills had been built from local materials, so the price of flour could be lowered to 3,500 pounds.[6]

The people of Rojava could not live on wheat alone, so the cantons had to obtain vegetables, fruit, and grains from elsewhere, especially from Latakya, Turkey, and from Damascus and other Syrian cities. But during that first hard winter of 2012–13, though grain was plentiful, flour—due to the lack of flour mills—was scarce. To avert a famine, several grain mills were constructed in 2013. Since that first winter, the food supply in all three cantons has been generally satisfactory. The economics commissions at all levels ensure that no one goes hungry and see to it that even the economically weakest are provided for as well as the many refugees. In 2014, Cizîrê was even able to export flour to the KRG. Kobanî's wheat production rose, so that by the end of 2013 it had an adequate supply of baked goods. Afrîn partially converted to wheat production in 2014. In early 2014, the FSA and Jabhat Al-Akrad expelled IS from Azaz, allowing Afrîn to better provide for itself.

As for oil, the refining of crude into diesel started in the summer of 2013, which helped stabilize Cizîrê economically. Diesel is used for automobiles, household generators, heating, small trades, and agricultural production. The councils organized the refining in amounts sufficient to alleviate hardships, and the price controls made it affordable. Today, a liter of diesel costs half as much as it did before the revolution, which has brought considerable relief to people's lives. The current refinery process, however, produces diesel of a lesser quality, which over the long run will damage generators, cars, and machinery, so the councils are looking for better refining methods.

In 2013 and 2014, all three cantons saw a building boom. The regime had forbidden the construction of houses of more than two stories within 15 miles (25 kilometers) of the Turkish border. But in the autumn of 2013, the two-story cap was lifted, and people were allowed to build up to four stories. New buildings were soon being constructed everywhere, as well as new levels added to existing one- and two-story buildings. In every city, you can see dozens or hundreds of construction sites, which are needed as more and more people have fled to Rojava from other parts of Syria and require living space.

The cement used in construction is partly fabricated in Rojava and partly imported. As we walked through Cizîrê's inner cities in May 2014, we saw that despite the scarcity, a great deal of economic activity was under way. A few businesses were closed, because they could not import enough goods or because fewer goods were available for sale. But the primary source of the economic vitality remained agriculture: every morning, in every city, hundreds of farmers arrived to sell their produce or buy necessary goods.

12.3 The Embargo

The Turkish government finds Democratic Autonomy in Rojava intolerable, inspired as it is by the writings of the PKK chief Abdullah Öcalan, and lying as it does just across the border. Soon after the 2012 liberation, Turkey closed all its border crossings to trade [see 12.3]. Certain urgently needed goods are smuggled into Rojava over the

Turkish border, but only in small quantities, and prices are usually very high. Smugglers work at risk to their lives—every week, there are reports of border traders and refugees shot by Turkish soldiers.

The KRG followed suit. South Kurdistan supports the embargo and works closely with Turkey to maintain it. While this fact may seem jarring at first, but even though President Barzanî often boasts of the KRG'S independence, it has actually long been a quasi-colony of Ankara. The KRG is financed by petrodollars, which it receives from Baghdad and then distributes among the leadership's minions. Apart from oil, the KRG produces almost nothing of economic value; it has no agriculture—even chickens are imported from Brazil. Most of the imports and investment capital arriving from abroad originate in Turkey.[7] As a result, the KRG leans heavily on Ankara politically and lets it call the tune on Rojava.

If Rojava's northern border is closed off by Turkey and its eastern border by the KRG, the south and west are impenetrable because of IS, Al-Nusra, and other armed non-state groups. Surrounding the three cantons, they exploit Rojava's isolation for profit. For a large bribe, they will allow fruit and vegetables, or other goods, to be trucked through its areas, but by the time these items reach Rojava, they are so expensive that few can afford them. So despite Rojava's price controls, an informal market exists where things can be purchased at exorbitant prices.

Nor do the Western powers support Rojava, which is after all a project to carve out a society outside capitalist modernity and Western interventionism. If Rojava succeeds, it will have political and social consequences throughout the Middle East and beyond. Since the strategy of the NATO states has been to thwart this effort, they too support the embargo.

The embargo's effects on the three cantons have been severe. Most dramatically, Rojava, with its wealth of wheat and oil, can't sell its products abroad. Farmers sit on their wheat and cotton. The DAAs have no money to pay their wages, let alone to meet the needs of ordinary people and refugees. Machines, medications, and general medical supplies and equipment are urgently needed.

The consequences of decoupling Rojava from the international market have not been entirely negative. It has forced the cantons to produce their own clothing and food and has allowed for the creation of cooperatives. Under pressure of the embargo, the need for everyone in Rojava to come together to organize daily life spurred on the MGRK council system. So it has been both a blessing and a curse. At the end of the day, however, given that machines and much else necessary for a functioning economy are lacking, the embargo must be ended as soon as possible.

12.4 The Social Economy

Democratic Confederalism aims to create a communalist economy. As Abdullah Öcalan observes, "In self-government, an alternative economic system is necessary, one that augments the resources of the society instead of exploiting them, and in that way satisfies the society's multitude of needs."[8]

Because of the Syrian state's treatment of Rojava, nothing like a modern capitalist economy developed here, and capitalism entrenched itself less in the people's mentality than elsewhere. Öcalan has observed of Kurdistan's economy: "While in the West the economy sometimes determines the holders of political power, in the Middle East political power is the deciding factor in the economy. The laws assumed to be intrinsic to economic life don't count in the local culture. On the one side are small households and family economies; on the other is the state-run economy. In between there are artisans and traders."[9]

Rojava's economic underdevelopment is simultaneously a great disadvantage and an opportunity. It allows the traditional social collectivism of the Kurdish people to be channeled positively to build a new, alternative economy. Indeed, integrating traditional structures is a typical approach of the Kurdish freedom movement, connecting tradition and emancipation.

That new economy is called the "social economy" and is distinguished from both the neoliberalism of capitalist modernity and from Real Socialism's state capitalism. According to Dr. Yousef, "The artificial creation of needs, the adventuristic search for new markets, and the bottomless greed for ever more gigantic profits widen the gap between rich and poor, and the army of those who live on the poverty level or die of hunger multiplies in size. Humanity can no longer bear such an economic policy. The greatest task is therefore the creation of an alternative economy, one that does not rest exclusively on the quest for profits but is oriented toward the just redistribution of wealth."[10]

Azize Aslan agrees: "Capitalism foregrounds exchange value, the production of things for the market. It rests entirely on the profit motive; production is not for the society but for the market. But a society that cannot determine its economic activities is helpless even to improve the lot of its own workforce. We are forced to work for pathetic wages, for miniscule compensation, but we do it anyway. We work in the informal sector without job security, without unionization, but we work regardless."[11]

"Historically, the economy developed separately from society," observes Dr. Dara Kurdaxi, a member of the economics commission in Afrîn. "That led to the establishment of exploitative states and finally economic liberalism. In contrast, state socialism, which diverged from its own economic ideas, made the economy part of the state and turned everything over to the state. But [state capitalism] is clearly not so different from multinational firms, trusts, and corporations ... We should have no capitalist system here—that system fails to respect the environment and perpetuates class contradictions and ultimately serves only capital ... We in Rojava must follow a different model."[12]

An economy was needed that would emancipate social consciousness from both capitalistic and feudal compulsions and so achieve a social revolution. The idea of extending democracy to economic life originated in discussions in TEV-DEM and other parts of the democratic self-government. It would be called the social economy.

The goal of a social economy, says Dr. Kurdaxi, is to achieve a democratized economy. "Economic development must have the society clearly as a goal ... Our system should be participatory, supporting natural resources and creating a strong infrastructure." The social economy was to be entrusted to the hands of the society, which would implement economic activities in the residential streets, villages, neighborhoods, district, and cantons.

In communalism, all resources, including factories, are self-governed through the communes. Every economic entity, as Murray Bookchin observes, is a "material constituent of its free institutional framework ... part of a larger whole that is controlled by the citizen body in assembly as citizens—not as 'workers,' 'farmers,' 'professionals,' or any other vocationally oriented special-interest groups."[13] "We are building a communal, social economy," Dozdar Hemo, Cizîrê's economics adviser, told us in 2014. "Everyone should have the opportunity to participate and, as a minimal first step, to achieve subsistence."[14]

12.5   Cooperatives

Once the idea of a social economy was settled upon, the council system became the mover of the process. About 80 percent of the land in Rojava had been nationalized under the Syrian regime. After the revolution, this formerly state-owned land was socialized: that is, it was transferred to the communes. "When the regime fled," Dozdar Hemo told us in Dêrîk, "we transferred the state-owned land—which actually belongs to the society—to the people." The communes in turn initiated the creation of the social economy by distributing it for agriculture cooperatives, especially "for the poor and for families of martyrs," as Hemo told us.[15]

In 2015, more than 2,500 hectares of formerly state-owned land were redistributed to the councils in Serêkaniyê alone, and more will follow.[16] "The bulk of the land," Hemo continues, "is going to the cooperatives— the exceptions are small areas, from one to four hectares, that individual families can also obtain. No new large landholdings are to emerge." The self-government, in deliberate contrast to the Ba'ath regime, spurns the use of force, so no large landholdings have been expropriated. About 20 percent of the land remains in the hands of large landholders.

"Through cooperatives and communes," Dr. Yousef observes, "we want to protect the rights of the simple people against the well-off. A down-to-earth economy should rest on redistribution and use, instead of orienting itself toward accumulation and the theft of surplus value and surplus product. Local economic institutions should damage neither the society nor nature."

The first cooperatives were rolled out in 2013. In Cizîrê, cooperatives planted 50,000 fruit trees in 2015 and attempts are being made to diversify agriculture by ecological criteria and to change the wheat monoculture. In Serêkaniyê, 25,000 *dunams* of land have been distributed to cooperatives so far. More land will be available when it is cleared of mines.

Self-sufficiency through agriculture is possible in Rojava in the summer; for winter agriculture, greenhouse cooperatives are being built. Near Rimelan, cooperative greenhouses now undertake farming even in the wintertime.[17]

Cooperatives are being organized in the cities as well. They have been formed for bread-baking, textile production, sewing and alterations, cheese-making and other dairy production, growing peanuts and lentils, and selling cleaning materials. By the end of 2015, a network of small cooperatives dotted Cizîrê.

Since Democratic Autonomy is an anti-centralist movement, its economy is based on local decentralized production. But Rojava has some large cooperatives, too, showing how a full-fledged cooperative system could work. For example, near Amûdê a cooperative of three villages produces groceries for more than two thousand participating households and is even able to sell a surplus on the market.

The diversity blossoms with every passing year, which is important because Rojava has set a goal of extending cooperatives to as many sectors of the economy as possible and of making them, in the near future, the dominant economic form.

Women's Cooperatives

On June 10, 2012, in Qamişlo, Yekîtiya Star's economics commission convened and decided to establish a women's economics commission in every city, to support the founding of women's cooperatives.

For women to run a business is something entirely new in Rojava—before the liberation, it was unthinkable, and only a few could work professionally as teachers, doctors, or lawyers. Most are still economically dependent on their husbands or families. "Women don't have land of their own," Silvan Afrîn, Yekîtiya Star's economic representative in Dêrik, explained to us, "and they have no opportunities to earn money. Our solution for both problems is women's cooperatives. We bring together, say, ten women and talk to them and find out what kinds of work they can do. We help them develop their projects until they are up and running. We have given land to landless women and helped them get started cultivating it."

During our May 2014 visit, accompanied by Silvan, we spent a day visiting cooperatives in Cizîrê. Below are sketches of a few of them.

Warşîn, a Sewing Cooperative in Qamişlo

One of Yekîtiya Star's largest projects is a sewing cooperative in Qamişlo. Twenty-three Kurdish and Arab women and two men, most of them refugees from Aleppo, Damascus, Raqqa, and Idlib, earn their livelihood at this cooperative, called Warşîn. "We came to Qamişlo," says Fatma Sihade, an Arab woman from Idlib, "because of the war in our city. I found work here, without discrimination, even though I'm Arab. It's a step toward a Syria in which Arabs and Kurds can live together in equality." Naima Bektaş, Warşîn's spokesperson, explains that the cooperative was founded to offer refugees a livelihood.

The factory got under way in October 2013, with two sewing machines and four workers. Now the 40 machines and 25 workers produce clothing for Cizîrê canton. They work eight hours a day and produce about two thousand garments every week. One of the machines is used to sew badges for Asayîş uniforms.

"We could produce clothing for all of Qamişlo," laments Naime Bektaş, but due to the embargo, "we can't obtain enough fabric." Aleppo, she continues, "was the center of the textile trade, but now IS controls the streets there. Our high-quality raw cotton used to be shipped to Aleppo. We don't have the machines to manufacture cotton fabric here. The fabrics you see here are flown in from Damascus. Because of the embargo, we can't sell the cotton, but we don't have the machines to work it either. So the growers produce less of it. Here in Rojava we produce only raw materials—there are no finishing or processing industries."

Figure 12.2   A sewing cooperative in Rimelan

"We urgently need generators, but they get seized at the South Kurdistan border. If we had more machines, we could provide other parts of Rojava with better-quality clothing at lower prices. There are many war profiteers—because of the embargo, they can set prices at their whim."

A Cheese Cooperative in Dêrîk

At a small dairy cooperative in Dêrîk, five women produce cheese and yogurt to sell in the markets. "We can provide for ourselves and our families," says Bermal, a co-worker at the cooperative. "Yekîtiya Star's economics commission supplies us with the milk. We give back part of our earnings. It's a very fair system." Gulbahar, another co-worker, adds, "We're also trying to preserve traditional methods of cheese production. The demand for our cheese is huge—we could sell a lot more."

A Lentil Cooperative Between Qamişlo and Tirbespî

Forty-two square miles (110 square kilometers) of formerly state-owned land that was socialized after the revolution are now in the hands of five cooperatives employing about 75 women in all. The cooperatives were established by Yekîtiya Star and are connected to the women's council. We visited one which produces lentils. It employs five women, who have invested in the coop, work the land, and now have disposable income.

A Women's Bakery in Serêkaniyê

In Serêkaniyê, a city devastated by war, a women's bakery has opened where six women produce about six hundred flatbreads a day. "After the liberation we set up this project with the help of the women's house (*mala jin*)," explains one young woman. "The bakery's previous owner was a gang member and fled to Turkey. We sell in the mornings from seven to ten. One flatbread costs ten pounds," or about five cents. The business belongs to the women, who founded it as a cooperative. "During the war we baked a lot of bread, to support the friends fighting at the front. Our situation is much better than it was under the regime, where opportunities for women to work were very limited. There are still barriers, and most Arab women don't work, due to their social situation. But our practices will influence them over time," the bakers predict confidently.

A Bakery in Derna Village

Between Qamişlo and Tirbespî lies the small village of Derna, where Yekîtiya Star has started another baking cooperative. It supplies six villages in the area with bread. The bakers begin in the morning and work a second shift in the afternoon. "Everything's made by hand—we don't use any machines," explains Gulinda, a village resident. One flatbread costs fifteen Syrian pounds (about eight cents). "That's very reasonable," says Silvan, who points out that this bakery is a humanitarian project supported by the women's movement.

The village of Derna comprises just over two hundred houses. "In 1963 we were dispossessed of all this land," Gulinda says. "We didn't have anything anymore. So now only women and children live here. Everyone else went away, much to our sorrow. Almost all the land was redistributed to build new Arab villages. Our village now has both an Arab name and a Kurdish name. The Arab villages were developed, but nothing was left for the Kurds." At the oven, which is fueled by diesel, eight women and four men stand working. "We have no machines, so we can supply only six villages," Silvan says. "With machines we could produce much more."

An Agriculture Cooperative near Amûdê

Outside Amûdê, we visit a farming cooperative. "We have cows, peanuts, and onions," explains Medya, of Yekîtiya Star in Amûdê. "The land belongs to a private owner. Yekîtiya Star brings the seeds, the owner provides diesel for the water pumps, and we supply our labor. We're trying to diversify the crops grown in Rojava so we can become more self-sufficient. At the moment we have some agrarian engineers here to analyze what can be grown in this soil. We're raising peanuts here now, for the first time. The same for lentils. Because of the embargo, fertilizer and pesticides are very expensive, but we got lucky—last winter was very cold, and so this year we don't need pesticides. Pesticides and fertilizers cost four times as much as they did before."

"The idea of cultivating peanuts here was Medya's," says Silvan, "and Yekîtiya Star supported it. Along with nuts, we want to produce vegetables like cauliflower for the market. They would do especially well in the wintertime. There's also an olive cooperative in Tirbespî with 480 trees. Thirty percent of the earnings go to Yekîtiya Star and 70 percent to the cooperative."

A Drugstore in Tirbespî

In Tirbespî, the local women's council has opened a small drugstore that's a cooperative, started by 15 women. Each of the women has invested 15,000 Syrian pounds (about $80). A few of their products are bought wholesale in Qamişlo. The women share the income. Next door they're going to open a clothing shop, then share those earnings. Two months earlier, there was a bomb attack in front of this row of shops, and one of the women from the cooperative was killed.

Women's Cooperatives in Amûdê

One of the women's movement's most ambitious projects is being built in Amûdê: a whole row of shops. There's already a dressmaking cooperative. The movement trained 21 women as dressmakers. They'll work at home, and the garments will be sold in one of the shops. A baklava shop is also in the works. "It's supported by Yekîtiya Star," says Nesmiya. "We're planning to open in a week." Besides that, "there's an oven, where we can bake bread. A cheesemaker is also planned. We've rented the building for a year."

These communes are only a drop in the bucket, as tens of thousands of women's jobs are needed, but they're a promising start. Kongreya Star may call to life more cooperatives, but they need financing. The existing cooperatives run on a shoestring. Everywhere machinery and other infrastructure is lacking. This would be a great area for international solidarity support.

12.6 Control of Production

What happens to the goods produced? "Of the proceeds from the cultivation of the land," Dozdar Hemo told us, "the democratic self-government takes 30 percent, and the cooperatives take 70 percent. In Girkê Legê, fifty families of martyrs who formed a cooperative signed a contract with the self-government: 30 percent to the self-government, and 70 to the cooperative."

If there is neither a market nor a state economy, another question arises: how is production to be controlled? After all, "in building the cooperatives it is also important to eliminate competitors and establish social equality." Models like the *kolkhoz* collective farms, or Mondragon, are rejected, just like the capitalist and statist planned ways of economic production. These models are criticized in Rojava as centralist. In Democratic Autonomy, communal control of the economy is the answer—control by the communes, upon which the MGRK council system rests.

Cooperatives must be connected to the council system; they are forbidden by law to become independent enterprises outside democratic control. "Our cooperatives are one hundred percent oriented toward the needs of society and are directly connected to the communes," a member of Cizîrê's economics ministry told us in November 2015. "The communes elect the cooperatives' leadership. The economic commissions at all levels support them and their work through education programs."

In Rojava's social economy, needs are determined not by state or capital but by the communes. Of course, one commune alone is not in a position to cover its own needs, so communes must network through their economics commissions [see 6.3], at the residential street, village, neighborhood, district, canton, and federation levels. The economics commissions at the communal level identify the communes' needs and pass them on to the relevant councils at the federation level. At other levels, the MGRK system makes it possible to determine the needs of different regions.

To satisfy the people's needs, industry is necessary. As of late 2015, debates are taking place over how to build ecological, democratic, and communal factories.[18] Ideas for the construction of ecological-democratic industry are being developed to cover all social needs. But due to the embargo, it seems a long way off, as the ongoing attacks on Rojava hinder its projects. Still, projects are under way in energy supply. Parts of Afrîn, for example, have been converted to solar energy.

12.7 Expanding the Cooperatives

Superficially the cooperatives may appear to be the temporary result of an emergency wartime administration, created to organize basic supplies. But as Hemo told us, "We're building cooperatives everywhere. People aren't waiting to see if someone else will fix their problem with electricity or water or anything else—they've gone ahead and organized it themselves. The councils can create cooperatives to resolve such issues."

Rather than administering scarcity, Rojava is systematically attempting to provide for the people's basic needs, for example, by building cooperative flour mills and bakeries. According to the Social Contract, staple foodstuffs and natural resources belong to the people, so their price is kept as low as possible. "We see even oil as a national resource for everyone," Hemo told us. "We don't want the price to go up." Diesel is sold at cost, and the revenue from oil sales goes to the self-government, which invests it in infrastructure. The oil wealth thus is used to advance agricultural cooperatives.

Other forms of trade and economy also exist in Rojava, but the social economy model is spreading fast. Now even the concept of self-defense includes the defense of the economy against outside interference.

The cooperative system is solving the problem of unemployment. "Through the communes and cooperatives and the needs-based economy," explains Dr. Yousuf, "each person can participate in production in his own way, and there will be no unemployment. Where communes are established, it will become clear that unemployment is a result of the capitalist system itself."[19] In Afrîn, according to Dr. Yousef, "before the revolution there were only a few jobs for the 450,000 residents. Now even though the population has doubled, in practical terms there is work for everyone."

Ultimately, every sector is to be organized cooperatively. "We're building cooperatives in road construction, in public service, in agriculture, in trade, in business—in all sectors," Hemo told us. "We especially support the self-government in guaranteeing the supply of water and electricity. At the moment, most of our projects are agricultural, but that's because we live in a primarily agricultural region. We also have building cooperatives, with the aim of giving everyone a chance, according to circumstances and their contribution, to have a house."

Discussions are also under way about the recognition and communalization of the work of reproduction—that is, the invisible, unpaid work that women do for the family, in the household. "We want that all 'invisible' work be socialized, beginning with housework," the economist Azize Aslan has said. "Why should women use washing machines at home? Why shouldn't there be a laundry for the village or the district? Why should there be no kindergarten or common kitchens? ... These are some of the ways the patriarchal, gendered separation of 'men's and women's work' can be discarded."[20]

Fundamentally, the Kurdish freedom movement advocates even further communalization. "Water, soil, and energy belong to the whole society and must be available for use by the whole society," says KCK co-chair Cemil Bayık. "As long as the society is the communal proprietor of these goods, no individual can exploit them. Moreover, such a society cannot become subject to economic domination. Therefore it must never give up control of water, land, and energy. Least of all should water, land, and energy belong to a state. A state that claims to control them is despotic and fascistic."

Moreover, these resources must be available to all free of charge, Bayık insists. "The Kurdish people should pay absolutely nothing for them. How can one sell water? Energy too is the property of the people of Kurdistan and can't be sold. Of course society must find ways to prevent waste, but water and energy are essential and are not to be sold. ... Even the oil belongs to all the people of Kurdistan."[21]

To ensure that society is able to make decisions about the use of water, soil, and energy, information about the society's needs are to be taken out of the hands of experts and socialized. Education is crucial for this purpose. "We school the people in how cooperatives can form a social economy," says Bayık. "We are establishing economics academies to advance this."

Democratic Autonomy's economic project is intended as a path toward an international alternative economy based on solidarity. "We've developed a model that the entire world will ultimately adopt, indeed must adopt," says Dr. Kurdaxi. "Sooner or later we will be successful, because our success will be the success of the society."

12.8   The Challenges Ahead

Even as the US-led coalition supports the YPG/YPJ in its fight against IS, the economic embargo against Rojava remains in place. Almost no humanitarian aid reaches Rojava. The troops of Rojava may be used to counter IS, it seems, but their social and political model is to be starved to death.

Still, the goal of constructing a non-exploitative economy and placing it under the communal, democratic control of society continues is to be actively supported. By working to achieve this goal, Rojava can become a model with international ramifications. Its experience in creating cooperatives, indispensable to a communal economy, is impressive.

Due to the circumstances, at least some of the economy will remain capitalistic for a while, but over the long term, it's important to ensure that the cooperatives do not become too large and do not behave like private enterprises and grow at one another's expense. That hasn't happened in Rojava, but in some international cases it has. In Rojava, such a negative development cannot be ruled out. It is important that they remain under the democratic control of the communes. A new draft of the Social Contract could set the terms for the cooperatives.

Enterprises at the district and cantonal levels currently organize petroleum production and distribution, the energy and water supply, traffic, waste disposal, most of the bread production, and public transport, among other things. These enterprises are under the control of the councils and the DAAs. They must be governed by law, securely embedded in the society, and perform entirely in service to the people.

Even though the councils administer these district- and cantonal-level enterprises, their workers must organize themselves in labor unions. As of May 2014, they had not yet done so, but they must be encouraged. Only a strong workforce with strong partnership rights can fulfill its social tasks while also improving working conditions. Even the economics commission of a cantonal council can make a wrong decision.

Similarly, transparency and democratic controls are important. The councils have already instituted some such mechanisms, but they should be implemented more directly. Let us not forget that in most states of the world, in the absence of transparency and democracy, public enterprises are guided by general interests far less than they should be. Economically strong enterprises can work against smaller, aspiring private firms in fulfilling so-called "market niches." The Social Contract forbids monopoly formation, but this provision must be enforced, and any tendency toward it spotted early.

Agricultural diversification must be pursued steadily, regardless of political developments. The embargo must be viewed as an opportunity for reorganizing agriculture outside the industrial-monoculture model. It's also necessary from an ecological standpoint.

New sources of energy are also needed. Lessons can be drawn from the enforced lower energy consumption that occurred in 2012, due to conflict. Instead of trying to restore pre-revolutionary levels of energy use through generators or power plants, the council system should permanently reduce energy use by adopting new policies in food production, transportation, and housing. Technically efficient measures can help to some extent, used in conjunction with means and natural elements. In 2014, this discussion remained insufficient, although a good start has been made.

If Turkey ever decides to lift the embargo—and with the growing success of the revolution, that could happen—a great challenge may arise. Rojava would be opened to the world market, and trade could take off, seemingly without limit. Goods produced in Rojava (petroleum, wheat, olives, olive oil, and more) could be sold abroad, bringing in much income. But at the same time, Rojava could be overwhelmed with an influx of commodities. Unsealing the border, then, would open possibilities but would also present dangers. How, should it happen, can Rojava protect the communal character of its economy? Which of Rojava's products should be exported, and by whom? How should the income be used? What products should be introduced from abroad, and in what amounts? How high should the taxes on imports be set? How can the cooperatives' production levels and structure be protected? Should foreign investment be permitted, and if so, which ones and in what forms?

Since 2012, Rojava has been developing, gradually, an exceptional economic form. Should the borders be opened to trade, the cooperatives and the public enterprises must be protected until the above questions have found answers. Nor should a border opening allow private enterprise to grow quickly in Rojava; rather, cooperatives and public enterprises should profit. Too often in history, revolutions have been lost not militarily but economically, as they became stripped of their meaning. That must not happen in Rojava. Fortunately, we have the advantage of being able to glean insights from the entire historical experience of revolutions.

Notes

1. Representatives of the MGRK and the local transitional government, interviews by author. See also Judit A. Szonyi, Eddy De Pauw, Roberto La Rovere, and Aden Aw-Hassan, "Poverty Mapping in Rural Syria for Enhanced Targeting," presentation to the conference of the International

Association of Agricultural Economists, Australia, August 12–18, 2006, http://bit.ly/1MEHqEJ.

2. "Syrien," Deutsche Gesellschaft für Internationale Zusammenarbeit GmbH (GIZ), 2014, http://bit.ly/1zTdrag.

3. Dr. Ahmad Yousef, interview by Sedad Yilmaz, "Wir wollen mit den Kooperativen und Kommunen die Rechte der einfachen Bevölkerung gegen die Wohlhabenden schützen," Kurdistan Report, no. 177 (January–February 2015), http://bit.ly/1QIsjuf. Unless otherwise noted, quotes from Dr. Yousef are taken from this source.

4. Ahmet Çimen, in ANF, July 17, 2014.

5. Remziye Mihemed, "Das Wirtschaftsmodell in Rojava, Gespräch mit Civaka Azad," Civaka Azad, February 16, 2014, http://bit.ly/1dXbkYq.

6. Yousef, "Wir wollen mit den Kooperativen," p. 16.

7. Soner Cagaptay, Christina Bache Fidan, and Ege Cansu Sacikara, "Turkey and the KRG: An Undeclared Economic Commonwealth," Washington Institute, March 16, 2015, http://bit.ly/28Uy2z6.

8. Abdullah Öcalan, Democratic Confederalism (2011), p. 21, http://bit.ly/1AUntIO.

9. Abdullah Öcalan, Jenseits von Staat, Macht, und Gewalt (Neuss, 2010), p. 268.

10. Dr. Ahmad Yousef, in ANF, November 9, 2014.

11. Azize Aslan, speech to the DTK's "Democratic Economy" conference, Amed, reported in "Hedef Komünal bir Ekonomi," Özgur Gündem, July 14, 2014, http://bit.ly/1DA8Ewu.

12. "Ekonomist Kurdaxi: Suriye karanlığa, Rojava aydınlığa gidiyor," ANF News, November 28, 2013, http://bit.ly/1PeVwOp. All quotes from Dr. Kurdaxi in this chapter come from this source.

13. Murray Bookchin, The Rise of Urbanization and the Decline of Citizenship (San Francisco, CA, 1987), p. 263.

14. Hemo means "subsistence" in the sense of self-sufficiency, without reliance on farm imports from other regions.

15. See also "Blick nach Kobanî—Reisebericht eines Aktivisten der Karakök Autonome," Libertäre Aktion Winterthur, http://bit.ly/1QA8eX6.

16. Personal research by the authors.

17. Members of the economics ministry of Cizîre canton to authors, November 2, 2015.

18. Ibid.

19. Yousef, "Wir wollen mit den Kooperativen," p. 16.

20. Aslan, speech to DTK conference.

21. Cemil Bayık, "Su, Toprak ve Enerji Komünlerini Kuralım," Yukesova Güncel, September 11, 2014, http://bit.ly/1Ta7bDV.

13

Ecological Challenges

Rojava's radical new society faces great ecological challenges: in oil and gas production and consumption, in agriculture and transportation, in waste disposal and wastewater treatment, and in housing construction. The Ba'ath regime's priority was to exploit the area's natural elements with the greatest efficiency, to maximize agricultural production over the long term, and to maintain basic public services with the lowest input. It scarcely contemplated the ecological consequences of these policies. The resulting negative impacts are a grave legacy, yet Rojava today is confronted with even further challenges as a result of war and embargo. The revolution's few positive effects have been surpassed overall by the accumulation of negative ones.

The Kurdish freedom movement began to analyze the deepening ecological crisis in the 1990s and associated it with hierarchical structures and capitalist modernity, especially with neoliberalism. In this respect, the movement stood out among most other leftist movements in Kurdistan and Turkey. The ecological dimension took its place in the political concept of Democratic Confederalism, developed in the 2000s. The paradigm announced in 2005 emphasized ecology as much as democracy and gender equality.

By focusing especially on species preservation and climate change, Democratic Confederalism brought ecological awareness into Kurdish society for the first time. While its early discourse on ecology was rather shallow, in the last few years it has grasped the reasons to transform life ecologically and now argues that principles of ecology must become essential to every aspect of a free society. All human beings are part of nature, and benefit from certain elements in nature, but they are not superior beings. The Kurdish freedom movement has criticized the high levels of global consumption of energy and materials, arguing that they should be much lower and equal for everyone.

In Rojava, general ecological awareness was no greater at the beginning of the revolution than in other societies in the Middle East. It remains rather limited, even as movement activists are striving to transform their society to be consistent with ecological consciousness.

13.1 The Destruction of Biodiversity

In antiquity, northern Syria was densely forested, but three thousand years of logging have stripped away the vast majority of trees. Especially since the mid-nineteenth century, the fast-growing local population has used wood on a large scale. In Afrîn, old-growth forests of holly oaks and pines still covered at least a third of the region when the Berlin-Baghdad Railway, operating from 1904 to 1921, took to felling huge swaths of trees to keep its steam locomotives running.[1] The forests were replaced with giant olive plantations, drastically narrowing the area's biodiversity. Kobanî, too, had oak forests, although less dense than Afrîn. They all disappeared for cultivation mainly of wheat but also barley, cotton, olives, and grapes.

Cizîrê had holly oak forests and even some wetlands until its lands were turned over entirely to wheat production.[2] Even eighty years ago outside Amûdê there was still a famous forest with wetlands, where gazelles roamed. Over time, these coveted animals had been all but decimated by hunting, and in the twentieth century, they became extinct. The last "natural trees" disappeared a half-century ago, and most plant and animal species disappeared from the canton. All land areas except those used for settlement, roadways, mining, and cattle ranching were given over to agriculture.

In the 1970s, to ensure that local farmers planted nothing but wheat, the Syrian state spread rumors that the tomatoes on the Turkish side of the border had developed a blight that could spread to Cizîrê and destroy all crops for years to come. So not only tomatoes but all fruits and vegetables were "voluntarily" avoided. Villagers were encouraged not to plant trees because that would mean forfeiting land area, and it would not be compensated. The very experience of living among trees was forgotten.

Present-day discussions start from the premise that Rojava's agriculture must be diversified for the sake of self-sufficiency. Crop diversification will enhance the soil and be better for plants and animals in general. Proposals are discussed for laying out a network of small forests, or even non-agricultural lands, in a connected habitat, or at least planting trees between farmlands, but unfortunately these proposals are still in the discussion phase. Neither political decision-makers nor villagers have much ecological consciousness; historical memory of trees is all but gone, and the ongoing war has brought many other concerns. If biodiversity is to be enhanced over the long term, political organizations will have to put tree and forest planting on the agenda, since farmers will not be quick to do it themselves. To its credit, in the spring of 2015, the new political system planted its first "national park" comprising diverse trees near Dêrîk city.

In the 1970s, the Syrian state began applying chemical fertilizers and pesticides to crops, which doubtless damaged both soil quality and groundwater. But the imposition of the embargo has forced most farmers to use fewer chemicals, applying them at only a quarter or a third of previous levels. The big landholders make much more use of chemicals since they can afford them. Some small farmers are reverting to traditional use of manure, but as of 2015, not many. Using organic wastes as fertilizer has helped protect the soil, the water, and nature, even if it has reduced production. Since Cizîrê grows more than enough wheat, a decline in harvests of up to 50 percent would not be a serious problem from a nutritional standpoint, although a way of compensating the affected farmers will have to be found.

Figure 13.1   Urban gardening at the economics ministry in Dêrîk

In late 2015, the tightening of the embargo caused the price of fertilizer to increase fourfold. As a result, many farmers chose to cultivate only part of their land or none at all. A serious drop in agricultural production was projected for 2016. Meanwhile plans are under way to overcome the lack of chemical fertilizer by establishing facilities in several districts to manufacture organic fertilizer locally, using wastes from cities and farms. This shift would not only make the economy more self-sufficient, it would improve the quality of agricultural products and soil and would enhance biodiversity.[3]

13.2 Water Crisis

In 2012–13, long-predicted water shortages became a reality. The Xabur River (Arabic, Al-Khabur), which originates in North Kurdistan, is fed by springs in Serêkaniyê, flows on to Hesekê, then empties into the Euphrates. However, the Xabur flows only for a few winter months; for the rest of the year, the bed is dry. The otherwise large Rumzian Creek, which flows from the Dêrîk area toward Hesekê, has water only five or six months of the year. Only the Çaxçax River, which originates in the Mardin mountains in North Kurdistan and flows near Nisêbîn and Qamişlo, has water nearly all year round.

In Cizîrê and Kobanî, the average water level in the rivers is declining, hampering the rivers' capacity to carry wastewater downstream. Moreover, the Çaxçax's water quality is horrendous, as the 100,000 inhabitants of Nisêbîn dump their untreated sewage into it. Anyone who bathes in it will unquestionably become sick. Yet quite a few farmers use water from the Çaxçax to irrigate their fields—we can easily imagine the health consequences.

The wastewater treatment facilities in Qamişlo and Serêkaniyê are currently out of service, so wastewater is now channeled directly from the sewage system into the Xabur and Çaxçax rivers without being treated. Nisêbîn was planning to build a new water treatment facility, but construction was halted due to financial difficulties, and more recently by the Turkish Army's destruction in the spring of 2016.

When we spoke to Qamişlo municipal officials in 2014, they seemed highly aware of the problem, but because of limited financial and technical means, the possibilities for cleaning up the river are few. Still, they are intent on at least cleaning up the trash that litters the banks of the riverbed within the city. People still throw garbage from the bridges and roadsides onto the riverbanks or directly into the riverbed, albeit less than in the past. Working with nearby inhabitants, shop owners, and schools, the Qamişlo municipality is preparing a campaign to remove the garbage. In other places that still have wastewater facilities, the personnel now responsible for water treatment lack the necessary technical knowledge, and maintenance is minimal.

In the summer, when water shortages occur in Qamişlo, water can fortunately be transferred via pipeline from Dêrîk, where a dam constructed many years ago still sustains a full reservoir. And drinking water is still available near the border with North Kurdistan, for example, in Serêkaniyê. Water extracted from Serêkaniyê is carried by a pipeline under YPG control.

Groundwater

For centuries, the people of Rojava have been extracting drinking water from underground reservoirs. The quality is good, even without much filtering. Afrîn and Dêrîk districts have the largest groundwater reserves.

But groundwater levels are falling. A few decades ago, it was sufficient to drill 10-20 meters below ground to extract water. According to our interview partners, it's now 100-200 meters—and the water pumps and the pipes are aging, which causes water loss and decreases water quality. Under the embargo, Rojava has no access to spare parts.

The most urgent groundwater crisis is in the Hesekê region and other southern areas. Historically, Hesekê (population around 300,000) extracted drinking water from underground, but in recent decades, due to industrial agriculture, the quality of its groundwater has declined drastically, because all the rivers and streams in Cizîrê converge in Hesekê, carrying the whole region's residues of chemical fertilizers, pesticides, and herbicides. Water tanks are now positioned on top of every building in Hesekê, to collect rainwater. Drinking water must be brought in from wells in the Serêkaniyê area and is distributed in Hesekê once every three days for six hours.

The Role of Turkey

Turkey controls the Euphrates River, which flows into the three cantons, by means of a comprehensive system of dams. Through the ongoing

Southeastern Anatolia Project (Güneydoğu Anadolu Projesı, GAP), it has built 24 dams and 17 hydroelectric plants to date on the Euphrates. One purpose of the dams is to create reservoirs for irrigation.[4] If you stand on a hill at Rojava's border with Turkey, you will see at a glance that the fields are much greener on the North Kurdistan side than on Rojava's. The reason is that for years the flow of the Euphrates has been declining, due to these dams. Turkey also diverts water for irrigation directly from rivers. This industrialized irrigation has reduced the quantity and quality of water that streams into Rojava.

Rojava also shares groundwater reservoirs with Turkey, but for the past 15 years, affordable and efficient motors have made it far easier for Turkey to extract groundwater. The Turkish state places no controls on wells that draw out the water for irrigation. As a result, the water table has been dramatically lowered, with potentially catastrophic consequences for Rojava. Even if some of the water used for irrigation seeps back into the earth, the water loss is significant.

In addition to Turkish water politics, climate change is also contributing to water scarcity. Since the end of 1990s, the catchment area of the Euphrates and Tigris (that is, North Kurdistan, Rojava, central-eastern Syria, Iraq, and western Iran) has seen 8–10 percent less precipitation, which further affects the riverbeds.[5]

Compared to North Kurdistan, Rojava uses less water per acre (the Syrian state manages water better than Turkey does), but the amounts of water extracted are still considerable and unsustainable in the long term. Here too, water policies have reduced the groundwater. For decades, Cizîrê obtained water for irrigation from some 3,000 wells. After the revolution, controls on wells were lifted, and nowadays the number of wells is not known; TEV-DEM activists who spoke to us were aware that the groundwater levels are declining, but they had no detailed implementation plans for managing groundwater use fairly.

In May 2016, the agriculture ministry of Kobanî canton decided to limit the number of wells to protect the supply.[6] This wise decision should be repeated, particularly in Cizîrê, and the limits should be strictly enforced and monitored.[7]

Even if Turkey and Rojava were to implement excellent water policies and even if the amount of rainfall were to suddenly soar, it would take decades to replenish the groundwater to approximate former levels. But Turkey will not easily adopt a social-ecological water policy—that would require an enormous political transformation. Rojava can contribute little by itself, because most of its groundwater comes from North Kurdistan. Still, the democratic self-government in Rojava can take some measures to ameliorate the problem, like regulating the number and capacity of wells.

In addition to introducing such controls, laws, and regulations, Rojava should work to raise awareness. Educating people that they must use less water and use it more efficiently will have much more impact than threatening to punish those who commit infractions. Discussions and seminars with farmers and other actors would be useful for long-term success.

Rojava also has to consider whether to remove some of its arable land from irrigation, particularly for raising wheat. A reduced water supply must not hinder the process of diversifying crops, but the new crops introduced should be those that require little or no irrigation. More efficient irrigation technologies and methods must also be discussed, even if the embargo makes them difficult to implement in the near term.

13.3 Waste Disposal

Other serious ecological problems are sanitation and waste disposal, which are also health issues. After the liberation, Rojava's waste disposal system, which had been maintained by the municipal administrations, ground to a halt in several cities. In Kobanî, Afrîn, Dêrîk, and Tirbespî, garbage collection continued without a significant break because after the MGRK took over the administrations, the municipal personnel stayed in place, but in Qamişlo problems persisted for several months. The Syrian state's administrators retreated to the state-controlled neighborhoods, with the result that in the fall and winter of 2012–13, the garbage in most Qamişlo neighborhoods lay uncollected. After a few weeks, however, the Revolutionary Youth organized a campaign to collect the garbage. Yekîtiya Star participated in the campaign, all of which helped raise awareness and accelerated the process of establishing a new municipal administration in Qamişlo and elsewhere.

By 2014, everyplace in Rojava had functioning services for trash collection and disposal. Pickup trucks, light trucks, and backhoes were repurposed as garbage trucks. As of May 2014, the Qamişlo municipal administration had seven vehicles available, but they didn't work as effectively as might be wished and needed repairs. The war and the embargo make it difficult to obtain garbage trucks and equipment. In other words, not much has changed in the system of waste collection and disposal.

The collected trash is brought to pits and deposited there and mostly incinerated. Almost all the pits now in use were dug before 2012. These unregulated dumpsites pose a serious health and ecological problem. The wastes may be contaminating the groundwater, and dumps situated near housing endanger the health of people and animals through airborne trash and noxious odors. In Qamişlo, we saw drinking water wells located less than a kilometer from a dumpsite. Cizîrê's largest dumpsite, which also accepts waste from some of the surrounding villages, is a great danger to the Qamişlo water supply. Doctors from the district health commission told us that children in the city are affected by waterborne illnesses at a greater than average rate. Qamişlo's garbage pits were dug in 1999, even though the potential danger was known. The drinking-water wells had been in use for over thirty years.

The municipal administration is discussing several solutions. The simplest would be to dig a new pit south of the city, away from the drinking-water wells. They have identified a suitable place, but two other villages would be directly affected.

An expensive but reasonable solution would be to finish the partially constructed waste incineration plant right next to the existing garbage dump. The war in Syria has stalled the project, but 75 percent could now be completed, sanitation experts told us. Even if the right construction firm or team could be found, of course, the embargo would prevent the necessary equipment from entering the cantons. But it's not clear which equipment and machines are needed. And the professionals needed to manage the plant are likely not available in Rojava.

There is, however, one positive aspect to the waste question: since the liberation, the embargo has diminished the flow of commodities into Rojava, from Turkey and South Kurdistan, so that the waste stream is considerably reduced. Moreover because of the scarcity economy, people reuse and repurpose goods, packaging, machines, cables, wood, and equipment—anything that can be recycled is. But some items are still coming into Rojava and are not recycled, especially plastic bags. In many city peripheries, thousands of plastic bags are scattered on the open ground, tossed around the wind. This was the case when we entered Hesekê by car.

13.4 Air Pollution

In Cizîrê, much diesel is refined and consumed, so the air quality in the cities is often filthy. Cars and buses now run on diesel, and because it is available, the number of automobiles and other vehicles has scarcely declined since the revolution. Moreover, the technology of refining crude oil has not returned to the same skilled level as before the revolution, which contributes to an increase in air pollution. Still more problematic are the many diesel generators that are used in shops and homes, providing five hours of power daily. These can often be heard and seen in the streets, contributing massively to air and noise pollution, and leading to serious health problems. The longer this situation persists, the graver the consequences will be.

13.5 Petroleum Production

The oil wells of Cizîrê lie between Tirbespî and Dêrîk, near the city of Rimelan. As elsewhere, the petroleum economy in Rojava has considerable ecological effects. The exploitation, transport, refining, and distribution of crude oil causes the contamination of soil and agricultural lands. Until 2011, the petroleum drilled in Cizîrê was refined outside Rojava, in Homs. The revolution gave Cizîrê the opportunity for oil refining, but it did so with simple means, scarcely meeting environmental standards, so the soil was again contaminated. At least as bad, the contaminated wastewater is disposed of in the Rumzian Creek. The volume is not great, but it is enough to pollute the whole creek. The creek now flows from Rimelan to Hesekê almost completely devoid of fish or any other species. For several dozen miles, the water cannot be used for irrigating fields. Children are endangered when they play in its waters.

The environmental minister of Cizîrê, Lokman Ahde, is trying to inform the public of the danger, and it is repeatedly emphasized that more would be done if the technical means and capacities were available.

Overall, the people of Cizîrê face a dilemma. They can continue to refine petroleum and thereby provide power and mobility for themselves and for defense, while risking the environment and people's health. Or they can renounce power, vehicles, severe ecological destruction, and defense. In the foreseeable future, this contradiction is not going to disappear, but the negative effects can be minimized in the short term, and the public can be informed about the risks. Suitable measures could be undertaken even with only small means and little money.

13.6 Outlook

Despite all of Rojava's challenges, the people have access to the basics of life. No one goes hungry, and everyone has access to water (if not always of good quality). Bread and oil are cheap. They enjoy fundamental rights. Solidarity prevails, from which everybody benefits. The people channel immense creativity into overcoming challenges, including agricultural diversity.

But the three cantons' limited technical and personnel capacities undoubtedly have seriously negative ecological impacts. Privately, people use diesel generators for electricity production, which has grave ecological and health effects, yet it will be impossible to ban them until sufficient clean electricity is available from another source. Today, families and communes organize educational efforts to limit their use. The war itself is a source of ecological destruction: even a defensive war causes harm to nature.

Some of these challenges have no short-term solutions. Meeting ecological challenges over the long term, including crucial changes in production and consumption, will require an educational efforts in schools, cooperatives, communes, and people's councils. Steps toward more comprehensive measures have been taken, resulting in many small projects and seminars around Rojava. In 2015, to spread ecological awareness, the first Ecology Academy was founded in Cizîrê.

But the challenging circumstances can be considered an opportunity to change production, consumption, transportation, and other aspects of society in an ecological way. The project to manufacture organic fertilizer should not be seen just as a method of coping with the embargo period—it must be planned and organized for the long term. The small "guerrilla gardens" in the courtyards of houses, and around school buildings, are crucial for developing food sovereignty. The public control over agricultural land must be considered an opportunity to increase biodiversity. The decreasing use of plastic in daily life and of waste in general is positive; after war and embargo, this level should be maintained. If the people become accustomed to having less and to healthy consumption, that aim could be achieved.

Rojava will never again enjoy access to the water in the amounts that were normal twenty or thirty years ago. It must learn from the water crises. Even if the Turkish state were somehow to dismantle all the dams and eliminate all the large-scale irrigation, people in the three cantons must use less water in general. Millions of people live downstream. Instituting agricultural methods that use less water would enhance Rojava's self-sufficiency and strengthen its own local economy. The revolution is at a point where it can make crucial decisions to create an ecological society, within the ideological framework of Democratic Confederalism.

Notes

1. Eugen Wirth, *Syrien, eine geographische Landeskunde* (Darmstadt, 1971).
2. Kadri Yıldırım, *Kürt Tarihi ve Coğrafyası 1 – Rojava* (Diyarbakir, 2015), pp. 213, 290, 314.
3. Rojava Plan, "Feed the Revolution," http://bit.ly/295ga9K.
4. These installations have submerged numerous villages and towns, including the ancient city of Zeugma. With the Ilisu Dam project, under construction near the ancient Kurdish city of Hasankeyf, Turkey intends to also control the waters of the Tigris. Hasankeyf, a site occupied since the Neolithic, is considered part of the world's cultural heritage. It will be flooded if the Ilisu Dam is completed. See Necattin Pirinccioglu, *Agenda 21*, May 22, 2006; and Daniela Setton and Heike Drillisch, *Zum Scheitern verurteilt: Der Ilisustaudamm im Südosten der Türkei* (Berlin, 2006).
5. Cyprus Institute, "Climate Change and Impacts in the Eastern Mediterranean and the Middle East," n.d., http://bit.ly/297DiTn; K. Tielbörger et al.; "Middle-Eastern Plant Communities Tolerate 9 Years of Drought in a Multi-site Climate Manipulation Experiment," *Nature Communications*, October 6, 2014, http://go.nature.com/1x6UbPP.
6. "Water Wells Are Not Drilled Without Permission," *ANHA*, May 23, 2016, http://bit.ly/290QHtn.
7. F. Hole and B. F. Zaitchik, "Policies, Plans, Practice, and Prospects: Irrigation in Northeastern Syria," *Land, Degradation and Development* 18, no. 2 (March–April 2007): 133–52.

14

Neighbors

During the uprising that began in March 2011, the Syrian insurgency had a strong Sunni dimension, comprising the country's majority-Sunni Arab population with its various factions.[1] The Free Syrian Army (FSA), formed on July 29, 2011, to overthrow Assad, grew rapidly as an alliance of diverse forces. As the uprising escalated into civil war, and as the regime perpetrated horrendous massacres, Syrians flocked to the FSA. In September 2011, the Movement of Free Officers joined the FSA, making it the largest armed opposition movement, with fighters from the military and the Sunni Arab population, but also from Turkey, Arabia, the Maghreb, and elsewhere, as well as some Christian and Kurdish groups. The FSA headquarters and most local groups were soon influenced by Western, Turkish, and Gulf States' intelligence services, and the FSA tried to gain dominance over the locally initiated defense committees in various Syrian cities. "States that had long planned to destabilize Syria, first and foremost the United States and Saudi Arabia," saw their opportunity.[2]

14.1 The Islamization of the Syrian Opposition

As the uprising against the Ba'ath regime took on a war footing, the opposition forces gradually came under the influence of the Muslim Brotherhood and its network of front organizations. The Syrian National Council (SNC) was founded on August 23, 2011, as an alternative government to the Ba'ath regime. Meeting in Istanbul, it was a product chiefly of Turkey, with support from NATO (including Turkey), Saudi Arabia, and Qatar.[3] Qatar was a promoter of the Muslim Brotherhood, and the SNC was dominated by the Brotherhood. As Petra Becker of the Foundation for Science and Politics observed, "78 of the 320 members of the SNC were members of the Muslim Brotherhood." In June 2012,

Bassam Ishak, a Syriac member of the SNC, led an effort to reform it to bring in "the whole range of identities in Syria and the whole spectrum of revolutionary forces." But the reform failed: "What we got was a tiny representation of minorities and a strong representation of the Islamic elements that had already begun to dominate the situation in Syria." Thereafter, the SNC as well as the groups that used the name FSA were mostly Islamist.[4]

In November 2012, the SNC participated in the creation of the National Coalition of Syrian Revolutions and Opposition Forces (NC), which was formed in order to strengthen the influence of the United States, NATO, and the Gulf States in Syria. Qatar hosted the meeting, which led to the further Islamization of the Syrian opposition forces. Saudi Arabia, Qatar, and Turkey obstructed every attempt to prevent that Islamization.[5] Despite the slaughter at Hama in 1982, "the Syrian Muslim Brotherhood stood firmly in the tradition of militant Islam."[6]

The West tolerated or ignored Islamization, as the Sunni alliance seemed the most promising lever against the Assad regime. It bears heavy responsibility for strengthening the jihadists in Syria. While direct support is hard to verify, the forces opposing Assad's regime interests and also Rojava's self-government were created by interest groups associated with the so-called "friends of Syria": Turkey and the Gulf States, especially Saudi Arabia and Qatar, the most vehement opponents of Iran.[7]

In Antakya, Turkey, in December 2012, the Supreme Military Council (SMC) was founded as a new command structure for the mainly non-democratic opposition forces. Here too in the council, jihadist forces gained dominance, as Salafist- and jihadist-oriented groups like the Syrian Islamic Liberation Front (SILF) joined.[8]

Jabhat Al-Nusra/Jabhat Fateh Al-Sham

Jabhat Al-Nusra li-Ahli ash-Sham (Support Front for the People of Syria) was formed by Abu Mohammed al-Jaulani, a Syrian loyal to the Al-Qaeda leader Ayman al-Zawahiri in late 2011. Together with thirteen Salafist groups, Al-Nusra strove to establish a radical Islamic emirate in the region. Al-Nusra openly acknowledged its affiliation with Al-Qaeda. By contrast with IS, most Al-Nusra fighters are Syrians.

The SMC developed a close cooperation with Al-Nusra.[9] In 2012, an international public outcry forced the United States to put Al-Nusra on the State Department's list of foreign terrorist organizations, which it had hesitated to do. Broad parts of the Syrian opposition also protested, including the then-president of the NC, Ahmad Moaz Al-Khatib Al-Hasani, who protested strenuously.[10]

By early 2013 Al-Nusra was the most powerful armed group in Syria. The FSA was in active collaboration with jihadists, and Al-Nusra developed ties with it. Abdul Jabbar Akidi—military head of the FSA from Aleppo and militarily responsible for the FSA in northern Syria and head of the Lîwa al-Tawhid (which is aligned with the Muslim Brotherhood and supported by Qatar)—was asked about Al-Nusra on March 29, 2013. "They are our partners," he said. "We see them differently from the way you in the West do. For us they are not terrorists! They want to drive out Assad."[11]

Some of the nationalistic Kurdish parties were also close to the FSA and strongly oriented toward Turkish politics, like the Peşveru ("Future") movement. Peşveru is strongly tied to the SNC and the FSA and rejects the Kurdish freedom movement. Its media in Europe is known for relativizing the crimes of the jihadists and for propagandizing against Rojava's self-government. *Kurdwatch*, a website based in Germany, shares personnel with the Peşveru movement and has close ties to the NC; it uses seemingly objective presentations to try to advance this party's positions to the European public.

On July 28, 2016, Al-Nusra split from Al-Qaeda and renamed itself Jabhat Fateh Al-Sham (Front for the Conquest of Syria). Turkey and Qatar had been promoting such a split since 2015, so that Al-Nusra could gain international legitimacy. The United States has said that the change of name and status will not alter its assessment of the group.

The Attack on Serêkaniyê

Rojava, for its part, was trying to avoid combat operations. The YPG was established as a shared multi-party defense force, but it tolerated no forces like the FSA that could draw the region into the civil war.[12] Al-Nusra and the FSA shared a common antagonism towards Rojava. The FSA commander Akidi stated the anti-Rojava policy: "The Kurds have created a state. We won't allow Syria to be dismembered," a typical anti-Kurdish argument also used in Turkey.[13] Supported by Turkey and NATO, Islamist forces became more aggressive against Rojava.

In November 2012, about 3,000 heavily armed jihadists—Al-Nusra and parts of the FSA, like the Syrian Islamic Liberation Front (SILF)—slipped over the Turkish-Syrian border at Ceylanpınar and attacked Serêkaniyê. The goal was to push on to Qamişlo and bring down the self-government in Cizîrê.[14] After four days of fighting, they occupied Serêkaniyê. The FSA touted the invasion as "the FSA's liberation of Ras Al-Ayn." But the "liberation" took the form of massacres, devastation, and the radical application of Sharia law. For seven months, they would occupy Serêkaniyê, during which Peşveru's Masaal Temmo Brigade collaborated with the SILF and Al-Nusra.[15]

In June 2013, as we have seen, the YPG/YPJ liberated Serêkaniyê [see 8.4] and expelled Al-Nusra and the FSA. When we visited the city in October 2013, dozens of witnesses—Sunni Arabs, Christians, Yezidis, and Kurds—described the jihadists' reign of terror to us. On many walls we saw "We have come to slaughter" written in blood. And in a courthouse that had been occupied by the jihadists, we found documents signed by Al-Nusra indicating that their forces had streamed by the thousands over the Turkish border.

On July 23, 2013, the US Congress approved weapons deliveries to the FSA.[16] On July 26, seventy FSA commanders met with SMC leadership in Antep (Dîlok), in Turkey, and issued a communiqué against Rojava. Abdul Jabbar Akidi stated, "As much war materiel as we have, everyone should have. Every time we listen to the PKK, they stab us in the back … From now on we will have no pity. We will have no mercy. As much as is humanly possible, we will yank them out by the roots."[17] The ANHA news agency reported hearing some say that the time had come to drive the Kurds from Syria and exterminate them. A video message from another member of the FSA military council, Abdulcabbar El-İkeli, also threatened the Kurdish people with annihilation.[18]

Over the course of July 31 and August 1, 2013, members of the FSA and Al-Nusra, together with the Kurdish Azadî Brigade (which adheres to the Azadî Party in the Kurdish National Council or ENKS), committed a massacre in Til Hasil and Til Aran, two towns near Aleppo that were not under the control of the Rojava self-government. The justification was that the villagers were associated with the leftist Kurdish PYD.[19] Survivors told one of the authors that members of Al-Nusra and the FSA, before attacking a neighborhood in Til Hasil, called the Kurds there "unbelievers" and alleged that they wanted to collaborate with the Assad regime. Another survivor told us, "Al-Nusra and FSA went into the neighborhood in Til Hasil and declaimed over mosque loudspeakers that Kurdish women, Kurdish houses, and Kurdish property were *halal*," or available for forcible appropriation. "Then they surrounded Til Hasil and Til Aran. No one could leave." Snipers opened fire on fleeing civilians. "They captured women, tortured and raped them. They looted. They even killed children. They didn't ask whether someone was an Apoist [supporter of Öcalan], it was enough to be a Kurd ... The first to be attacked were those who worked with the *mala gel*."[20] Some seventy people were killed, although the exact number could not be determined. Hundreds were captured.

According to reports of survivors, militias of the ENKS, the KDP's offshoot party in Syria, participated in the massacres of Til Hasil and Til Aran.[21]

Almost daily while we were in Cizîrê, we heard reports of murderous attacks by a fast-growing jihadist group, called at that time ISIS, usually against civilians. On May 29, 2014, it overran three villages in the Serêkaniyê region that were allegedly Ezidi but were actually inhabited by Arab refugees. ISIS slaughtered fifteen people, including seven children.[22] Images of this grisly massacre in the Kurdish media kept us awake at night. Gulistan Osman, of Yekîtiya Star, told us about "a youth from Dêrîk whose throat was cut by the jihadists. His mother hasn't slept since that night. Now whenever she sees or hears about a knife, she almost goes out of her mind."

Although dozens of eyewitnesses to the massacre could very clearly report what happened, the South Kurdistan parties and their Syrian counterparts called the killings isolated combat deaths.[23] On September 9, 2013, when the German government was asked about the jihadist massacres in Syria in general and in Til Hasil and Til Aran in particular, its response was: "No substantial information is available on the question."[24] It said it was "deeply concerned about the situation" there and was seeking information from sources close to the KDP. From 2011 to June 2014, the attacks on Rojava by the FSA and its allied forces, including Al-Nusra, and by ISIS were greeted by international silence. It was an indication that the world considered the attacks something to be tolerated.

14.2   Islamic State (IS)

In August 2013, ISIS (the Islamic State in Iraq and the Levant) began its triumphal march through Syria, overrunning the city of Raqqa. In June 2014, it captured Iraq's second largest city, Mosul, the commercial center of Iraq and the most important stop on the road to Syria. On June 28, the first day of Ramadan, it renamed itself Islamic State (IS) and proclaimed itself the worldwide caliphate, evoking the Islamic expansion in the seventh and eight centuries. IS seeks to take over "greater Syria" (Bilad as-Şam), by which it means present-day Syria, Lebanon, Jordan, and Palestine, as the nucleus of a restored Islamic world empire. By using the term "caliphate," it appeals to the desires of many Muslims for cultural authenticity, religious purity, and political unity, after a century of Western domination and plunder of the Middle East.[25]

IS had its roots in the US-led invasion of Iraq. In August 2003, the Jordanian Abu Musab Al-Zarqawi founded a group—Jama'at al-Tawhid wal-Jihad (Monotheism and Jihad)—that targeted the coalition forces as well as Iraqi Shiites. Several former officers of Saddam Hussein who had been radicalized during the war joined the jihadists. In October 2006, Al-Qaeda in Iraq teamed up with several Sunni tribes and other insurgents and founded the Mutayibeen Coalition, who then proclaimed themselves the Islamic State of Iraq (ISI; in Arabic, Al-dawla al-Islamija fi-l-Iraq).[26] In 2010, Abu Bakr Al-Baghdadi, an Iraqi, took over the leadership.

In September 2014, videos circulated over the Internet, showing IS people in moving cars shooting pedestrians and drivers with semi-automatic weapons, while *nasheed* (battle songs, in this case for jihad) played in the background. A few days later, images of hundreds of bullet-riddled Iraqi soldiers were shown on the IS Internet page.[27] IS demands that recruits submit to a strict set of rules, but it sends the alluring message that everyone who joins will personally have a stake in the creation of a new world. "After Til Koçer was liberated," YPJ commander Rûken Jîrik observed, "we inspected the corpses of the Islamists, and we could see that they came from Afghanistan, Libya, Pakistan, Turkey, and Europe. Most came from North Africa, from Turkey, but also from Chechnya, from Europe. One was even Chinese." According to the YPG, of the 587 jihadists who were captured in 2013, only 91 were of Syrian origin.[28]

IS was said to have 25,000–100,000 armed fighters in the Middle East, of whom almost half came from other parts of the world. YPJ fighters at Serêkaniyê told us that most of the IS fighters there were mercenaries, and some were children.[29] "ISIS fighters go to death without fear," YPJ fighter Axîn Amed told us. "They fight without knowing anything about the country where they are fighting." Indeed their very lack of connection to the indigenous people makes them pitiless and unrestrained. The commander at Til Xenzir, the westernmost YPG outpost in Cizîrê in May 2014, told us that some of the jihadists they captured thought they had been fighting Israel. Some YPJ fighters expressed pity for such naïveté, "but what are we to do with a sixteen-year-old who has cut the throats of five of our young people?" wondered Axîn Amed.

Jihadists proceed with special brutality against competing Salafist and jihadist groups, even fighters within their own ranks can be brutally murdered: "Those who want to leave the groups are mercilessly slaughtered by high-ranking members of the *dawlah* [state]," reported one deserter who managed to escape.[30]

The Battle for Kobanî

On September 15, 2014, IS attacked the self-governing canton of Kobanî, with the goal of taking over all of northern Syria. They used modern weapons systems, including heavy weapons looted from US stores in Mosul and some fifty tanks. IS quickly overran more than three hundred villages and part of the city, committing mass murder. As hundreds of thousands fled, IS confidently announced that it would take Kobanî within two weeks.

For more than two years, Kobanî had been fending off attacks by jihadists, but the world finally noticed this battle. The international press stationed itself on a hill on the Turkish side of the border, so-called "Press Hill," the better to follow the IS attack. Only a hundred or so meters away, a few thousand fighters of the YPG/YPJ, as well as civilians, were waging a determined resistance against an opponent that no army had previously been able to stop. They had hardly any heavy weapons. Turkey deployed tanks to the border, seemingly ready to help IS at a moment's notice.

The Kurdish side asked for only one thing: that a corridor be opened so that aid could reach Kobanî, which was otherwise completely cut off. Since IS surrounded it on three sides, the corridor would have to run through Turkey. But the Turkish government refused to create a safe passage or to allow necessary aid deliveries, foodstuffs, medications, and construction materials, into the city. Those who arrived to try to help were repeatedly obstructed by the Turkish military and police with gas grenades and live weapons. The aid organization Medico International had to spend months fighting with the authorities to allow in a few ambulances. PYD co-chair Salih Muslim explains succinctly: "The Turks suffer from Kurdophobia, that's all there is to it."[31]

To many, IS seemed unstoppable, and IS tried to instill panic and resignation in the people of Kobanî. The Erdoğan government predicted that Kobanî would fall, as did the US Secretary of State John Kerry. Yet the YPG/YPJ kept fighting. At one point, a platoon of nine YPG/YPJ fighters took a stand against IS in Zerzûri, a village a few miles from Kobanî. They held off a huge IS force for more than 32 hours. When IS started to take the school, they blew themselves up, so as not to fall into IS hands. Their dedication inspired the resistance at Kobanî. Other fighters followed suit, like Arîn Mirkan, who stopped an IS tank with her own body and explosives on the Miştenur hill.

Even as the world's respect for the defenders of Kobanî grew, IS received protection and aid from Turkey.[32] IS fighters were able to pass over the border with little difficulty. Erdoğan proposed the creation of a "buffer zone," to extend from Afrîn and Aleppo, over Raqqa, and to Hesekê—that is, through all of Rojava. It would eliminate the self-government and put Rojava under Turkish control. He lumped together the PYD, the YPG, Rojava, and the PKK and equated them all with IS as "terrorist." The United States rejected the proposal.

Given Kobanî's desperate situation, millions of sympathizers demonstrated in Turkish and Kurdish cities to break the governments' silence. On October 6–8, the Turkish state attacked the demonstrators brutally, killing more than forty. The European media reported that they had been protesting Turkey's inaction in Syria, but the opposite was actually true: they were demanding that Turkey cease its active support for IS.[33]

Finally, public pressure to aid the defenders of Kobanî grew so intense that the United States could no longer ignore it. The recently formed international coalition, joined symbolically by Qatar and Saudi Arabia, started to bomb IS in Kobanî and to airdrop weapons to the YPG/YPJ. Erdoğan, pressed to provide help, twice allowed about 140 KDP

Peshmerga to travel through Turkey with a few heavy weapons for the defense of Kobanî. Arriving in October and December 2014, they joined the YPG, the YPJ, and Burkan Al-Firat in defending Kobanî.

On January 27, after four months of heavy fighting, Kobanî liberated itself. After only a few more days, most of the 365 villages were freed. Kurds everywhere rejoiced, but the inhabitants of Kobanî paid a high price. At least five hundred YPG/YPJ fighters had been killed, and almost every family had a member who was martyred. Some 80 percent of the buildings in the city were destroyed.

The resistance of Kobanî transformed the war against IS by shattering its myth of invincibility. "The West must ask itself why it has so long sat on its hands while its allies delivered weapons to Syria that ended up in the hands of extremists," noted editor Rainer Hermann of the *Frankfurter Allgemeine Zeitung*. "It must finally recognize what is at stake in Syria and change its policy."[34]

Figure 14.1   Celebration of YPG/YPJ fighters in Kobanî in October 2015

As the rebuilding process slowly got under way, IS perpetrated a huge massacre. On June 26, 2015, two groups of IS attacked Kobanî from the south while a third group entered the city directly through the Turkish border post of Murşitpinar. Their goal was to gain control of the city, supported by thousands of IS fighters from across the Euphrates River to the west. The IS terrorists had shaved and donned YPG and Burkan Al-Firat uniforms; they entered houses in Kobanî and, one after another, killed more than 288 civilians, many of them children. The massacre was aimed at terrifying the people of Kobanî and intimidating their supporters so that they would leave.

The massacre would not have been possible without Turkish support, as IS used the official border crossing.[35] One eyewitness exclaimed, "How can it be that five cars with IS Dushkas [machine guns] pass the official Turkish border crossing and nobody is stopping them? The IS and the AKP act out of the same mindset."[36] Not only did the IS terrorists enter Kobanî from the Turkish border, but afterward some of them returned there as well.

In the villages, the jihadists had left behind mines, rendering agricultural production nearly impossible. Nearly every week people died from stepping on mines or other explosives left by IS. Since Kobanî and Cizîrê were geographically connected in June 2015, most of Kobanî's food supply has had to come from its sister canton to the east.

Needless to say, the existence of hostile groups around Rojava constitutes part of the embargo, enforcing its international economic and political isolation [see 12.4].

14.3   The Kurdish Regional Government (KRG)

Since the attacks by the jihadists were directed against all Kurds, the YPG wanted to bury intramural hostilities and unite all Kurds against the jihadists; in June 2014, the YPG had declared itself ready to defend South Kurdistan alongside the Peshmerga. One declaration read: "We of the YPG have been struggling against these extremist groups (in Rojava) for more than eighteen months now. We have often heard that the IS gangs' goal is to exterminate the Kurdish people. We have gained valuable experience in our resistance against these gangs, and our fighters have fought heroically." The YPG appealed to all the peoples of Kurdistan to affirm their unity and struggle against the common foe, regardless of party.[37]

But it was not to be. Barzanî's KDP exhibits, says writer Dilar Dirik, an "active policy of exclusion and hostility toward the Kurds in Turkey, Syria, and Iran."[38] Indeed, it shares responsibility for the embargo against Rojava, alternatively loosening and tightening it based on its own political interests. It opens and closes the pontoon bridge crossing at Semalka at will. In February 2014, the KDP even decided to dig a 20-mile-long trench along its border with Rojava, ostensibly in defense against jihadists but in reality to prevent cross-border trade and to complete the embargo.

Figure 14.2   Syriacs join a demonstration against the ditch dug by the KPD to reinforce the embargo

The KRG enjoys touting its independence from Baghdad, but in reality it is dependent on Turkey and the United States. Its system, fundamentally different from that of Rojava, is basically one of patronage, in which the two largest governing parties—the KDP and the PUK—distribute the wealth generated by petroleum to their supporters. As Dirik observes, the governing KDP defines freedom as "capitalist economic growth, idealized by 'independent' petroleum sales, luxury hotels, and shopping centers, while actively supporting the borders drawn [in the 1920s] and thereby contributing to the oppression of the Kurds." Ninety-five percent of the economy is based on the income from oil, most of which it sells to Turkey. It is fostering a neo-feudal project to transform oil-wealthy KRG into a "new Dubai." The KRG, particularly the KDP, has a strong interest in controlling the oil fields around Rimelan.

Barzanî's KDP is trying to establish a Kurdish capitalist-patriarchal nation-state and to strengthen its alliance with Turkey. Democratic Autonomy constitutes a challenge to the KRG's system—and so must be destroyed at all costs. KRG residents who adhere to neither the KDP nor the PUK are socially excluded. The system requires a highly developed security apparatus to maintain itself, and it has repeatedly used violence and repression against protesters, accompanied, according to a 2013 Human Rights Watch report, by severe limitations on press freedom.[39] The KDP has long tried to destabilize Rojava in other ways as well. In January 2014, a car bomb detonated in the center of Dêrîk, in front of the Kongreya Star office. A father and child were killed, and panic spread in the city. At that point, the KDP opened the border to South Kurdistan, so that many could flee. When we entered a few months later, Berîvan of Kongreya Star explained to us that because of the embargo, educated people, doctors and engineers have left the region, to find better-paying jobs in South Kurdistan.

The KDP's hostility was proved when Beshir Abdulmecid Mussa, a cadre of Abdulhakim Bashar's KDP-S, was arrested while trying to prepare bomb attacks in Rojava against the self-administration. He confessed fully and explained in detail that he worked for the secret service of the KDP in South Kurdistan.[40] In late May 2014, the KDP shut down the border crossing at Til Koçer, where we had entered Rojava.

In August 2014, IS expanded unchecked in northern Iraq. Most Peshmerga were unwilling or unable to stop them. PKK fighters, together with PUK Peshmerga, installed themselves in a few cities. Since the 1990s, Maxmur (Makhmur, 25 miles or 40 kilometers from Hewlêr/Erbil) has been home to a large camp of refugees from North Kurdistan. In August 2014, IS attacked Maxmur, bringing Hêwler into danger. KDP Peshmerga failed to fend off the jihadists and fled. Only the PKK fighters were able to repel them. The PKK supported PUK Peshmerga in the successful defense of the multi-ethnic metropolis of Kirkuk.[41]

According to the KRG's constitution, Barzanî is supreme commander of the Peshmerga Army. In the summer of 2014, as we have seen [see 8.9], when IS invaded Şengal to destroy the Ezidis, the Peshmerga failed to live up to their responsibility to protect them. In fact, the KDP withdrew its 11,000 Peshmerga and left the Ezidi population nearly defenseless [see 14.9], which could have led to a massacre of 10,000 Ezidis. But the YPG, the YPJ, and the PKK rescued tens of thousands of Ezidis from Şengal.

According to Kurdish National Congress co-chair Nilüfer Koç, Barzanî bears responsibility: "The IS attacks on Şengal, Maxmur, and Rabia ... demonstrated that he is unable to defend the country, even though the Peshmerga is said to comprise 200,000 men. Not only the Peshmerga but also the security forces are controlled by the executive, so the political decision-makers must bear responsibility."[42]

The Peshmerga of the other party, the PUK, were self-critical about the previous surrender to the IS invasion. The governor of Kirkuk, Najmeldin Karim, admitted that the KDP's earlier accusations that the PYD and YPG were "antidemocratic" had been false: "We did not understand the PYD or the YPG, and we made a mistake. While they have resisted ISIS for years, we, with an army of one million Iraqi soldiers, could not even hold out for a few hours."[43]

During the battle for Kobanî, the United States publicly pressured the KRG to correct its policy and offer at least symbolic support for the YPG and YPJ against ISIS. In November 2014, Barzanî relaxed the embargo somewhat, and the KRG allowed some goods to pass over the border into Rojava. Then in the wake of the successful defense of Kobanî in 2014, as well as the PKK's successful defense of Maxmur, the KDP was forced to rethink its policy. A united front emerged against IS, encompassing the Peshmerga, the KDP and the PUK, and fighters from the HPG, YJA Star, the YPG, and the YPJ. And recently even the ENKS has had no choice but to work with the Rojava self-government, as laid out in the power-sharing Dohuk Agreement in October 22, 2014.

But concord could not last. For a few months in 2015, the KRG put Mount Şengal under an embargo to prevent the people from declaring Democratic Autonomy. KDP Peshmerga blocked roads to keep the other Kurdish forces away from the region, and tightened the embargo again.

Then in November 2015, working together, YPG/YPJ, PKK, Peshmerga, and local Ezidi forces jointly liberated the city of Şengal from IS once and for all. Afterwards, Barzanî denied that the YPG, the YPJ, or the PKK had participated, giving full credit to the Peshmerga.[44]

It was in that context that in December 2015 the KDP accepted a contingent of several thousand Turkish soldiers into the Mosul region.

14.4 Turkey Under the AKP

If Rojava's border with the KRG is sometimes permeable, its border with Turkey is all but impenetrable. With the liberation of 2012, Rojava joined the PKK in Turkey's gunsights. When residents of Afrîn try to cross the border, they have been killed by Turkish troops. Afrîn's cantonal government has now forbidden residents to leave without official permission, which seems a gesture to keep them from running to their doom, either at the Turkish border, in the Mediterranean, or in Europe. While we were in Rojava in May 2014, Turkish soldiers shot the mother of two children who hoped to make her way to Europe, where her partner awaited her. Other border crossers, smugglers, and refugees have met similar fates. Between January and May 2016, more than thirty people from Syria, including Rojava, were killed by Turkish soldiers.[45]

Support for Jihadists

If the Turkish border is closed to people from Rojava, it is open to jihadists who, under the eyes of the Turkish soldiers, easily cross into Turkey to resupply themselves, then cross back over to return to the war. The Syrian-Turkish border is one of the most closely monitored in the world, yet thousands of IS and Al-Nusra armed jihadists cross unhindered, to access logistics, transport, accommodation, and training opportunities in Turkey. We saw that clearly in October 2015, in a visit to the newly liberated city of Girê Spî (Til Abyad). Turkey had formerly provided electricity to the city, but once the YPG/YPJ liberated it in June 2015, it cut the electricity.

Under the prime minister, then president Recep Tayyip Erdoğan and the ruling AKP party, Turkey is engaged in a "neo-Ottoman" project of gaining authoritarian power and orienting Turkey toward former Ottoman areas rather than toward the West, as in previous decades. It is very friendly to Salafi jihadists. And eager to strengthen its position in its conflict with the Kurdish freedom movement in North Kurdistan, it was ready to use any means to annihilate Rojava.

In Rojava's early years, Turkey was linked to the Muslim Brotherhood in the Syrian National Council. The AKP invited then Egyptian president Mohamed Morsi to attend its congresses. But in July 2013, Morsi was ousted in a military coup, which weakened the general position of the Muslim Brotherhood in the Middle East. As a result, it lost influence in the FSA's Supreme Military Council and in the NC.[46]

Turkey went on to provide support for jihadist groups. The interior minister, Muammer Güler, directed the provincial governor of Hatay to provide the jihadist fighters with logistical support, transportation, and training.[47] That directive was fulfilled, with the support of Turkish intelligence.[48] The pattern has been repeated many times.

Turkey provided weapons to the Al-Qaeda affiliate Al-Nusra, and as we saw, it allowed Al-Nusra to invade Serêkaniyê over its border.[49] On January 19, 2014, in Antep, a truck was stopped and found to be transporting grenades for the MİT (Turkish intelligence) into the border town of Reyhanlı. The truck driver admitted that once there, he was to hand over the weapons to Al-Nusra.[50] In 2015, Al-Nusra, as part of the Jaish Al-Fatah alliance, as well as Turkish troops, attacked Afrîn.[51]

Figure 14.3   Discovery in a former IS training camp: the inscription says "Saudi Arabia and Turkey hand in hand"

Islamic State

Turkey's connections with IS are numerous, starting at least with the Karkamiş refugee camp near Antep (in Kurdish, Dîlok), which was used for the training of IS fighters.[52] A considerable amount of weapons and munitions have been smuggled across the border. Wounded jihadists routinely receive medical treatment in Turkey—they are even transported by Turkish ambulances from battle areas, treated, and then returned to resume fighting.[53] IS can bring huge amounts of oil into Turkey as well as cultural artifacts to sell. This trade, illegal according to the UN, is vital for the IS economy and for its ability to hold regions in Syria and Iraq. In the war against IS, as at Kobanî, Turkey is the logistical hinterland.[54]

In 2014, Prime Minister Ahmet Davutoğlu said that IS jihadists were not terrorists but merely "young men driven by anger."[55] When the YPG/YPJ liberated Girê Spî (Til Abyad) from IS, they found that Turkey had left 24 tons of ammonium nitrate at the border town of Akçakale, where the jihadists were to pick it up; officially designated as fertilizer, on the pretext of being humanitarian aid, it was likely intended for IS for military use. Turkey then set up a 700-meter zone just north of the border where everyone who enters from Rojava is shot. Civilians working their fields around Girê Spî have been attacked by Turkish heavy weapons.

Ahrar Al-Sham

Ahrar Al-Sham (Islamic Movement of the Free Men of the Levant), which emerged in 2011, is one of the largest opposition groups in Syria. An affiliate of Al-Qaeda, it too is supported by Turkey, Saudi Arabia, and Qatar. Researcher Guido Steinberg defines Ahrar Al-Sham as "ideologically very close" to Al-Nusra and also Salafist. It is organizationally connected to it through Jaish Al-Fatah, an alliance coordinated by Al-Nusra which controls the area around Idlib, west of Aleppo.[56]

Jaish Al-Fatah

Jaish Al-Fatah (Army of Conquest), formed in 2015, is a jihadist alliance led by Jabhat Al-Nusra and Ahrar Al-Sham, both affiliated with Al-Qaeda. Jaish Al-Fatah receives support from Turkey, Saudi Arabia, and Qatar. It captured the Syrian city of Idlib on March 28, 2015, and much of the province thereafter, in the area around Aleppo and Afrîn.[57] That made it a factor in the region, where it is now intent on constituting the "moderate opposition" and alternative to IS. (It introduced the Turkish lira as currency in the areas under its control.) The US think tank Atlantic Council, which has strong ties to the Obama administration, has advised the US government to collaborate with Jaish Al-Fatah against IS.[58]

Jaish Al-Islam

Jaish Al-Islam (Army of Islam) was founded in 2012 under the name Liwa Al-Islam by Zahran Alloush, the son of a Syrian sheikh in Saudi exile. It was renamed in 2013, and is particularly strong in southern Syria. Like AAS and JAF, it is supported by Qatar, Saudi Arabia, and Turkey. It would like to form an Islamic state and impose Sharia law.

14.5 Democratic Autonomy in North Kurdistan

Meanwhile at least since 2009, Kurds have worked to establish Democratic Autonomy in North Kurdistan. They implemented neighborhood councils, district councils, women's councils, ecology councils, youth councils, and others, creating Democratic Autonomy in many cities. And as in Rojava, they built women's liberation into the council system.[59] In many places, courts and mediation commissions, affiliated with the councils, have prevented patriarchal violence and punished forced and polygamous marriages. As a result of a broad educational program, the people increasingly find themselves in solidarity with the movement's ethical values, so that in many places acts of violence against women or children are now considered shameful. No one may participate in the institutions of Democratic Autonomy if they are known to perpetrate domestic violence.

But conditions in North Kurdistan differ fundamentally from those in Rojava, because the north is under the state control of Turkey, which has tried to extinguish the Kurdish freedom movement for some 35 years—arresting thousands of activists and politicians, and waging wars and carrying out massacres. In the 1990s, state forces destroyed more than 4,000 rural villages and expelled up to 3 million residents, murdering more than 17,000 civilians. Under these conditions, the Kurdish freedom movement had to go underground to organize its radical democratic institutions.

Above ground, Kurdish parliamentary parties have sprung up over the past three decades, one after the other. They were unable to gain seats in the Turkish Parliament because the hurdle was deliberately set high, at 10 percent, to present a solid obstacle to the emergence of Kurdish parliamentarianism. Yet even though they were repeatedly banned, new parties would emerge, winning increasing support in elections, especially in the Kurdish regions. In March 2009, the Democratic Society Party (DTP) won majorities in most Kurdish municipalities. In 2011, the successor party, called the BDP, gained electoral success as well.

These outcomes led the AKP government to inflict a wave of repression against the Kurdish movement, known as the anti-KCK operation. It charged more than 9,000 people from civil society groups, the municipal government, the press, and the labor unions with terrorism and imprisoned them for years. Anyone who held a position as mayor or councilor for the DTP/BDP, or was involved in civil society work and in the neighborhood councils, could find themselves locked in prison. The prisons became overcrowded.

In 2012, the establishment of the Peoples' Democratic Party (HDP) was founded in order to connect emancipatory forces throughout Turkey to represent and to create a unified opposition. The HDP is allied with the Democratic Regions Party (DBP), which organizes at the local level in North Kurdistan.

In the Turkish parliamentary elections on June 7, 2015, the HDP easily overcame the 10 percent threshold, gaining 13 percent of the vote. With parliamentary representation, it was poised to frustrate Erdoğan's drive for a presidential dictatorship. The Democratic Autonomy model clearly has many supporters in Turkey, both Kurdish and non-Kurdish.

Turkey's War on North Kurdistan

The Turkish state could not tolerate the HDP's electoral success and called for a new "snap" election in November. To ensure that the HDP's percentage would decline, it whipped up a frenzy of anti-Kurdish prejudice, with the result that more than a hundred HDP offices around the country were attacked.

During that summer, the collaboration between IS and Turkey became even more obvious. In July, young solidarity activists from the Turkish and Kurdish left-wing movement gathered in Suruç, en route to help reconstruction efforts in Kobanî. On July 20, an IS jihadist set off a bomb that murdered 34 of them and wounded more than a hundred. The day before, the murderer had been released from police custody and was on a police watch list.

On July 22, Ankara agreed to let the United States use İncirlik Air Base for the campaign against IS. The Turkish state thereby joined the coalition against "terrorism," but by "terrorism" it meant Kurdish politicians and activists, including the PKK. It proceeded to bomb the Qandil Mountains, while scarcely moving against IS at all.

On October 10, 2015, leftist organizations were demonstrating in Ankara in favor of peace negotiations between the PKK and the Turkish state. Two bombs went off, killing 103 and wounding four hundred. One of the two suicide bombers was the younger brother of the bomber of Suruç; both were linked to IS.[60]

The AKP's anti-Kurdish campaign proved successful in that in the November snap election, the HDP percentage fell from 13 to 10.8 percent, large enough for the party to stay in Parliament but not enough to block the AKP's drive toward authoritarian presidentialism.

In the late summer and fall of 2015, Kurdish activists in Cizre, Botan, Gever, Şirnex, and other Kurdish cities that had councils discussed how to respond to this renewed repression. Many decided to declare Democratic Autonomy.[61]

The youth movement refused to accept a recurrence of 2009, so in December 2015, the autonomous and clandestine youth organizations YDG-H and YDG-K declared liberated areas in several cities and created Civil Defense Units, or Yekineyen Parastina Sivil (-Jin), modeled on the YPG and YPJ in Rojava, to fight the Turkish security forces.[62] Their shift to armed self-defense had broad social acceptance. They dug trenches and erected barricades in Cizre, Colemerg, Gever, Nisêbîn, Silopi, Silvan, Varto, and Yüksekova, as well as the Diyarbakir neighborhood of Sur.

The Turkish state responded by imposing 24-hour curfews on these cities. Under the curfews, no one was permitted to step outdoors even to get supplies. The towns and villages were hermetically sealed by the police and the army, so no one from outside could enter, not even ambulances.

Turkish armed forces entered with tanks and attacked with heavy weapons. Soldiers and police broke down doors and invaded homes, then went up to the roofs and stationed snipers who could shoot with impunity. Bodies lay in the streets where they had been shot, their families unable to retrieve them. Şoreşger Dêrik, of the Dicle neighborhood of Şirnex, told one of the authors that the armed forces "attack us without respite. Against this occupying power we dug ditches—in order to live … Here it's not only the YPS that resists. The people fight together, shoulder to shoulder … We have faced massacres. We say it's enough."

Through artillery fire and aerial bombardment, Turkish armed forces carried out massacres in the occupied and besieged cities, murdering hundreds of civilians. The level of destruction is about the same as in the 1990s, says Muharrem Erbey, former chairman of the Human Rights Association (İHD), but "the methods have changed ... Before, people were killed secretly, today they are shot in public. Indeed, today the situation is more dangerous than in the nineties. At that time everything happened in secret, today everything is public, in front of the eyes of the families, and the perpetrators do not even bother to run away, because they can rely on their impunity."[63]

The behavior of the police is even coming to resemble that of jihadists, in the use of psychological warfare, in the gross abuses, and even in iconography. Special police units were formed called Esadullah Teams (Lions of Allah) who terrorize the population. These bearded men, says Muharrem Erbey, "previously comprised the death squads of Turkish nationalists and right-wing extremists but now have an Islamic appearance, growing their beards and writing nationalistic, sexist phrases, words with Islamic references on the walls."

It is done on the pretext of fighting the "terrorists" of the PKK. Says Şerife, a resident of Diyarbakir, "The Turkish prime minister and the president of the republic say that PKK is here, but in Sur we are not PKK we are the people. We defend ourselves and our neighborhood along with our children. We are the people, and we are the ones who take up positions here. We do not fear death. Whatever happens, we have nothing more to lose."

At the time of writing, the destruction continues. Some cities have been under curfew for months. But the communes will continue to spread, and the deep desire for a change in society through Democratic Autonomy will not be easily crushed.

14.6   Turkmen Militias

Turkey's AKP government, with its neo-Ottoman ambitions, craves the destruction of the Kurdish movement on both sides of its border. The YPG/YPJ liberation of Girê Spî (Til Abyad) on June 16, 2015, was a setback for the AKP, because the result was to geographically connect Cizîrê and Kobanî. Since then Turkey has repeatedly shelled and attacked rural areas around Girê Spî.[64]

But the unification of Afrîn and Kobanî is to be prevented at all costs. The Turkish state is now doing everything it can to keep Kobanî and

Afrîn separate by holding the corridor between them. It is clear who Turkey regards as its main enemy in the region.

Turkey has shelled the corridor repeatedly. In Jarabulus, an IS stronghold and a border crossing connecting IS with Turkey, residents are asking for help against IS rule, but when the YPG/YPG tried to cross the river in the spring of 2016, Turkish artillery shelled them, and Turkish planes bombed them.

Here Turkey has found another force to carry out the task of keeping Afrîn and Kobanî separate: the Turkmen militias. In the nineteenth century, after the Ottoman Empire lost the Russo-Turkish war of 1877–78, it settled some of the war refugees in Syria. Syrian Turkmens today are the remnant of these people, who remained in Syria after the collapse of the Ottoman Empire. They have little or no direct connection to the republic of Turkmenistan, in Central Asia.

Syrian Turkmens number some 100,000–200,000, living in Aleppo, Damascus, Homs, Latakya, and the three cantons. In the strip of land between Afrîn and Kobanî lie some 150 Turkmen villages. These areas are controlled by IS in its shifting alliances with other Salafi groups like Jabhat Al-Nusra and Ahrar Al-Sham. Among them, the Turkish government circulates propaganda defaming the YPJ/YPG, to mobilize the villagers to either flee or join the militias. They spread the lie, for example, that the YPG was responsible for bombings in western Turkey that were actually carried out by the PKK split-off TAK, which acknowledged responsibility.

Turkmens play a role not only in neo-Ottoman ideology but in Turanism, a pan-Turkic mythology that posits a Turkish-speaking "empire" in Central Asia that allegedly once stretched from Finland to Mongolia and that must one day rise again. A nationalistic pseudo-science, it is an ideological component of the Turkish far right, promoted by the Nationalist Movement Party (MHP) and the neo-fascist Grey Wolves (Ulku Ocakları).

Turkmen militias were formed in 2015 and now comprise about 10,000 fighters, mainly Turkish military veterans, special forces, and far-right cadres. They operate under the neo-Ottomanist banner of the Sultan Murat Brigade, a creation of not only Turkey but Saudi Arabia and the KDP.[65] The brigade works closely with Jaish Al-Fatah and has shared operational centers with Jabhat Al-Nusra.[66] It also cooperates with IS and has ties to Turkish intelligence.[67] The Sultan Murat Brigade's operations, allied with Jaish Al-Fatah and IS around Jarabulus, are the de facto realization of the Turkish so-called "buffer zone." According to the *ANHA* news agency, on April 14, 2016, weapons were transported over the border at Kilis, under the observation of Turkish intelligence. Uzbek and Turkmen fighters waited on the border to be brought to Azaz to strengthen Turkey's "occupation zone."

14.6 The SDF and the Jihadists

Even though radical Islamists like Ahrar Al-Sham and Jaish Al-Islam are linked closely to the Al-Nusra Front, NATO countries continue to view them as an allegedly moderate opposition. The negotiation process at Geneva to discuss the future of Syria, set up by the international powers, began its third attempt at negotiation in January and February 2016. Ahrar Al-Sham and Jaish Al-Islam were included as participants—in fact, Mohammed Alloush of Jaish Al-Islam is on the negotiating committee.[68] But the Rojava self-government and the PYD were specifically excluded, to accommodate the anti-Kurdish hysteria of Turkey's AKP.

The three cantons did not allow themselves to go on the political defensive. It was in response to their exclusion from Geneva that on March 17 they declared the Federal System of Rojava/Northern Syria [*see* 6.9], as a step toward a multi-ethnic and multi-religious alternative in Syria. It followed on the heels of the founding of the Syrian Defense Forces (SDF) on November 11, 2015.

In June 2016, the SDF cut the road between Jarabulus and Raqqa, starting a massive offensive on Manbij. Hussein Koçer, a commander both in the YPG and in the SDF, said these forces are determined to "liberate the whole of Syrian soil from Daesh [IS] terrorists."[69] But obstructing this liberation, as always, is Turkey, which delivers weapons and has even bombed the YPG/YPJ/SDF directly, in Jarabulus and in Girê Spî. While the United States supports the SDF through light weapons drops and air strikes, it does not take a clear position concerning Turkey or even Ahrar Al-Sham and the Al-Nusra Front, which control large parts of Idlib province as well as North Aleppo and are attacking non-Sunni villages. The YPG/YPJ are fighting these groups with all their might.

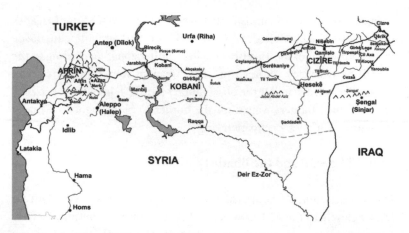

Figure 14.4 The war front as of July 31, 2016

Aleppo

In Aleppo, the Kurdish neighborhood of Şêx Maqsud is still self-governed in a direct-democratic manner, even with a reduced population. But it has repeatedly been the target of attacks. Starting in early 2016, jihadist militias intensively attacked the neighborhood with heavy weapons and missiles. Ahrar Al-Sham and Jaish Al-Islam used chemical weapons.[70] Kurdish units of the ENKS parties have participated in attacks on Şêx Maqsud—on the side of the jihadist militias, with so-called "Rojava Peshmerga" as party militias. A recently discovered letter from Ahrar Al-Sham to Jabhat Al-Nusra dated January 4, 2016, if authentic, establishes that the KDP and the ENKS, with help of the AKP and Turkish intelligence, sent military units toward Aleppo.[71] More than a hundred civilians have perished in these attacks as of this writing in July. Meanwhile when the SDF frees Arab populations in the area around Manbij, the people cheer.[72]

In March 2016, the KRG closed the Semalka border crossing altogether, even to journalists.[73] In June, after protests in South Kurdistan, the KDP announced it would reopen, but in reality it severely limits crossings by people and the transport of food supplies.

The embargo against Rojava—by the KRG, by Turkey, and by the jihadists—must end, and the revolutionary forces must be strengthened, so that the project for a democratic Middle East can be implemented.

Notes

1. Aron Lund, "Syria's Salafi Insurgents: The Rise of the Syrian Islamic Front," UI Occasional Papers no. 17, March 2013, http://bit.ly/1GpDnem; Emile Hokayem, *Syria's Uprising and the Fracturing of the Levant* (New York, 2013), loc. 303ff.

2. Karin Leukefeld, "Vom Aufstand zum Krieg," in Edlinger and Tyma Kraitt, eds., *Syrien. Hintergründe, Analysen, Berichte* (Vienna, 2013), p. 62.

3. The SNC was founded unofficially on that date; its official founding was in Tunis/Gammarth on December 18, 2011.

4. Bassam Ishak, interview by Michael Knapp, "Den Wunsch des Volkes nach einem demokratischen, pluralistischen und säkularen Syrien verwirklichen," *Civaka Azad*, June 4, 2014, http://bit.ly/1It9Y2m.

5. Petra Becker, "Die syrische Muslimbruderschaft bleibt ein wichtiger Akteur," *SWP-Aktuell*, no. 52 (August 2013), p. 2, http://bit.ly/1QJtzoa.

6. Charles R. Lister, *The Syrian Jihad: Al-Qaeda, the Islamic State and the Evolution of an Insurgency* (New York, 2016), p. 26.

7. See Armbruster, *Brennpunkt Nahost*, loc. 1590.

8. Lund, "Syria's Salafi Insurgents," p. 12.

9. In the press, the SMC is usually perceived as the FSA.

10. Hazem al-Amine, "Jabhat Al-Nusra and the Syrian Opposition's Failure," *Al-Monitor*, November 22, 2014, http://bit.ly/1B7lNvg; "Syria Opposition Urges US to Reconsider Al-Nusra Move," *Hurriyet Daily News*, December 12, 2012, http://bit.ly/1IGXcQM.

11. Jörg Armbruster, *Brennpunkt Nahost: Die Zerstörung Syriens und das Versagen des Westens* (Frankfurt, 2013), loc. 1290.

12. Anja Flach, *Frauen in der kurdischen Guerilla: Motivation, Identität und Geschlechterverhältnis* (Cologne, 2007).

13. Mutlu Çiviroğlu, "Nusra'nin Amaci Devlet Kurmakti," *Yukesova Haber*, August 9, 2013, http://bit.ly/1C1Qbm2.

14. Nils Metzger, "In Syriens Kurdengebieten herrscht ein brüchiger Friede," *Die Zeit*, March 4, 2013, http://bit.ly/1S8Vo4R.

15. Ronahi TV published a video that shows the collaboration between Al-Nusra and the Mashaal Temmo Brigade in Serêkaniyê. Because the video evidence has source problems, it must be mentioned that witnesses support our interpretation of the video. Plana Dagirkirina, *YouTube*, November. 23, 2012, http://bit.ly/1IxSCBB. Brigade leader Usama Al-Hilali resurfaced in May 2013, when he fought alongside Al-Nusra against the YPG: Rodi Khalil, "Recent Fighting in Til Tamir Escalates," *Kurdish Blogger*, May 3, 2013, http://bit.ly/1GAVcJo.

16. Tabassum Zakaria and Suzan Cornwell, "U.S. Congressional Hurdles Lifted on Arming Syrian Rebels," *AraNews*, July 23, 2013, http://bit.ly/1QssAqr.

17. "ÖSO Komutanı: PKK'nın kökünü kurutacağız," *Sabah*, August 8, 2013, http://bit.ly/1B6sYnM.

18. "Freie syrische Armee und Islamisten erklären den KurdInnen den Krieg," *Civaka Azad*, August 4, 2013, http://bit.ly/1Rpfta7; "Two Turkish Intelligence (MIT) Agents Killed in Syria," *Ekurd Daily*, August 17, 2013, http://bit.ly/291sVOo; "Massacre in Aleppo Continues," *Alliance for Kurdish Rights*, August 4, 2013, http://bit.ly/28YphTQ.

19. "Kürtlere saldırı kararı Antep'te alındı!" *ANF News*, August 2, 2013, http://bit.ly/28YphTQ.

20. Survivors of Til Hasil und Til Haran, unpublished interview by author, Qamişlo, October 2013.

21. Ibid.

22. "ISIS Propaganda: 'Wir haben Yeziden getötet, keine Sunniten!'—Klarstellung," Êzîdî Press, May 31, 2014, ezidipress.com/?p=2120, which contains a list of those killed.

23. ENKS representatives, including Hakim Bashar, conversation with authors, October 2013.

24. "Antwort der Bundesregierung auf die Kleine Anfrage ..." *Deutscher Bundestag*, September 10, 2013, Drucksache 17/14738, http://bit.ly/1GB6mOl.

25. Stephan Rosiny, "'Des Kalifen neue Kleider': Der Islamische Staat in Iraq und Syrien," *GIGA Focus: Nahost*, no. 6 (2014), http://bit.ly/1BawoYf. GIGA is the German Institute of Global and Area Studies.

26. Daniel Steinvorth, "Eine Söldnerarmee im Dienste des 'Kalifen,'" *Neue Zürcher Zeitung*, November 16, 2015, http://bit.ly/1RhcC1Z.

27. "The Failed Crusade," *Dabiq*, no. 4, http://bit.ly/1HErIte.

28. Michael Knapp, "Ausschließlich zum Schutz der Bevölkerung agieren," *Kurdistan Report*, no. 172 (March–April 2014), http://bit.ly/1QpZ4lc.

29. Abu Mohammed, "Syrian Children the Fuel of Bombing," *Raqqa News*, October 6, 2015, http://bit.ly/1SUkvrN.

30. Abu Hassan Karimov al Azeri, former ISIS member, interview, May 9, 2014, blog, http://bit.ly/1B7xJNL; Sherko Omer, "'It Was Never My Intention to Join ISIS: Interview with a Former Member of Islamic State," *Newsweek*, November 6, 2014, http://bit.ly/1FJXaS9.

31. Salih Muslim, interview by Özlem Topcu, "Die Türken leiden unter Kurdophobie," *Die Zeit*, October 14, 2014, http://bit.ly/1G5rNR7.

32. David L. Phillips, "Research Paper: ISIS-Turkey Links," *Huffington Post*, March 7, 2016, http://huff.to/1Iaatvo; Barney Guiton, "'ISIS Sees Turkey as Its Ally': Former Islamic State Member Reveals Turkish Army Cooperation," *Newsweek* (European edition), November 7, 2014, http://bit.ly/1GfVQsK; "Turkey Supports IS, Wants to Revive Ottoman Empire—Syria's UN Envoy," *RT*, December 30, 2015, http://bit.ly/1JINlpO.

33. Hannah Strange, "Battle for Kobane Rages and Protests Against Turkey's 'Inaction' End in Kurdish Deaths," *VICE News*, October 8, 2014, http://bit.ly/291K4sR.

34. Rainer Hermann, "Terrorstaat Irak," *Frankfurter Allgemeine Zeitung*, June 11, 2014, http://bit.ly/1G5hOLP.

35. Eyewitnesses at Kobanî to author, October 31, 2015.

36. Ibid.

37. "Rojava YPG Proposes Joint Action with South Kurdistan Peshmerga Against ISIS Terrorists," *Kurdistan Tribune*, June 10, 2014, http://bit.ly/1IRT53u.

38. Dilar Dirik, "Islamischer Staat, kurdische (Un-)abhängigkeit und das Versagen des Nationalstaatsparadigmas," *Kurdistan Report*, no. 175 (September-October 2014), http://bit.ly/1Gb7h4E.

39. "Iraqi Kurdistan: Free Speech Under Attack," *Human Rights Watch*, February 10, 2013, http://bit.ly/1B3xF1z.

40. Anja Flach and Michael Knapp, "Der Fall Beshir Abdulmecid Mussa—Starke Hinweise auf Verstrickung der südkurdische regierung in Bombenanschläge in Rojava," May 26, 2014, http://bit.ly/1Ua98MK.

41. *Millyet.com.tr*, August 13, 2014, http://bit.ly/1B3y8kp.

42. Songül Karabulut and Nilüfer Koç, "Gute Zeiten für die Kurden—schlechte Zeiten für die Türkei," *Kurdistan Report*, no. 176 (November-December 2014), http://bit.ly/1cJKJol.

43. Governor of Kirkuk, "IŞİD'le savaşan YPG'ye karşı hata ettik," *DIHA*, June 12, 2014.

44. Markus Bickel, "Die Schmach von Sindschar sitz tief," *Frankfurtur Allgemeine Zeitung*, November 25, 2015, http://bit.ly/1YBBcKa.

45. According to the Syrian Observatory for Human Rights, in Anna Reimann and Raniah Salloum, "Syrische Flüchtlinge in der Türkei: An der Grenze droht der Tod," *Spiegel*, May 11, 2016, http://bit.ly/28XL8z5.

46. Aron Lund, "Syria's Salafi Insurgents: The Rise of the Syrian Islamic Front," UI Occasional Papers no. 17, March 2013, http://bit.ly/1GpDnem.

47. "Lekolin genelgeye ulaştı," *Yeni Özgur Politika*, July 27, 2014.

48. Jörg Armbruster, *Brennpunkt Nahost: Die Zerstörung Syriens und das Versagen des Westens* (Frankfurt, 2013), loc. 1766.

49. "Turkey 'Protects & Supplies' Al-Nusra Camps at Its Border—Syria's YPG to RT," *RT*, March 4, 2016, http://bit.ly/1OV2PrS; Kim Sengupta, "Turkey and Saudi Arabia Alarm the West by Backing Islamist Extremists the Americans had bombed in Syria," *Independent*, May 12, 2015, http://ind.pn/1jLcHMT.

50. Nick Brauns, "An der Brust der AKP," *Kurdistan Report*, no. 175 (September-October 2014), http://bit.ly/1IWHvnG.

51. "Turkey Strikes Kurdish City of Afrin Northern Syria, Civilian Casualties Reported," *Aranews*, February 19, 2016, http://bit.ly/1UcnyOJ; "Syria Calls on UN to Condemn Turkish Attacks on Kurds," *Al Jazeera*, February 15, 2016, http://bit.ly/1VhEXnx.

52. As documented by the human rights organization İnsan Hakları Derneği (IHD), "İHD raporu: IŞİD Türkiye'yi lojistik üs olarak kullanıyor," *DIHA*, July 25, 2014.

53. "IŞİD militanları Türkiye'de tedavi ediliyor mu?," *Radikal*, September 24, 2014, http://bit.ly/1QJqc9C.

54. David L. Phillips, "Research Paper: ISIS-Turkey Links," *Huffington Post*, March 7, 2016, http://huff.to/1Iaatvo; Barney Guiton, "'ISIS Sees Turkey as Its Ally': Former Islamic State Member Reveals Turkish Army Cooperation," *Newsweek* (European edition), November 7, 2014, http://bit.ly/1GfVQsK.

55. "Davutoğlu Says ISIL Is Driven by Anger, Avoids Calling It Terrorist," *Today's Zaman*, August 7, 2014, http://bit.ly/1kb6rxY.

56. Guido Steinberg, "Ahrar ash-Sham: Die syrischen Taliban," *SWP-Aktuell*, April 28, 2016.

57. Wladimir van Wilgenburg, "The Rise of Jaysh al-Fateh in Northern Syria," *Terrorism Monitor* 13, no. 12 (June 12, 2015), http://bit.ly/28TDaT0; Alessandrai Masi, "Jabhat Al-Nusra's Win in Idlib," *International Business Times*, March 31, 2015, http://bit.ly/291rfmo.

58. "Chuck Hagel," *Atlantic Council*, March 28, 2015, http://bit.ly/1mv6FBW; Mohammed Alaa Ghanem, "Syria: An Opportunity in Idlib," *Atlantic Council*, April 3, 2015, http://bit.ly/1NFKCiC.

59. TATORT Kurdistan, *Democratic Autonomy in North Kurdistan*, trans. Janet Biehl (Porsgrunn, Norway, 2013).

60. "Ankara Suicide Bomber was Brother of Suspect in Previous Attack, Turkey Says," *Guardian*, October 19, 2015, http://bit.ly/29660WA.

61. "Resistance Is On for Young Women of Silvan," *JINHA*, August 22, 2015, http://bit.ly/297XwLG; "Self-government Means an End to Police Killings," *JINHA*, August 25, 2015, http://bit.ly/29jfPoc; "Kurds Decide on Self-Government," *JINHA*, August 19, 2015, http://bit.ly/2992EAH; "140 Communes Formed in Cizre," *Kurdish Info*, September 24, 2015, http://bit.ly/29jgzST.

62. "YDG-K Cizre'de düğ"nevini basıp evlenmek istemeyen kız çocuğunu aldı," *Siyasi Haber*, November 10, 2015, http://bit.ly/1P3ALHO. These organizations performed other services as well, such as liberating girls from forced marriage: Mahmut Bozarslan, "With Spread of IS-like Tactics, Urban Warfare in Turkey Grows Bloodier," *Al-Monitor*, March 7, 2016, http://bit.ly/29970qK.

63. "The Current Situation of the HDP And DBP: Construction and Defence," interview with Muharram Erbey, *Kurdish Question*, March 25, 2016, http://bit.ly/295ktz4.

64. "Turkey Confirms Shelling Kurdish Fighters in Syria," *BBC*, October 27, 2015, http://bbc.in/29c0PC4.

65. "MHP'li eski başkanın oğlu IŞİD'le savaşıyor," *Hurriyet*, July 9, 2014, http://bit.ly/1Np91bZ.

66. "Halep'te Ansar Al-Seria Operasyon Odasi Kuruldu," *Türkmen Ajans*, July 2, 2015, http://bit.ly/1QDtTlR.

67. Michael Knapp, "Spiel mit dem Feuer," *Kurdistan Report*, no. 181 (September–October 2015), http://bit.ly/1RyBtOJ.

68. Karen Zraick, "Syria Talks Are complicated by Competing Opposition groups," *New York Times*, January 29, 2016, http://nyti.ms/298QsS1.

69. "Kurdish Commander: Syrian Democratic Forces Prepared to Liberate the Whole Country from Radical Groups," *ARA News*, November 20, 2015, http://bit.ly/1J3e5B2.

70. "YPG Says Islamists Fired Chemical Weapons at Kurdish Neighborhood of Aleppo," *Rudaw*, March 9, 2016, http://bit.ly/2963jPy; "Amnesty: Attacks on Aleppo's Kurdish Section Amount to 'War Crimes,'" *Rudaw*, May 13, 2016, http://bit.ly/29413Yd; "'Chemical Gas Attack' on Kurdish-held Area of Aleppo Says Kurdish Red Crescent," *International Business Times*, April 7, 2016, http://bit.ly/29413Yd.

71. "Act of Aggression by KDP-ENKS-MIT," *ANHA*, March 14, 2016, http://bit.ly/29h8nWp.

72. "Village Rejoices After Being Freed from IS," AJ+ Facebook Page, June 2016, http://bit.ly/29h88dT.

73. "Rojava Officials Negotiate with Iraqi Kurds over Reopening Semalka Border Crossing," *AraNews*, May 26, 2016, http://bit.ly/28WQV3q.

15

Prospects

15.1 Rojava and Hegemonic Powers

The Middle East is a place where the spheres of interest of the various global hegemonic powers collide. Local and regional forces are forced to serve one or another international power bloc as subordinated forces or even directly as vassals.

Syria has become an arena where the NATO states and their Sunni allies, on the one hand, and Russia, China, Iran and their Shia allies, on the other, carry out a struggle for hegemony. "Every powerful country has its own plans for Syria," Ilham Ahmed summarized for us in 2014.[1] "We're not just talking here about an uprising of the people or a civil war. External powers play an important role. The war has a Russian front and a European front. Each of these powers is trying to install a system that fits its preconceptions, and they're all terrified of losing influence in Syria. Because if they did, they would lose influence in the whole Middle East, and so they'd forfeit any piece of the pie they might otherwise get."[2] The formation of sectarian blocs is symptomatic of the Middle East's tragic history. Geopolitical conflicts are carried out at ethnic and religious-sectarian levels, as various peoples are inflamed against each other to fight. Nilüfer Koç of the Kurdish National Congress calls the current civil war in Syria "a pure power struggle ... Al-Qaeda, the Al-Nusra Front, the so-called Islamic State, Hamas, and Hezbollah are fighting a proxy war in the name of the larger powers."[3]

Since the early 1980s, the Kurdish freedom movement has picked its way through this minefield with great skill, without allowing itself to be exploited by any of the warring hegemonic powers. Step by step, the Kurdish movement works to achieve its goal of a gender-liberated, communal-economic, radical-democratic, and ecologically aware society. It uses every contested space and period to expand its structures.

Even though the YPG/YPJ are at their peak effectiveness, the Kurdish freedom movement is ready for an equitable peaceful solution. It will fight the forces of the Turkish state only in active self-defense. Patiently, the movement claims rights, fights for them, and expands them.

Some leftists are skeptical about the rise of the pro-Kurdish parliamentary parties in Turkey, but we believe they have great importance. According to Dr. Kamran Matin of Sussex University, these parties, "combined with the PKK's military prowess, its organizational efficiency, and its control over parts of the Qandil Mountains, have allowed the Kurdish freedom movement in Turkey to set in motion a high-level, complex diplomacy that uses the international and regional contradictions advantageously for its own progressive social-political aims. The results have been impressive. It forced the state with the second-largest army in NATO into a peace or 'solution' process, whose very existence constitutes an unprecedented democratic achievement in Turkish politics."[4]

Despite the disappointing electoral results of November 1, 2015, the pro-Kurdish and leftist HDP still received almost 11 percent of the vote, and the movement now considers diplomacy and a peaceful solution to be its basic aims. The HDP's social importance is to bring people from different cultures and also different leftist parties together into an alliance trying to overcome racism and patriarchy. Parts of the left in Turkey and in Europe fail to grasp this approach and regard the Kurdish freedom movement's repeated efforts to achieve peace as a "betrayal" of revolutionary ideals. This dogmatic, traditionalist, Eurocentric, and nationalistic outlook mistakes war for revolution, and strategy for tactics. It would condemn a movement whose main goal is to protect the lives of all people in this region.

Another debate emerged among leftists in October 2014, when public opinion forced the US-led coalition against IS to collaborate in the defense of Kobanî in a limited way. People in Rojava welcomed this development. That US support has since increased is a positive fact for the struggle against IS, but it also carries dangers for the Kurdish freedom movement, for the forces of capitalist modernity will try to absorb it. Still, opportunities for tactical and operative alliances exist. The YPG and YPJ of the three self-governing cantons represent the strongest forces on the ground against IS, and the Syrian Democratic Forces (SDF) associated with the Federal System of Rojava/Northern Syria, became a factor in the Syrian-wide process in March 2016. None of the regional and international powers can now overlook Rojava.

Once Russia got involved in the Syrian war, some thought it necessary for Rojava to choose between it and the United States, but here too Rojava follows its own third path. In the practical battle against IS, it will not be exploited by foreign interests. As KCK chief Cemil Bayık told BBC Türkce, "We are on the side neither of Russia nor the United States … Whoever won't accept us, we won't accept them. No one can make a merely tactical alliance with the Kurds anymore. Those days are over. Whoever still says, 'Let's use the Kurds, they're good warriors, let them fight and so achieve our economic and military interests'—that person is mistaken. The Kurds are not the same as yesterday. The Kurds have now taken their destiny into their own hands. Now whoever makes strategic ties with us can win."

To be sure, this refusal can complicate the situation in Rojava. Parts of the international coalition work with the SDF against IS, yet are silent on the daily attacks by Turkey on Rojava. Still, in our eyes, Rojava is a revolutionary anti-fascist project whose significance is in no way secondary to that of the Spanish Republic of the 1930s. The states of the capitalist West abandoned the people of Spain and thereby helped Franco's fascism prevail. They considered Franco more acceptable than the Spanish Revolution and thereby contributed to the destruction of the revolution and helped fascism achieve victory.

Let's consider the current debate over military support for the YPG/YPJ in the light of this history. Few would likely have protested if the Americans had sent weapons to the Spanish Republic. What did not happen in Spain, became the case in Rojava, which initially seems contradictory. In Kobanî, a leftist project faced the prospect of annihilation by IS fascism, which had serious international support. Today, as in 1936–37, it is imperative for all humanists to pressure their governments, especially those that would prefer to see Rojava destroyed, to support Rojava and withdraw their backing from IS and its allies. The US and Peshmerga efforts on behalf of Kobanî are solely the result of the YPG/YPJ's vigorous defense of Kobanî and international pressure by the media and by people protesting in Europe, in Turkey, and all over the world, and other far-reaching US considerations. IS, as Cemil Bayık puts it, was "created by those" who now offer their help.[5]

Kamran Matin explains the meaning of Rojava for Western leftists: "Considering the malicious anti-leftist Turkish government's open resistance, and the US-led coalition's reluctance to stand with the YPG/YPJ—which could be overcome only by the pressure of pro-Kurdish public opinion in Europe—the success of the Western Left in pressuring the US-led coalition to provide unconditional support for the defenders of Kobanî, with military-logistical aid, was actually an important tactical victory for the left's overall anti-imperialist strategy ... Therefore the Left should not, nor can it allow itself to, absolutely exclude Western military aid for the defenders of Kobanî. It should rather concentrate on the concrete conditions and circumstances of such support and on supporting the larger political project and movement for which Kobanî stands, and it should carefully examine the likely implications of the deployment of even such limited aid for a democratic, leftist project in the region that undermines the goals of these helpers."[6]

For the self-governing cantons to achieve international recognition would be of enormous significance. Rojava's democratic-autonomous administrations, in the meantime, maintain some diplomatic contacts, but international aid organizations are still being officially prevented from providing support for refugees in Rojava. The humanitarian organizations require that the Syrian state approve all aid, but such approval is impossible for Rojava, even though it is seeking autonomous status within a democratized Syria and not the creation of its own nation-state or annexation to South Kurdistan. In June 2014 and in April 2016, when the Syrian presidential and parliamentary elections were held, regime supporters living in the neighborhoods of Qamişlo voted, but Rojava's self-government boycotted the elections on the grounds that the cantons did not recognize the regime as long as the regime didn't recognize the cantons.

A similar conditionality was observable in the negotiations over participation at the Geneva II conference in January 2014 and Geneva III in January 2016. Their purpose was to bring together the nationalistic Syrian National Coalition, the Islamist-jihadist opposition alliance, and the Syrian government to hammer out a solution to the civil war. Rojava's transitional government sought to participate, but Turkey adhered to its anti-Kurdish line, requiring the Kurds to join the "the opposition." This requirement did nothing but perpetuate Turkey's and Syria's policy of enforced assimilation, which it also applies to the Syriacs and other social groups.

As Sabri Ok, of the KCK executive council, observed, "They say the Kurds can go to Geneva only without an identity. This is an injustice and an insult to the Kurds ... There will be no solution in Syria without the Kurds."[7] Without the Kurds, the much-heralded Geneva talks were condemned from the outset to fail. The West has made it clear that it would only involve the right "opposition" in the talks, although while the United States supported Turkey's position in 2014, in 2016 it stayed more neutral, due to its tactical military cooperation with the YPG/YPJ and Turkey's dangerous role in Syria's war.

US military support for Rojava derives from the fact that IS has become a threat to the world. While Turkey and Saudi Arabia were pushing IS, the United States kept silent, and it would be naïve to think it did not foresee the upcoming threat. In the summer of 2014, opinion changed: IS must be stopped.

A hegemonic political power like the United States thinks that if it cannot marginalize, criminalize, or destroy an alternative movement, then a collaboration at a certain level or at a crucial time may be useful, to make this movement dependent and to change the revolutionary/ emancipatory content. We met many Rojava activists who were aware of this risk and stated that they could maintain themselves successfully in a position of independence.

For the success of the revolution, TEV-DEM member Aldar Xelîl observes, Rojava must not depend on foreign powers but remain grounded in the people: "The regime, the opposition, but also the international powers, can support you today when it's in their interest, but tomorrow, when the power relations have changed, they can change their mind. So we are building only on the support of the people. With the people and with their forces, we will build our own future."[8]

15.2 Solutions Within Syria

The Kurdish freedom movement, as we have seen, has its own ideas about the future of Syria, having advocated a peaceful democratic solution ever since the creation of the NCC in the summer of 2011. In January 2014, the three cantons announced the Social Contract, which says they regard themselves as part of a democratic Syria; the same is true of the Federal System of Rojava/Northern Syria, declared in March 2016. Nowhere does the Social Contract speak of a achieving an independent state, either as a long-term goal or even as an option. Rather, following the concept of Democratic Confederalism, the Kurdish movement is trying to implement a comprehensive democratic political solution within Syria's existing borders, without accepting existing nation-states and patriarchy.

Hence after January 2014, one of the main tasks of the democratic-autonomous administrations was to seek recognition for Rojava's social model throughout Syria. They requested a dialogue with most of the forces within Syria except Al-Nusra, IS, and other political extremists. In response, the Assad regime and the nationalistic-Islamist opposition remained conspicuously silent, even downplaying Rojava's accomplishments. Its defense forces' victory at Kobanî in 2015, however, opened a whole new chapter. Even as conditions in the rest of Syria deteriorated, Rojava had moved forward and inflicted the first major defeat on IS. Thereafter Arabs, Syriacs, Turkmens, and Kurds went on to cooperate in the liberation of Girê Spî (Til Abyad) and other areas. Because Rojava stood out, more political forces began to speak to the democratic-autonomous administrations. The formation of the SDF in October 2015 and the Syrian Democratic Council (MDS) in December 2015 is a beacon of hope for the whole region. Cities far from Rojava are now adopting Democratic Autonomy: in September 2015, the Druze city of As Suwayda, in southern Syria, declared its own democratic self-administration, and delegations from As Suwayda traveled to Rojava to exchange support and information. The Democratic Autonomy model is maturing.

Although many parties and organizations joined the MDS, several forces have ideas that are compatible with Democratic Autonomy—for example, the Local Coordinating Committees. Even though they have been repressed in the course of the bloody war, they remain a potential strategic partner with Rojava. Another possible partner is the Syrian Women's Initiative, founded in 2013 and comprising Kurdish, Arab, and Syriac women, but it will not be easy for this initiative to gain a foothold outside Rojava. Indeed, the Rojava self-government will accept nothing less than a strongly decentralized, democratic, and multicultural administration for itself; Rojava urges that its freedoms and achievements be broadly accepted and legally established in Syria as a whole.

Considering the continuing brutal war and the millions of refugees inside and outside the country, most people consider a democratic political solution to be unrealistic. But if Rojava stabilizes militarily, politically, and socially, if IS is beaten back significantly, and if the Ba'ath regime and the other Islamist-jihadist forces remain weak, that could change. When the importance of Rojava is recognized, when other democratic forces in Syria become stronger, and when the belligerent parties and their international supporters become war-weary or their conflict becomes too expensive, peaceful political solutions may finally make it onto the agenda. Maybe 2016 is too early, but we are in the Middle East, where developments may change very fast, under certain conditions.

But in 2016, peace is not in sight. The exclusion of the PYD and the Rojava self-government from the Geneva III process the situation. A ceasefire was declared, which obviously did not apply to the self-government, which is systematically attacked by the National Coalition and the Syrian regime. After the exclusion from Geneva III, the declaration of the Federal System of Rojava/Northern Syria introduced a new dimension for building a multi-identity, democratic Syria. The liberation of the corridor between Kobanî and Afrîn has the potential to empower the region's population. It will be a free space for self-government, and no annexation will take place, because the model of Democratic Autonomy acts through persuasion and is voluntary, in contrast to the forces of capitalist modernity and the nation-state.

Just as the liberation of the corridor between Cizîrê and Kobanî, and the breaking of IS's reign of terror there, relieved the besieged region, so does Afrîn need relief. Thousands of refugees from Aleppo, Azaz, and the other places have arrived in Afrîn, where they are provided for. The liberation of this region will take place in coordination with the people there.

But all the warring parties responded negatively to the announcement of the Federal System: Turkey, the Syrian government, and the Syrian opposition. This is because as unitary nation-states that are threatened by the new model, even as enemies otherwise, they can act together against Rojava.

15.3 International Solidarity

Whenever we asked activists in Rojava what the best form of solidarity would be, the most common answer we got was "Build a strong revolutionary movement in your own country." That response caused us to reconsider the very concept of solidarity. In the history of the Western Left, solidarity has often amounted to a subject-object relationship, in which the "object" of solidarity is tied to the metropolises' longings and needs for strong emancipatory movements. But this form of solidarity reproduces the colonial perspective on southern, traditionally non-industrialized, and historically exploited countries. Metropolitan leftists sometimes see themselves as helping the "poor" in these regions—but the "help" they offer serves as a projection screen. Since expectations go unfulfilled, both sides of the solidarity exchange end up disappointed.

This problem arose in most solidarity movements in the last decade. But solidarity, activists in Rojava say, means building solidarity movements together, movements that can learn from and support one another. The victory over IS at Kobanî was a victory of the Rojava project and thus would constitute a strong leftist alternative in an important region. The fight for Kobanî brought Rojava onto Western TV screens, and international solidarity grew rapidly. The willingness of Western governments to let Kobanî fall brought millions of people around the world into the streets and made non-intervention impossible.

But for many, the question of greatest importance was not only state intervention but also defense of the revolution. Volunteers from Australia and Germany joined the battle against IS—some have fallen, some are still fighting, and others have started campaigns for Rojava's reconstruction, for supplying medical aid, and for infrastructure projects. These people have come into the crosshairs of those who want to cut off Rojava from all support, as it did for the 34 young socialists killed by the bombing in Suruç, while they were preparing to build a house for orphans in Kobanî. This cruel attack, as well as the policy of embargo, showed that while it was possible to drop bombs on IS, it's impossible to drop food and medicine into Kobanî. From the perspective of capitalist modernity, a revolutionary alternative in the Middle East would shock the ruling regimes and have unforeseeable consequences in Europe and the rest of the world. Not for nothing are the hegemonic powers, even the Ba'ath and Erdoğan regimes, despite their deep differences, united when it comes to preventing or annihilating the Rojava project.

For leftists, solidarity with Rojava is not a question of benevolence but a necessity. At the moment, Rojava needs not only material support but also professionals of every kind. It needs doctors, engineers, lawyers, artisans, agricultural engineers, and people who are ready to work to build Democratic Autonomy. Interested people should first educate themselves about the political content that underlies the Rojava model. That could transform the current clamor into a long-term movement that advances radical democracy, gender liberation, environmental awareness, and a cooperative economy, mediated by Democratic Autonomy, and as an alternative to capitalist modernity.

Since the autumn of 2014, emergency appeals have gone out to Europe, especially for medical and humanitarian aid, asking for donations. Rather than participate in donation campaigns of bourgeois and state-oriented charities, some prefer to work with institutions in active solidarity with Rojava. But important donation campaigns to support women's institutions and women's cooperatives are under way. Equally important are campaigns to collect "weapons for Kobanî," to preserve the independence of the YPG/YPJ from Western military support. The defense of Kobanî inspired an abundance of initiatives for the reconstruction of Kobanî and other projects.

As of December 2015, more than 187,000 of the Kobanî's former 450,000 inhabitants have returned. The people have made efforts to clear the city: 1.4 million tons of rubble have been removed, with scant technical support. But due to the embargo, the reconstruction isn't proceeding fast enough to supply all the returnees. Beritan, an activist from Kobanî, explained, "International solidarity gave us a lot of confidence, and many people came back. We had high hopes for the reconstruction. But now winter is coming, and nothing has happened yet. Thousands of people have to live in tents."[9]

Solidarity should be understood not only as a technical concept. For the defenders of Kobanî, it had great meaning that on November 1, 2014, from Berlin to Melbourne, from Tehran to Kabul, people poured into the streets to demonstrate on behalf of Rojava. A movement in solidarity with Rojava must not neglect the international context and must therefore criticize the policies of Germany, NATO, and other international powers. One of the central demands must be to lift Germany's ban on the PKK, to remove the PKK from lists of "foreign terrorist organizations" maintained by the European Union and the United States, and to end weapons exports to Turkey, Saudi Arabia, Qatar, and other Middle Eastern states.

Figure 15.1   Civilians and YPG/YPJ fighters in a pickup after a demonstration

15.4   Communalism or Barbarism

"We know every day will be a little better," Asya Abdullah, PYD co-chair, has written. "Our society will continue to resist out of sheer conviction that it must take its fate into its own hands. The longer the resistance continues, the more experience we will accumulate in this struggle. Currently the people of Syria are undergoing great difficulties, but we see those troubles as the price of freedom."[10]

Revolutions are not finished on the day the progressive force gains control over an area. In fact, they only begin on that day. Revolutions fail when a revolutionary party holds on to power and excludes the broad population from decision making and thereby open a cleavage between itself and them. Over many years of discussions, the democratic movement in Rojava—the MGRK and TEV-DEM, and its main initiator, the PYD—criticized state socialism and discussed how to avoid repeating its mistakes.

In Rojava, the will of the councils is expressed not by parties but by broadly engaged activists and at higher levels by representatives directly elected by the people. The movement is trying to organize the entire population from below and integrate everyone into the direct-democratic decision-making processes. Identifying the commune as the basic unit of council and grass-roots democracy transforms social relations in favor of women and makes a state superfluous. Ecological efforts are everywhere now, with their critique of existing economic relations.

Of course, many problems and challenges remain for Rojava, mostly because the decades-long Ba'ath dictatorship kept people politically inexperienced and because conservative social structures run deep. Even the most engaged activists make mistakes; ways of thinking that are anchored in the old system will not be overcome in a day or even a year. The process will take many years or even decades. But the great advantage of the people of Rojava is that even before the revolution, they already had decades of experiences with people's and women's organizing. If the PYD and the YPG had not already existed, then the liberation could probably not have happened. The progressive women's and democratic organizations would have been shoved aside, as they were in Egypt, Yemen, Tunisia, Egypt, and Libya. The Islamists or a reactionary force like the KDP would likely have seized power in Rojava.

Revolutions fail also because of attacks from outside. Today the Islamists, showered with weapons and money from the Gulf States and Turkey, are trying to crush the nonviolent revolution. People die every day now defending their villages and cities against the Islamists, and the economic problems are enormous. In a small region divided into three non-contiguous parts, it is almost impossible to organize complete autarchy. Food has become expensive, and electricity and running water are often lacking.

But the will to solve these problems is strong. Every day, the reactionary and fascist forces are pushed back a little bit further; the people in Rojava will not give up either their hard-earned values or their homeland. By creating strong organizations, by explaining their vision of a better life, and by using their organizations to put their ideas into practice, women and other components of civil society are grasping a lever to ensure that they will not be crushed in the future. Also crucial is their belief that the revolution will be victorious, that it will inspire all of Syria and the Middle East and beyond. Many people in Rojava defend with conviction the accomplishments of their revolution as a model for the whole region.

What spurs them on is the knowledge that there is no objective alternative for the Middle East, a profoundly heterogeneous region. Or to put it another way: communalism or barbarism. The Kurdish freedom movement repeatedly recovers from its setbacks and advances further. Although North Kurdistan has suffered through repeated waves of repression, people here have promoted and strengthened Democratic Autonomy there, as they have in the Maxmur refugee camp and the Medya Defense Zones of South Kurdistan. The revolution is a force that will win over the minds and hearts of the people. "We love life so much that we're willing to die for it," a PKK founder, Mazlum Doğan, once said. In Rojava, the people must now reinvent themselves. Schools, administrations, courts, economic production, and so on—all are in upheaval, and all must be radically reordered, even as the society defends itself militarily. Rojava's revolutionary and liberatory project needs our unreserved solidarity. The survival of its revolution is also the survival of hope for a free, communal life and a gender-liberated, ecological society. Those of us in an alienated society can look to Rojava in order to rethink life in our own societies and take heart.

Notes

1. Ilham Ahmed is currently co-president of the Syrian Democratic Council (MSD).
2. "Die Revolution in Westkurdistan—Teil 2," *Civaka Azad*, n.d., http://bit.ly/1R84Y8g.
3. Nilüfer Koç, "Die Rückkehr des hegemonialen Krieges in Kurdistan," *Kurdistan Report*, no. 175 (September-October 2014), http://bit.ly/1MFMmcs.
4. Dr. Kamran Matin, "Kobanê: Was steckt alles in diesem Namen?" *Kurdistan Report*, 176 (November-December 2014), http://bit.ly/1cmEuj8.
5. Cemil Bayık, "IŞİD'i büyüten güçler kurtarıcı olmak istiyor!" *Yüksekova Haber*, August 24, 2014, http://bit.ly/1O3JOpi.
6. Matin, "Kobanê: Was steckt alles in diesem Namen?"
7. Sabri Ok, "If Kurds Are Not Recognized As a Third Party They'll Reject Geneva: PKK," *Firat News*, reprinted in *EKurd Daily*, Jan.uary 16, 2014, http://bit.ly/1KjPFUI.
8. Quoted in Mako Qoçgirî, "Aus der Kraft der eigenen Bevölkerung—Die Revolution in Rojava schreitet voran" *Kurdistan Report*, 172 (March-April 2014), http://bit.ly/1IrNfGz.
9. Personal conversation, October 31, 2015.
10. Asya Abdullah, interview by Pinar Öğünç, "Ohne die Freiheit der Frau keine Demokratie," *Radikal*, August 22, 2013, http://bit.ly/1QovIQD.

Afterword: The Philosophy of Democratic Autonomy

Asya Abdullah

We are all born with a sex and a skin color, and we are born into a religion, a language, and cultural and ethnic affiliations. Despite these differences, like flowers in the same garden, we all share ethical and humane principles. Love, sympathy, family, justice, and trust are values cherished by all societies, and all reject betrayal, oppression, and exploitation. Yet from early prehistory up to the present, monarchs, despots, and tyrants have endeavored to mold people for their own benefit and to destroy the natural underpinning of society. The powerful, even as they tout the words "justice" and "right," try to strangle society and lay waste to nature. The governed, for their part, regard laws as curses and resent that politics has become the art of deception. Achieving real justice would have to mean enhancing relations among individuals, society, and nature instead of crushing them.

The powerful, in order to legitimize their hegemony over the governed, weaken the society they rule, divide people into classes and groups, alienate them from one another, and encourage them to fight one another. Individualism has become egoism, to the point that no one can trust anyone else. The powerful stir up mistrust among peoples, spur competition and foster injustice; meanwhile people, hoping to establish even a frail lone union or small local association, have sacrificed their lives by the hundreds, rising up dozens of times in history and fighting to reclaim their basic rights from the despots.

The process of state building, a system that extends into both nature and society, has become a means by which rulers achieve their exploitative ends. The state's oppressive interventions into society became permanent, and relationships between humanity and nature followed suit. So has humanity become ever more alienated from itself as well as from nature.

The state fragments society into the smallest units, and state-fix-ated thinking propels humanity into a profound social, political, and economic crisis from top to bottom. The capitalist system considers itself unassailable, but people who live within it no longer believe in it. Its consequences are natural catastrophes, diseases of civilization, poverty, psychological disturbances, capitalist exploitation, and war, all of which dominate people's lives. Despite enormous scientific and technological progress, no one has yet found a way to rescue people from this chaos and destruction. The system's own refusal to change is leading us to an uncertain future.

For the sake of our very survival, we have to develop alternative models, to find a way out of a situation that is propelling us toward unspeakable social and ecological catastrophes. Many writers, philosophers, academics, and theorists have endeavored to explain to the general public the necessity of building a democratic model, one that includes nature but does not exploit it, one in which people can control their own lives, in which sexual inequality is overcome, in which ethnic and religious wars come to an end, in which bridges of peace are constructed among groups of people, and in which poverty and exploitation are no more.

Legend has it that when Pandora opened her box, she let loose all the evils into the world. Terrified, she slammed it shut, but hope remained inside. Rojava is like the hope that is hidden in the Pandora's box of the Middle East. It is a hope that can save our people from the darkness of war. Democratic Autonomy, which is being established throughout the cantons of Rojava as a part of Syria, has the fundamental aim of shriveling the state system, based as it is on power, and of creating a way for all ethnic and religious groups in the society to flourish. Every such group should be free to develop according to its own social character and to create its own organizational structures.

Democratic Autonomy has been implemented in Rojava's cantons, in the legislative and executive councils, in the supreme electoral commission, in the district councils, the neighborhood councils, the communes, the municipal administrations, and the women's councils. All individuals and institutions have equal rights and duties in the eyes of the constitutional court. In every canton, people have the right to form, by their own free will, councils and commissions to carry out cantonal tasks. Arabs, Armenians, Assyrians, Chechens, Circassians, Kurds, Roma, and Turkmens varying by religion as Christian, Muslim, and Ezidi, live cheek-by-jowl alongside one another; the region is diverse in every respect. And amid this diversity, a free and just social order has been built. The administration of Cizîrê canton has affirmed that people of every religious belief and every ethnic background may participate at all levels of the self-government. The democratic institutions established in Rojava's cantons include people from the streets, the villages, the neighborhoods, and the cities. By virtue of this breadth, a consciousness of democratic political culture is coming to life.

In Rojava, not one line will be drawn around any patch of soil on the basis of ethnicity, language, religion, or culture. A common life without borders, implementing a common self-government, will end the enmity among the groups of people, enmity that was originally created by the modern nation-state. By organizing everyone in the society for political decision making through the communal system, from the street to the village to the neighborhood to the city, and by fostering the conscious-ness about how these institutions can work, we hope to reach the level where the people can decide what will help them and what will harm them. By this means, we can prevent differences among the constituent groups from sharpening in conflict and instead contribute to a communal common life.

In the Middle East, the nation-state has become a model of pain, destruction, massacre, and repression for many religious and ethnic groups. Here, the nation-state was established on the assumption of ethnic homogeneity. Dictatorial and totalitarian regimes ignored the differences among peoples, in the name of protecting the system itself: monarchical rule. Its basic paradigm was profit—for one's self, one's family, or one's tribe.

At length, the peoples of the Middle East and North Africa have finally rebelled against these regimes. In Rojava, we were part of an uprising against such a regime. But instead of choosing destruction and violence, we chose a third path. Things, we decided, would no longer be as they had once been. We discussed what direction to take. And we developed self-government through Democratic Autonomy as an alternative model to the unitary and militaristic nation-state.

Democratic Autonomy does not try to attach specific ethnicities to specific patches of earth. Rather, it conceives the land as a place where everyone can live freely in their own identity. The Democratic Nation model embraces Kurdish, Arab, Turkmen, Armenian, Syriac, and all peoples of the society who with their languages, religions, and cultures are invited to participate actively through their own freely built institutions in the administration of the region. It has been said that chaos generated by sectarianism is Syria's fate, that no other future is possible. But it is against the background of this propaganda that the Democratic Nation and Democratic Autonomy are coming to fruition in Rojava. A new model of self-government on the basis of freedom and equality is emerging to replace the homogenizing, repressive, and freedom-limiting modern capitalist state. The Middle East has been a region of religious fundamentalism and nationalistic, centralized states, where religious, cultural, and ethnic enmities give rise to massacres and genocides; in that context, the freedom created by Democratic Autonomy will not only foster political consciousness in all parts of society but will vanquish, through common self-defense, all those who attack its communal, solidarity focused coexistence.

Women are subject to discrimination more than any other group in the Middle East. The world's democratic systems, touting their vaunted "defense of democracy," have never yet been able to bring about the liberation of women to the extent that has been done in Rojava. In Democratic Autonomy, the equality of the sexes finds expression in the practice of dual leadership, a principle of "positive discrimination" that will remain in place until that system and the organization of women are completed. In every institution in Rojava, women must make up at least 40 percent of participants. Women play an active role in every part of Rojava, from defending themselves and seeing to their society's security, to redressing problems in the family, to exercising leadership. In the Middle East, patriarchy and traditional family structures exert great pressure on women, but in Democratic Autonomy self-government is giving rise to a new social order. In the cantons of Rojava, women represent the subject as they struggle against the patriarchy of traditional society, with its underage marriage, polygamy, and more. In the cantons, the aim is to cast off the patriarchal mentality and liberate women in all respects. Even the smallest institutions of the society support the development of strong women's solidarity. In women's councils, cooperatives, academies, and centers, women participate as subjects in all aspects of the process of building a free life. Wherever there are people's councils, women's councils have been formed as well. The women on the councils report to all women in Rojava on the goals and purposes of the revolution. Women's cooperatives and workshops educate women for trades and thereby shore up their economic independence. Women are leading actors in Democratic Autonomy and play a responsible role developing it, implementing it, and protecting it.

In the rest of Syria, let it be said that the unitary, monistic politics of the regime led to a loss of all tolerance among the population groups. Over long years, the regime fostered a climate of mistrust and uncertainty among all the constituent groups. Each of the Syrian population groups is allotted a separate, demarcated district. In a demographic sense, we exist side by side but separate from one another. Up to the present in the Middle East, centralistic, monist, and nationalistic state systems have repeatedly tried to recast our diverse society in terms of homogeneity. They have seen variety not as enriching but as problematic.

We often hear throughout our region of a "problem of minorities." Massacres and genocides are committed against minorities, and yes, there have been a few "ethnic cleansings." But now the Kurds have risen up to challenge this policy of massacre and genocide. Our society is diverse, like a mosaic, and the monistic state principle is entirely unsuited for it and cannot be implemented no matter how much force is exerted.

So in Rojava, our project is a matter of allowing all who make up this mosaic to live together. Rojava models the fact that the destructive, monistic systems don't function. Consider that in the so-called "Arab Spring," in Tunisia and Egypt, a system of majority democracy was attempted. The underlying mindset was "When I win the election, when the people elect me, I will be able to do anything, including change the laws." They were speaking of a system in which there was no participation. Rojava is the opposite. It is participatory and consensus-oriented and includes all people with their distinctive languages, identities, and individualities. That is how Rojava represents a new hope for the Middle East. Even as Syria descended into a firestorm, Rojava, on the fringes of the war, in a climate of peace, witnessed the rise of a just system.

A few factors can explain how it happened. One of the most important is the attitude and the logic of the system being built: the will to guarantee the participation of women, who constitute the majority of Rojava's society. Today, the feudal attitude in Rojava has been weakened and is structurally collapsing. But women have the largest proportion of illiteracy; there is conservatism, but it is grounded in tradition, not religion. All these factors have led to the development of Rojava's new system. But most important was the political ideology and organizing efforts to bring women to the foreground. Democratic Autonomy makes it easy for women to participate.

The cantons have also adopted the model of a communal economy, in which social use is central, as opposed to the capitalist model, which maximizes profits and lays waste to nature. Through communal organizing, the citizens grow in consciousness and sensibility; they internalize respect for nature and a sense of ethical responsibility. Economy, a humane outlook, and ecology cannot be separated from one another. Democratic Autonomy understands them as complementary and envisions an economic system beyond domination and exploitation, in which the interconnections between people and nature are mutually understood and reinforced. Rojava's cantons aid the cooperatives, organizing from the bottom up, and ensure that all factories and enterprises are under the control of the people. In this way, resources can be justly distributed, inequalities in distribution overcome, and a just economic order can be developed. In Democratic Autonomy, the will of the people is the fulcrum of economic decision making. The cantons' democratic institutions should include the whole population and create a sense of belonging and responsibility among citizens and prevent destructive practices.

By building Democratic Autonomy in Rojava, we are creating a decentralized, democratic system; extended to Syria, it could be the basis for a democracy in which people of all ethnicities, identities, and languages contribute and in which women have their own voice in all areas of self-government and life. For that, we continue our fight. Our object is freedom, peace, equality, and justice. To the battle for these values, we are prepared to give our all. Today, the nameless heroes of Kobanî are also defending these values. Their armed struggle draws strength from their purposefulness, their determination, and their ethical values. Freedom, defended by them, will prevail.

November 18, 2014, Kobanî, Rojava

Glossary

ENKS (Encûmena Niştimanî ya Kurdî li Sûrieyê)—the Kurdish National Council in Syria. Founded in October 2011, this coalition of Syrian Kurdish parties is dominated by the KDP-S and the PUK-S.

FSA—Free Syrian Army. A loose coalition of armed groups, originally made up of deserters from the Syrian Army. It is the military arm of the SNC, based in Turkey.

Gorran. A political party in South Kurdistan. It was founded in 2009 to oppose the two-party KDP and PUK governing coalition.

heval. The Kurdish word for "friend," in the sense of "comrade."

Hewlêr Agreement. An agreement between the PYD and the ENKS, signed in Hewlêr (Erbil) on July 12, 2012, to cooperate and share power in Rojava through the Supreme Kurdish Council (SKC).

HPG (Hêzên Parastina Gel)—People's Defense Forces. Founded in 2000, the HPG, the successor to the ARGK, is the guerrilla army of the PKK and a force for legitimate self-defense.

Jabhat Al-Akrad, Kurdish Front. A Kurdish defense force that aims to protect Kurdish people outside Rojava. It has worked with the FSA, among other things on the expulsion of IS from Azaz. On August 16, 2013, it was excluded from the military council of the FSA of Aleppo because of its presumed connection to the PKK.

KCK (Koma Civakên Kurdistan)—Union of Kurdish Communities. A supranational coalition of Kurdish communities that brings together radical democratic self-governing institutions. Originating in the PKK, it seeks to implement Democratic Confederalism and defend the Kurdish people.

KDP (Partîya Demokratiya Kurdistanê)—Democratic Party of Kurdistan. The ruling party in the KRG (in Northern Iraq/South Kurdistan). Founded in April 1946, it has been led by Massoud Barzanî since 1979. It has its own security forces and military. It controls the region around Hewlêr (Erbil) and operates through offshoots in the other parts of Kurdistan.

KDP-S (Partiya Demokrat a Kurdî li Sûriyê). The Syrian sister party of the KDP and a leading party in the ENKS.

KNK (Kongreya Neteweyî ya Kurdistanê)—Kurdistan National Congress. An alliance of Kurdish parties, civil society associations, and exile organizations founded in May 1999 and headquartered in Brussels.

KRG, Kurdish Regional Government. The government of South Kurdistan, in northern Iraq,

Kurdistan. The four parts of Kurdistan are (1) North Kurdistan, in southeastern Turkey, also known as Bakur; (2) West Kurdistan, in northern Syria, also known as Rojava; (3) South Kurdistan, in northern Iraq, also known as the KRG, and (4) East Kurdistan, in northwestern Iran, also known as Başur.

Medya Defense Zones. Located in the mountains of northwestern Iraq, the zones encompass Qandil, Xinere, Xakurke, and Behdinan, all near the borders of Iran and Turkey. Covering some 970 square miles (2,050 square kilometers), they have been controlled by the PKK since the 1990s.

MFS (Mawtbo Folhoyo Suryoyo)—Syriac Military Council. A Syriac defense force associated with the YPG/YPJ.

MGRK (Meclîsa Gela Rojavayê Kurdistanê)—People's Council of West Kurdistan. The council structure in Rojava and Syria, founded in the summer of 2011. It comprises four levels of councils; TEV-DEM is its board at the two upper levels.

NC, National Coalition of Syrian Revolutions and Opposition Forces. A Syrian opposition group comprising 60 representatives of various groups, including two women. It was founded in November 11, 2012, in Doha, Qatar. In the executive committee are, among others, Abdulhakim Bashar of the KDP-S.

PAJK (Partiya Azadiya Jinên Kurdistanê, or PAJK)—Party of Liberation of the Women of Kurdistan. Founded in 2004 in North Kurdistan.

PKK (Partiya Karkerên Kurdistan)—Kurdistan Workers' Party. Founded on November 27, 1978, the PKK has fought ever since for the self-determination and democratic rights for Kurds in Turkey, Syria, Iran, and Iraq. Since August 15, 1984, it has been in armed struggle against the Turkish state. Since the beginning of the 1990s, it has intensively sought a political solution. Its principal figure is Abdullah Öcalan. In the 1990s and 2000s, it developed the concepts of Democratic Autonomy and Democratic Confederalism, which are the foundational concepts for Rojava's self-government.

PUK (Yekîtiya Nîştmanî Kurdistan)—Patriotic Union of Kurdistan. A Kurdish party in South Kurdistan led by Jalal Talabani. It shares power with the KDP. Its power base is in the Soranî-speaking area around Sulaimaniya.

PUK-S (Partiya Demokrat a Pêsverû ya Kurdî li Sûriyê). The Syrian sister party of the PUK.

PYD (Partiya Yekîtiya Demokrat)—Party of Democratic Unity. Founded in 2003, the largest political party in Rojava. Advocating Democratic Autonomy, it is based in the council system. By its charter, it is a member of the Union of Kurdistan Communities (KCK Rojava). It has no organizational ties to the PKK but shares its goal of building grass-roots democracy through people's and women's councils.

SDF (in Arabic, Qūwāt Sūriyā ad-dīmuqrāṭīya; in Kurdish, Hêzên Sûriya Demokratîk)—Syrian Democratic Forces. A military alliance, founded on October 10, 2015, comprising Kurds, Arabs, Syriacs, and others, with the goal of liberating Syria from IS and establishing a self-governing democratic Syria. Among its thirty forces are the YPG/ YPJ, the Syrian Arab Coalition, the Al-Sanadid Forces, the Syriac Military Council, and the Burkan Al-Fırat Operations Center.

SKC (Desteya Bilind a Kurd)—Supreme Kurdish Council. Created by the Hewlêr Agreement of July 12, 2012, a governing board for Rojava comprising equal representation for the PYD and the ENKS.

SMC, Supreme Military Council. The successor organization of the FSA, founded in December 15, 2012, in Turkey as a result of the Doha Conference. Several jihadist groups participate in this broad military alliance.

SNC, Syrian National Council. A council that considers itself a Syrian government in exile. It is tied to Turkey and the Gulf States and is dominated by the Muslim Brotherhood.

TEV-DEM (Tevgera Civaka Demokratik)—Movement for a Democratic Society. The coordinating organ of the MGRK, existing at the upper levels of the three cantons' council system. It also encompasses the supporting political parties, diverse NGOs, social movements, and professional and trade organizations.

Yekîtiya Star, Star Union of Women. The umbrella women's organization in Rojava that has established women's councils, academies, and other institutions in Rojava. *Star* is a reference to the goddess Ishtar. In early 2016, its name was changed to Kongreya Star.

YJA Star (Yekîtîya Jinên Azad)—Ishtar Unit of Free Women. The women's guerrilla army in North Kurdistan, founded as YAJK in 1993.

YPG (Yekîneyên Parastina Gel)—People's Protection Units. The main defense force of Rojava. It was formerly mixed gender but after the split-off of the YPJ in 2013, it is all male.

YPJ (Yekîneyên Parastina Jinê)—Women's Protection Units. The women's defense force of Rojava, created in 2013.

About the Authors

Anja Flach an ethnologist and member of the Rojbîn women's council in Hamburg, is the author most recently of *Frauen in der kurdischen Guerilla. Motivation, Identität und Geschlechterverhältnis in der Frauenarmee der PKK* (2007).

Ercan Ayboğa, while living in Germany, worked as an environmental engineer and co-founded Campaign TATORT Kurdistan. In North Kurdistan, he has been an activist for many years in the Initiative to Save Hasankeyf against the Ilisu dam and in the Mesopotamian ecology movement.

Michael Knapp, an activist with the Berlin Kurdistan Solidarity Committee, is a historian who studies radical democracy and social movements.

Index

Abdo, Meysa, 61, 138
Abdullah, Asya (PYD co-chair), 52, 61, 69, 70, 77, 78, 259, 262, 267
Abdulselam, Mamoste, 86, 87, 89
academies, 181: military, 134, 136, 148–51; Asayîş, 173; cultural, 126; economics, 207; ecology, 220; health, 190; PKK, 37; women's, 70–1, 75, 136, 148–51, 183, 271. *See also* education
Academy for Kurdish Language, History and Literature, 175, 177, 179–81
Afendi, Aysa 48
Afrîn (canton), xxiii, 2, 7, 96, 183; agriculture in, 107, 192, 195; attacks on, 135, 159, 236, 237; DAA in, 114–5, 192; defense of, 140, 235; districts in, 121n1; economy in, 194, 206; education in, 177, 180; energy in, 205; Ezidis in, 21–2, 156; forestation in, 107, 212; groundwater in, 215; health care in, 187; isolation of, 91, 117, 241–2, 256; justice in, 166, 167; liberation of, 55–6; Manbij and, 157, 229, 241–2, 256; MGRK system in, 87, 96, 98, 109, 110, 116, 118, 120; refugees in, 4, 101–2; in Social Contract 112–13; waste disposal in, 217; women in, 67–8, 69, 137
Afrîn (city and district in Afrîn canton), 4, 136
Afrîn, Silvan, 47, 51, 88, 93, 146, 200, 203

Agirî, Dr., 185–9
agriculture, xxviii, 9, 14, 195–6; cooperatives in, 199–200, 203, 206, 208; as dominant economy in, Rojava 23, 195, 212, 215; irrigation in, 9, 10, 154, 203, 213, 214, 216–17, 219, 221; olive cultivation in, 4, 107, 192, 203, 209, 212; wheat cultivation in, xxx, 4, 6, 8, 154, 192–6, 199, 209, 212–13, 217
Ahde, Lokman, 219
Ahmed, Abdulselam, 91
Ahmed, Ilham, 53, 56, 63, 67, 68, 71, 75, 76, 80, 250, 261n1
Ahrar Al-Sham, xxiv, 156, 159, 237, 242, 243–4
Akidi, Abdul Jabbar, 224
Akîf, Dorşîn, 71
Akobian, Dajad, 27
AKP (Turkish ruling party), xxiv, 231, 234–6, 239, 241, 243, 244
Aktaş, Yûhanna, 26
Al Azam, Hussein Taza, 7
Al-Baghdadi, Abu Bakr, 227
Al-Hasani, Ahmad Moaz Al-Khatib, 224
Al-Qaeda, 28, 102, 223, 224, 227, 236, 237, 250
Al-Sanadid Forces, 156, 162n32, 270
Al-Zarqawi, Abu Musab, 227
Aleppo, 2, 4, 201; Arabs in, 23; Armenians in, 5, 26; Ba'ath regime and, 48; economy of, 201; education in, 177; Nawar in, 33; MGRK system in, 84, 91, 95–102;

273